1·75

HOW TO FIND OUT ABOUT THE VICTORIAN PERIOD

HOW TO FIND OUT ABOUT
THE VICTORIAN PERIOD

A Guide to Sources of Information

BY

LIONEL MADDEN

Bibliographer to the Victorian Studies Centre
University of Leicester

PERGAMON PRESS

Oxford · New York · Toronto
Sydney · Braunschweig

Pergamon Press Ltd., Headington Hill Hall, Oxford

Pergamon Press Inc., Maxwell House, Fairview Park, Elmsford, New York 10523

Pergamon of Canada Ltd., 207 Queen's Quay West, Toronto 1

Pergamon Press (Aust.) Pty. Ltd., 19a Boundary Street, Rushcutters Bay, N.S.W. 2011, Australia

Vieweg & Sohn GmbH, Burgplatz 1, Braunschweig

First edition 1970

Library of Congress Catalog Card No. 74-116777

Printed in Great Britain by A. Wheaton & Co., Exeter

08 015833 1 (flexicover)
08 015834 X (hard cover)

*To the staff and students of
the Victorian Studies Centre
in the University of Leicester*

Contents

List of Illustrations		ix
Preface		xi
Chapter 1.	Introductory: The Study of the Victorian Period	1
Chapter 2.	General Guides to the Literature	4
Chapter 3.	Victorian Periodicals and Newspapers	22
Chapter 4.	Guides to Special Collections and Source Materials	39
Chapter 5.	Philosophy	49
Chapter 6.	The Christian Church	54
Chapter 7.	Social and Economic Life and Thought	60
Chapter 8.	Education	73
Chapter 9.	Science	84
Chapter 10.	The Visual Arts	100
Chapter 11.	Music Literature	122
Chapter 12.	English Literature	129
Chapter 13.	History	145
Chapter 14.	General Biographical Works	158
Index		169

List of Illustrations

FIG. 1. T. Besterman, *A World Bibliography of Bibliographies* 5
(By kind permission of Rowman & Littlefield Inc.)

FIG. 2. *Bibliographic Index* 7
(By kind permission of the H. W. Wilson Co.)

FIG. 3. British Museum, *General Catalogue of Printed Books* 9
(By courtesy of the Trustees of the British Museum)

FIG. 4. *British National Bibliography* 11
(By kind permission of the Council of the British National
Bibliography Ltd.)

FIG. 5. *Cumulative Book Index* 12
(By kind permission of the H. W. Wilson Co.)

FIG. 6. *British Humanities Index* 14
(By kind permission of the Library Association)

FIG. 7. *Victorian Studies* ("Victorian Bibliography", Section I) 15
(By kind permission of the Editors)

FIG. 8. *Victorian Studies* ("Victorian Bibliography", Sections III–IV) 16
(By kind permission of the Editors)

FIG. 9. *Index to British Theses* 19
(By kind permission of Aslib)

FIG. 10. S. Halkett and J. Laing, *Dictionary of Anonymous and
Pseudonymous English Literature* 20
(By kind permission of Oliver & Boyd Ltd.)

FIG. 11. *Victorian Periodicals Newsletter* 24
(By kind permission of the Editor)

FIG. 12. *Tercentenary Handlist of English and Welsh Newspapers,
Magazines and Reviews* 26
(By kind permission of *The Times* (The Times Newspapers
Ltd.))

FIG. 13. *British Union-Catalogue of Periodicals* 27
(By kind permission of Butterworths)

FIG. 14. *Poole's Index to Periodical Literature* 29
(By kind permission of Peter Smith)

FIG. 15. W. E. Houghton, *The Wellesley Index to Victorian Periodicals*
(Tabular Listing) 32
(By kind permission of Routledge and Kegan Paul Ltd.)

FIG. 16. W. E. Houghton, *The Wellesley Index to Victorian Periodicals*
(Bibliographies of Contributors) 33
(By kind permission of Routledge and Kegan Paul Ltd.)

FIG. 17. A. Boyle, *An Index to the Annuals*   35
          (By kind permission of Andrew Boyle Ltd.)
FIG. 18. P. and G. Ford, *Select List of British Parliamentary Papers,*
          1833–1899   43
          (By kind permission of Basil Blackwell (Publishing) and Irish
          University Press)
FIG. 19. H. Temperley and L. M. Penson, *A Century of Diplomatic Blue*
          Books, 1814–1914   45
          (By kind permission of Cambridge University Press)
FIG. 20. *Guide to the Contents of the Public Record Office*   47
          (By kind permission of the Controller of Her Majesty's
          Stationery Office)
FIG. 21. *London Bibliography of the Social Sciences*   62
          (By kind permission of the British Library of Political and
          Economic Science)
FIG. 22. G. Ottley, *A Bibliography of British Railway History* 66
          (By kind permission of George Allen & Unwin Ltd.)
FIG. 23. *Journal of Transport History*   67
          (By kind permission of Leicester University Press)
FIG. 24. *Urban History Newsletter*   69
          (By kind permission of the Editor)
FIG. 25. *Scientific Research in British Universities and Colleges*
          (Part III: *Social Sciences*)   70
          (By kind permission of the Controller of Her Majesty's
          Stationery Office)
FIG. 26. S. K. Kimmance, *A Guide to the Literature of Education* 74
          (By kind permission of the Librarian, University of London
          Institute of Education)
FIG. 27. C. W. J. Higson, *Sources for the History of Education* 76
          (By kind permission of the Library Association)
FIG. 28. *British Education Index*   80
          (By kind permission of the Library Association)
FIG. 29. A. Christophers, *An Index to Nineteenth Century British*
          Educational Biography   82
          (By kind permission of the Librarian, University of London
          Institute of Education)
FIG. 30. *Isis* ("Critical bibliography of the history of science") 87
          (By kind permission of the Editor)
FIG. 31. *Technology and Culture* ("Current bibliography in the history
          of technology")   88
          (By kind permission of the Editor and University of Chicago
          Press)
FIG. 32. *Current Work in the History of Medicine*   94
          (By kind permission of the Wellcome Institute of the History
          of Medicine)
FIG. 33. M. W. Chamberlin, *Guide to Art Reference Books*   101
          (By kind permission of the American Library Association)

FIG. 34. N. Carrick, *How to Find Out About the Arts* (1965)   102
(By kind permission of Pergamon Press Ltd.)
FIG. 35. *Art Index*   106
(By kind permission of the H. W. Wilson Co.)
FIG. 36. D. L. Smith, *How to Find Out in Architecture and Building* 114
(1967) (By kind permission of Pergamon Press Ltd.)
FIG. 37. J. H. Davies, *Musicalia* (1966)   123
(By kind permission of Pergamon Press Ltd.)
FIG. 38. *British Catalogue of Music*   126
(By kind permission of the Council of the British National
Bibliography Ltd.)
FIG. 39. F. W. Bateson, *A Guide to English Literature*   131
(By kind permission of Longmans, Green & Co. Ltd. and
Doubleday & Co., Inc.)
FIG. 40. W. E. Fredeman, *Pre-Raphaelitism: a bibliocritical study* 133
(By kind permission of Harvard University Press)
FIG. 41. R. D. Altick and W. R. Matthews, *Guide to Doctoral Disserta-
tions in Victorian Literature, 1886–1958*   138
(By kind permission of University of Illinois Press)
FIG. 42. *Victorian Poetry* ("The Year's Work in Victorian Poetry") 140
(By kind permission of the Editor)
FIG. 43. *Annals of English Literature, 1475–1950*   142
(By kind permission of the Clarendon Press, Oxford)
FIG. 44. American Historical Association, *Guide to Historical Literature* 147
(By kind permission of the Macmillan Co. Copyright 1931 by
the Macmillan Co. renewed 1959 by American Historical
Review)
FIG. 45. J. Roach, *A Bibliography of Modern History*   148
(By kind permission of Cambridge University Press)
FIG. 46. C. Gross, *A Bibliography of British Municipal History*   153
(By kind permission of Leicester University Press)
FIG. 47. W. Kellaway, *Bibliography of Historical Works Issued in the
United Kingdom, 1961–1965*   155
(By kind permission of the University of London Institute of
Historical Research)
FIG. 48. *Biography Index*   160
(By kind permission of the H. W. Wilson Co.)

Preface

THIS book is intended as an introductory guide to essential sources of information for the study of the Victorian period in Britain. It is designed for all people interested in Victorian studies, including students engaged on dissertations or on interdisciplinary courses of study and for librarians organizing collections and information services. It confines its attention to works of reference and does not attempt to provide a reading list of the best scholarly writings within each subject field. Such a work, though desirable, would have to be undertaken for the Victorian age not by a single individual but as a joint enterprise by a group of specialists. At present the reader must turn for such guidance to the more detailed handbooks noted in the text.

The study of the Victorian period frequently fails to conform to traditional subject divisions. Because of this the student will often find himself faced with the problem of seeking information within a variety of fields of interest. This book aims to provide him with an initial outline of the most significant reference sources which will enable him efficiently to organize his bibliographical investigations of materials relevant to his own research. It surveys not only those guides which are specifically devoted to the Victorian period but also the many general reference works which are valuable for Victorian studies as for other disciplines.

Throughout the book, details of place, publisher, and date are included for works mentioned. The place is omitted, however, when the work is published in London. In citations of periodicals, dates indicate the years officially covered by the periodical, not the actual dates of publication.

I am grateful for the help I have received during the writing of this book from my wife, from Dr. G. Chandler, the editor of the series, and from many colleagues and correspondents. In the University of Leicester I should like to acknowledge advice given by Dr. W. H. Brock, Professor Philip Collins, Miss Priscilla Metcalf, and Professor H. A. D. Miles.

CHAPTER 1

Introductory: The Study
of the Victorian Period

THE study of the Victorian period has now become widespread. This is due to several differing impulses. The normal revolution of fashionable taste has made many of its aesthetic achievements admirable to contemporary eyes. Concepts of Victorian attitudes to life, sometimes in the form of creative or comforting myths, are adopted by those who are dissatisfied with life in the twentieth century. The popular shift from denigration to adulation of the Victorians finds expression in the increasing flow of "coffee table" books which offer by pictures or quotations views of a society at once fascinating and mysteriously unreal to the present age.

Along with fashionable interest in a vanished age has developed a serious study of the Victorians, a strenuous attempt to define the extent of their achievement and to assess its relevance to contemporary life and thought. Inevitably, the nineteenth century provides an essential background for the understanding of the structure of modern society. The shape of modern political and social thought, the revolution in religious attitudes, the development of a scientific methodology and outlook, the technological advances and the aesthetic and cultural ideals of twentieth-century Britain, all derive much of their character from the dynamic changes which took place during the Victorian period.

In his inaugural lecture, *The Impress of the Moving Age* (Leicester, Univ. Pr., 1965), Philip Collins notes that "many of the problems confronting Victorian society remain with us". He

1

quotes Edward Thompson's pertinent observation that "the greater part of the world today is still undergoing problems of industrialization, and of the formation of democratic institutions, analogous in many ways to our own experience during the Industrial Revolution. Causes which were lost in England might, in Asia or Africa, yet be won." The study of the Victorian age is relevant both as an essential historical background to contemporary British life and a valuable perspective for the analysis of problems which are still of major importance in the modern world.

The impulse towards serious study of the Victorians has itself contributed towards the breaking down of traditional disciplines of study. For an age so various, in which individuals regularly engaged in many fields of action and from which a multitude of original source materials survive, it is necessary to adopt new techniques of analysis and to seek broader perspectives as a basis for assessment. The editors of the first volume of *Victorian Studies* in 1957, after stating that the periodical hoped "to capture something of the life of that era, to discuss its events and personalities, and to interpret and appraise its achievement", lent strong support to the concept of interdisciplinary studies by expressing their conviction that "This hope is more likely to be realized through the co-ordination of academic disciplines than in departmental isolation". A Victorian Studies Association, recently formed in Ontario, voiced a similar interdisciplinary approach in the first number of its *Newsletter* (March 1968).

Recognition of the value of interdisciplinary study of the Victorian period has been acknowledged in several British universities. A Victorian Studies Centre has been established in the University of Leicester to provide teaching for postgraduate students and to promote research on an interdisciplinary basis. Other universities have inaugurated courses involving an interdisciplinary approach to the period. This is, of course, by no means to claim that the concept of interdisciplinary study has evolved solely from ideas advanced by students of the Victorian period. It forms part of a much wider movement of educational thought. It is perhaps true to say that its adoption by many students of this period indicates a recognition of its particular suitability for the examination of the life and thought of the nineteenth century.

An interdisciplinary approach to the Victorian period has inevitably made students increasingly aware of the limitations of their knowledge about those areas of study in which they have received no formal training. In addition to procedural problems arising from the different approaches adopted by scholars in different fields, students are faced with the more elementary difficulty of identifying the basic reference works in a variety of subject areas.

The present book attempts to outline some of the essential sources of information for the general study of the period and for research into specific areas of Victorian history and achievement. Although selection in a work of this type must necessarily be at times open to debate, it is hoped that the most significant materials have been included. It is, of course, inevitable that some information will be quickly outdated as new works and new editions of old works are published. This is particularly true in the field of Victorian studies where an enormous amount of research is currently in progress. It is hoped, however, that this book will indicate how much bibliographical work still remains to be undertaken. The wealth of source materials and commentary requires much greater organization to ensure that it is effectively used. In particular, there is a great need for closer analysis and codification of information about manuscript materials, periodicals, newspapers, and ephemeral publications. There is, too, a continuing need for biographical information about figures of local eminence.

Despite such deficiencies, however, it is clear that a serious attempt is now being made to increase the tools available for the student. The following chapters offer both a guide to the reference works that already exist or are in active preparation and an implicit commentary on basic guides that still need to be supplied.

CHAPTER 2

General Guides to the Literature

Reference Sources

In common with all other research workers the student of the Victorian period will commence his search for printed materials with certain basic general guides. Among books which attempt to survey the whole field of reference work, the most significant are A. J. Walford, *Guide to Reference Material* (2nd edn., Library Association, 1966–), and C. M. Winchell, *Guide to Reference Books* (8th edn., Chicago, American Library Association, 1967). Both these works list sources of information on all subjects and provide useful annotations indicating the scope of the items listed. The user will note that Walford tends to emphasize British and Winchell American publications.

A convenient guide to the latest reference sources is provided by *New Tools for Reference Librarians* (Oxford, Maxwell, 1962/3–). G. Chandler, *How to Find Out* (3rd edn., Oxford, Pergamon Press, 1967), is a useful concise general introduction to sources of information.

Bibliographies

At the commencement of any project on the Victorian period it will be necessary to establish whether a bibliographical listing of the subject already exists. The most important general guide to bibliographies is T. Besterman, *A World Bibliography of Bibliographies* (4th edn., Lausanne, Societas Bibliographica, 1965–6). This 5-volume work lists in a single alphabetical sequence of subjects some 117,000 separately published bibliographies (see Fig. 1). The *Index Bibliographicus* (4th edn., The Hague, Fédération

4

TEXTILES

F. R. TAYLOR, Dyes, dyeing and textile printing. Library association: Special subject list (no.6): 1956. pp.12. [143.]*

TEXTILE wastes. Public library of South Australia: Research service: [Adelaide] 1958. ff.9. [137.]*

ZEITSCHRIFTEN-VERZEICHNIS zum dokumentationsdienst faserstoffe und textiltechnik. Deutsche akademie der wissenschaften: Bücherei der dokumentalisten (no.11): Berlin 1959. pp.121. [238.]*

Thackeray, William Makepeace.

[RICHARD HERNE SHEPHERD], The bibliography of Thackeray. [1880]. pp.viii.62. [225.]
a second edition appears in W. M. Thackeray, Sultan stork (1887), pp.219-260.

CHARLES PLUMPTRE JOHNSON, Hints to collectors of original editions of the works of William Makepeace Thackeray. 1885. pp.48. [37.]

CHARLES PLUMPTRE JOHNSON, The early writings of William Makepeace Thackeray. 1888. pp. xiv.64. [100.]

WILLIAM MAKEPEACE THACKERAY. . . . A list of books and of references to periodicals in the Brooklyn public library. Brooklyn 1911. pp.52. [500.]

CATALOGUE of an exhibition commemorating the hundredth anniversary of the birth of William Makepeace Thackeray. Grolier club: New York 1912. pp.viii.106. [150.]
— [another edition]. 1912. pp.xii.142. [150.]
260 copies printed.

[H. S. VAN DUZER and EDWARD TURNBULL], A Thackeray library. First editions and first publications . . . collected by Henry Sayre Van Duzer. New York 1919. pp.xiii.199. [750.]
175 copies privately printed.

JOHN D[OZIER] GORDAN, William Makepeace Thackeray. An exhibition from the Berg collection. First editions, manuscripts, autograph letters and drawings. Public library: New York 1947. pp.[ii].39. [200.]

THANET.

SIAM. Far eastern book and journal list Public library: Newark, N.J. [1922]. si [21.]

BETH DICKERSON [and others], Bibliog Thailand. A selected list of books and art annotations. Cornell university: Depar far eastern studies: Southeast Asia progr paper (no.20): Ithaca 1956. ff.iv.64.5. [4]

LIST of Thai government plublicat covering the years B.E. 2497 (1954), (1955), B.E. 2499 (1956). National library ment of fine arts: Bangkok [1957]. [850.]*

JOHN BROWN MASON and H. CARROL Thailand bibliography. University of Libraries: Department of reference an graphy: Bibliographic series (no.4): G 1958. pp.vii.247. [2500.]*

LIST of Thai government publiccati Thammasat university: Institute of publi istration: Research division: Bangko ff.[i].4.43. [1250.]*

SUGGESTED reading list on Thailand. assistance institute: Library: Arlington, ' pp.36. [350.]*

Thallium.

MARTHA DOAN, Index to the liter thallium, 1861-1896. Smithsonian in Miscellaneous collections (no.1171). W. 1899. pp.26. [300.]

FRANCIS F[ARNHAM] HEYROTH, Thal review and summary of medical literatur health service: Public health reports: Sup (no.197): Washington 1947. pp.[ii].23. [

Thälmann, Ernst.

[HEINZ GITTIG], Ernst Thälmann, kär frieden und freiheit. Auswahlverzeich schriften über Ernst Thälmann. Arbeits gesellschaftswissenschaftlichen beratun

FIG. 1. T. Besterman, *A World Bibliography of Bibliographies*. (Copyright: Rowman & Littlefield Inc.)

Internationale de Documentation, 1959–) is a directory of the more important currently published abstracting and bibliographical services. This edition is planned to be completed in 4 volumes.

The *Bibliographic Index: a cumulative bibliography of bibliographies* (New York, Wilson, 1937–) is a periodical devoted to listing bibliographies which are published separately, together with those published in books and periodicals (see Fig. 2). Entries are arranged alphabetically by subject. About 1500 periodicals are examined for bibliographical material.

It is worthy of note that many useful bibliographies by librarians were formerly submitted to the University of London in partial fulfilment of the requirements for the Postgraduate Diploma in Librarianship. Copies are deposited in the University of London Library and the Library of University College, London. The bibliographies have been listed in the Occasional Publications of the School of Librarianship and Archives in University College, London. It is now common for librarians seeking to qualify for Fellowship of the Library Association to undertake bibliographical projects. Details of these are recorded in the *Library Association Record*.

Library Catalogues

Despite the evident value of bibliographies they are, inevitably, rarely completely comprehensive or wholly up to date. The information which they supply must be checked and supplemented by reference both to the catalogues of major libraries and to the guides to the most recent books, periodical articles, and theses. For the study of the Victorian age the holdings of the library of the British Museum are of major importance. The strenuous efforts of Panizzi to compel publishers to deposit copies of new books in accordance with the requirements of the Copyright Act ensured that the British Museum's coverage of Victorian works, though by no means complete, is much more extensive than it would have been under less energetic direction.

BIBLIOGRAPHIC INDEX 1967   67

DETENTION camps. See Concentration camps
DETERGENTS. See Cleaning compositions
DETERMINATION of sex. See Sex determina-
  tion and control
DETERRENCE (strategy)
  Green, Philip. Deadly logic; the theory of
    nuclear deterrence. Ohio state univ. press
    '66 p329-44 annot
DEUTERONOMY, Book of. See Bible, Old Test-
  ament—Deuteronomy
DEVELOPMENT. See Embryology; Evolution;
  Growth
DEVELOPMENTAL psychology. See Genetic
  psychology
DEVIL
    See also
  Demonology
DE WETTE, Wilhelm Martin Leberecht, 1780-
  1849)
  Smend, Rudolf. Wilhelm Martin Leberecht de
    Wettes arbeit am Alten und Neuen Testa-
    ment. Helbing & Lichtenhahn '58 p 189-
    203
DIABETES
  Ralli, Elaine Pandia. Management of the dia-
    betic patient; a practical guide: Putnam '65
    p 195-200
DIAGENESIS
    See also
  Rocks, Crystalline and metamorphic
DIAGNOSIS
  Current diagnosis & treatment, 1966 [-1967]
  Lange medical '66-'67 2v incl bibliog
    See also
  Biopsy
  Mental illness—Diagnosis
  Urine—Analysis and pathology
DIAGNOSTIC psychological testing. See Clini-
  cal psychology

DICHLOROBENZONITRILE. See Dichlobenil
DICHLOROPROPIONIC acid. See Dalapon
DICKENS, Charles, 1812-1870
  Collins, Wilkie, and Brannan, Robert Louis,
    eds. Under the management of Mr Charles
    Dickens; his production of The frozen deep.
    Cornell univ. press '66 p 161-73
  Fielding, Kenneth Joshua. Charles Dickens
    [repd, with additions to bibliog] (Bibliog
    ser, of sups; to British bk. news, no37)
    Longmans '66 p41-52 annot
  Mariani, Giulianna. La crítica social en las
    novelas de Dickens. The author? '60 p231-92
DICKINSON, Emily, 1830-1886
  Ford, Thomas W. Heaven beguiles the tired;
    death in the poetry of Emily Dickinson.
    Univ. of Ala. press '66 p 197-202
  Pickard, John B. Emily Dickinson: an introd.
    and interpretation. Holt '67 p 127-30
DICTATORS
  Hamill, Hugh M. ed. Dictatorship in Spanish
    America. Knopf '65 p235-42
    See also
  Totalitarianism
DICTION. See Articulation (speech)
DICTIONARIES
  Whittaker, Kenneth. Dictionaries. (Readers
    guide ser) Bingley '66 88p
  See also subhead Dictionaries under the
    following subjects
  Agriculture
  Indic languages
  Medicine
  Science
DIDELPHYIDAE. See Opossums
DIDERICHSEN, Paul, 1905-1964
  Diderichsen, Paul. Helhed og struktur; ud-
    valgte sprogvidenskabelige afhandlinger. Se-
    lected linguistic papers with detailed Eng-
    lish summaries. Gad '66 p387-97
DIDIER, Noël

FIG. 2. *Bibliographic Index.* (Copyright: the H. W. Wilson Co.)

The *General Catalogue of Printed Books* (Fig. 3) constitutes a complete author catalogue of the British Museum's holdings to 1955. The *General Catalogue* totals 263 volumes. This has been supplemented by a catalogue of works received during the period 1956–65 and further supplements are planned. The *General Catalogue* represents primarily an author sequence but also includes references for books written about authors. Thus the entry for Charles Dickens includes a list of works about him contained in the library in addition to the complete record of the library's holdings of editions of his writings. A *Subject Index* has been compiled for books published and added to the library since 1881. For books before this date there is a valuable guide by R. A. Peddie. The first volume was published with the title *Subject Index of Books Published Before 1880* (Grafton, 1933). Three further volumes were published with a slight change of title as *Subject Index of Books Published up to and Including 1880* (Grafton, 1935–48). The 4 volumes were reprinted by H. Pordes in 1962.

The author catalogue of the Library of Congress in Washington has been published as *A Catalog of Books Represented by Library of Congress Printed Cards*. From 1953 monographs not in the Library of Congress but reported by other American libraries have been included and the work has been entitled *The National Union Catalog*. A subject catalogue to the library has been published from 1950.

It should be noted that both the British Museum and the Library of Congress author catalogues include details of periodicals in stock. Library of Congress lists these directly under title, but the British Museum groups them under the general heading "Periodical publications" which is subdivided by place of publication.

Among other libraries rich in Victorian material which have published catalogues of their collections, the London Library should be noted. The revised printed catalogue and supplements were published between 1909 and 1955 and at present comprise an author catalogue in 5 volumes and a subject catalogue in 4 volumes.

495

BRADDON (Lawrence)

—— [Another copy.] few ms. notes [by Dr. Thomas Birch]. **1093. c. 58.**
Imperfect ; wanting the frontispiece.

—— The Form of a Petition submitted to the Consideration and Correction of those Noblemen and Gentlemen who desire to Subscribe what Sums shall be necessary for Relieving, Reforming and Employing the Poor : but first to begin only with the poor of those three parishes, of St. Martins in the Fields, St. James's, and St. Annes Westminster, *etc.* [By L. Braddon.] pp. 40. 1722. 8⁰. *See* Saint Martin in the Fields, *Parish of.*
T.1814.(12.)

—— The Miseries of the Poor are a National Sin . . . but by making them happy, we shall remove that guilt . . . and pay old debts without new taxes, *etc.* pp. xxxiii. xlviii. 158. *T. Warner: London,* 1717. 8⁰. **1141. d. 33.**

—— Murther will out. [Two letters, signed : L. B., i.e. L. Braddon, relative to the death of Arthur Capel, Earl of Essex.] pp. 8. [1692.] 4⁰. *See* B., L. **115. h. 35.**

—— Particular Answers to the most material Objections made to the Proposal humbly presented to his Majesty, for relieving, reforming and employing all the poor of Great Britain. pp. x. 9–104. [*London,*] 1722. 8⁰.
1027. i. 18. (7.)

—— The Tryal of Laurence Braddon and Hugh Speke, Gent. upon an information of high-misdemeanor, subornation and spreading false reports to raise a belief . . . that the late Earl of Essex did not murther himself in the Tower . . . Before . . . Sir George Jeffreys, *etc.* pp. 78. *Benjamin Tooke: London,* 1684. fol. **515. l. 6. (5.)**

—— [Another copy.] **1418. k. 4.**

BRADDON (M. G.) *See* Braddon, afterwards Maxwell (Mary E.)

BRADDON, afterwards **MAXWELL** (Mary Elizabeth) *See* Arabian Nights. [*Abridgments, Selections, etc.— English.*] Aladdin ; or the Wonderful Lamp . . . Revised by M. E. Braddon, *etc.* [1880.] 8⁰. **12807. i. 28.**

—— *See* Periodical Publications.—*London.* Belgravia, *etc.* [vol. 1–28. Conducted by M. E. Braddon.] 1866, *etc.* 8⁰. **P.P. 6004. gn.**

—— *See* Periodical Publications.—London.—*Belgravia.* The Belgravia Annual, *etc.* [1868–76. Edited by M. E. Braddon.] [1867, *etc.*] 8⁰. **P.P.6004.gn.**

—— *See* Periodical Publications.—*London.* The Mistletoe Bough. Edited by M. E. Braddon. 1878, *etc.* 8⁰.
P.P. 6700. b.

BRADDON, afterwa

—— Aurora Floyd . . . *London,* 1863. 8⁰.

—— Eighth edition. Secret " [i.e. M. E *See* Floyd (Aurora

—— Aurora Floyd. ' Derosne, *etc.* 2 ton

—— [Aurora Floyd.] Marenicza. pp. 38?

Imperfect ; wanti:

—— *See* Hazlewo drama [based title], *etc.* [186 *Plays.* vol. 58.

—— *See* Suter (W . . . Adapted f same title, *etc.* *of Plays.* vol. ?

—— " Beyond These ' *London,* 1910. 8⁰.

—— Birds of Prey . . Secret " [i.e. M. E Birds.

—— Les Oiseaux de p Bernard-Derosne.

—— Boscastle, Cornw printed from The *Launceston,* 1881.

—— The Captain of th *London,* 1862. 8⁰.

—— Le Capitaine du Bernard Derosne, *et*

—— Charlotte's Inheri Audley's Secret " [i. 3 vol. 1868. 8⁰.

—— L'Héritage de Cl Charles Bernard-Der

—— The Christmas F Townsend. pp. 261 1894. 8⁰.

Fig. 3. British Museum, *General Catalogue of Printed Books.* (Copyright: Trustees of the British Museum.)

Books

The publication of new books in Britain and Ireland was recorded in the nineteenth century by the annual *English Catalogue of Books*. For the period from 1837 to 1889 the catalogue lists works under author and title and there is a separate consolidated 4-volume subject index. After this date, authors, titles, and subjects are presented in a single alphabetical sequence. In 1914 a volume covering 1801–36 was issued with the same arrangement. This catalogue was originally published by S. Low and has been continued by the Publishers' Circular.

From 1950 new books published in Britain have been listed in the *British National Bibliography* (Council of the British National Bibliography), which is issued weekly with regular monthly, quarterly, half-yearly and annual cumulations. Entries, which are compiled from books deposited in the British Museum under the Copyright Act, are arranged by subject according to a version of the Dewey Classification and indexed by author, title, and subject (Fig. 4). The index is cumulated at 5-yearly intervals. The *Cumulative Book Index* (New York, Wilson, 1898–) attempts to list all books in the English language published anywhere in the world (Fig. 5). Entries are listed by author, title, and subject in a single alphabetical sequence. The work is issued monthly with regular cumulations.

The reader who wishes to keep himself informed of new books about the Victorian period should cultivate the habit of checking regularly both the *British National Bibliography* and the *Cumulative Book Index*.

Periodical Articles

It is, of course, much more difficult to trace relevant new periodical articles on the period. Among general indexes of twentieth-century articles in British periodicals, the major tool for the humanities is the *British Humanities Index* (Library

Berrill, Norman John. The life of the ocean. *McGraw-H.*, 40/6. 574.5263t (B67-18513)

Berrisford, Judith Mary. The far-from-home cats. *Hutchinson*, 12/6. 823.91J (B67-6564)

Berry, Ann. Primary English course transition book teachers' manual. *See* Gagg, John Colton.

Berry, Brian Joe Lobley. Geography of market centers and retail distribution. *Prentice-H.*, 16/-(Pbk.). 331.[1] (B67-24568)

Berry, C. J. An experimental investigation of the interaction between a forward-facing step and a laminar boundary layer in supersonic, low-density flow. *See* Great Britain. *Aeronautical Research Council.*

Berry, C. J. Experiments with cones in low-density flows at mach numbers near 2. *See* Great Britain. *Aeronautical Research Council.*

Berry, Cyril John James. Home brewed beers and stouts. 2nd ed. *North Croye, The Avenue, Andover(Hants.), 'Amateur Winemaker,'* 5/-(Pbk.). 641.37[1] (B67-24198)

Berry, Cyril John James. 130 new winemaking recipes. 2nd ed. *North Croye, The Avenue, Andover(Hants.), 'Amateur Winemaker,'* 5/-(Pbk.). 641.37[1] (B67-24200)

Berry, Donald Michael, & others. *See* Box, Philip George, & others.

Berry, Erick, pseud. [i.e. Allena Best]. The springing of the rice. *Collier-M.*, 12/6. 823.91J (B67-2673)

Berry, Frederick Almet Fulghum, ed. Geology of petroleum. *See* Levorsen, Arville Irving.

Berry, Harrison M. & others. *See* Ennis, LeRoy Massey, & others.

Berry, James, (b.1842). Tales of the West of Ireland; ed. by Gertrude M. Horgan. *O.U.P.*, 30/-. 630.1437 t/10 (B67-2036)

Berry, John Pearson. Evans secondary English course for

Best from 'Fantasy & Science Fiction.' *See* 'Magazine of Fantasy & Science Fiction'.

Best laid schemes—!. *See* Meyer, Henry J.

Best man's duties. *See* Heaton, Vernon.

Best of Beardsley. *See* Beardsley, Aubrey.

Best of both worlds?. *See* Hunter, Guy.

Best of 'Granta,' 1889-1966. *See* 'Granta.'

Best of 'Olympia.' *See* 'Olympia Magazine.'

Best of sci-fi. *Mayflower.*
4; ed. by Judith Merril. 5/-(Pbk.). 823.91FS (B67-12182)

Best of sci-fi. *See* Anual S-F.

Best sellers of literature (Pan):
Blackmore, Richard Doddridge. *Lorna Doone.*
Trollope, Anthony. *The last chronicle of Barset.*

Best s.f. stories from 'New Worlds'. *See* New Worlds Science Fiction.

Best secret service stories. *Faber.*
3; ed. by John Welcome. 21/-. 823.91FS (B67-2672)

Best smuggling stories. *See* Welcome, John, comp.

Best stories of the South Seas. *See* Snow, Philip, comp.

Best spy stories. *See* Welcome, John, comp.

Best true adventure stories. *See* Bryans, Robin.

Beste, Joan, & Read, Eileen. Deptoment. *70 Gloucester Pl., W.1, Imperial Soc. of Teachers of Dancing,* 7/6. 395 (B67-7368)

Bester, Alfred. The dark side of the earth. *In* Bester, Alfred Omnibus.

Bester, Alfred. The demolished man. *In* Bester, Alfred. Omnibus.

Bester, Alfred. The life and death of a satellite. *Sidgwick & J.*, 18/-. 629.1388 (B67-21858)

Bester, Alfred. Omnibus. *Sidgwick & J.*, 30/-. 823.91FS (B67-9788)

Bester, Alfred. Tiger! Tiger! *In* Bester, Alfred. Omnibus.

Betteridge, Anne, p For works of this Newman, Marg Potter, Margare

Betteridge, Don, pr of this author pu Newman, Bern

Betteridge, Harold See Cassell & C.

Betterment levy :

Betterment levy. S
Betterment levy. S
Betterment levy (O
Betterment levy, a Britain. Housin,

Betterment levy an Bryan, & Nutley,

Betterment levy (S Development De,

Betley, Joseph Har 1906-1939. Rou Pbk. 12/6.

Bettina, pseud. [i O.U.P., 16/-.

Bettinas hemlighet
Bettina's secret.

Betting : Criminal
Betting : Horse ra
Betting : Sports :
Betting, Gaming & See Great Britain

Betts, Alan. The 798.48

FIG. 4. *British National Bibliography.* (Copyright: the Council of the British National Bibliography Ltd.)

Diagnosis—*Continued*
Vakil, R. J. and Golwalla, A. F. Clinical diagnosis. 2d ed Rs 35 (85s) '67 Asia pub.
See also
Children—Diseases—Diagnosis
Diagnosis, Differential
Electrodiagnosis
Medicine—Practice
Pain
Pathology
Radiesthesia
Diagnosis, Differential
French, H. ed. Index of differential diagnosis. 9th ed $24 '67 Williams & Wilkins; £6 15s Wright, J.
Diagnosis, Radioscopic
Caffey, J. P. and Silverman, F. N. Pediatric X-ray diagnosis. 5th ed $39.50 '67 Year bk. medical
Felson, B. and Wiot, J. F. Case of the day. $8.50 '67 Thomas, C.C.
Schinz, H. R. and others. Roentgen diagnosis. 2d ed v5 $55 '67 Grune
Diagnosis, Surgical
Bailey, H. Demonstrations of physical signs in clinical surgery. 14th ed $16.75 '67 Williams & Wilkins; 75s Wright, J.
See also
Electrodiagnosis
Diagnostic and remedial reading for classroom and clinic. Wilson, R. M. $5.95 Merrill
Diagnostic procedures in gastroenterology. Bockus, C. H. ed. $19.75 Mosby
The dialect of Dentdale in the West Riding of Yorkshire. Hedevind, B. 60kr Almqvist
Dialectic (logic). See Logic
Dialectical materialism
Jordan, Z. A. The evolution of dialectical materialism. 60s '67 Macmillan (London)
Osbert, R. Marxism and psychoanalysis. pa $1.95 '67 Dell
Plekhanov, G. V. Essays in the history of materialism. $8 '67 Fertig
Somerville, J. The philosophy of Marxism. pa $2.25 '67 Random house
Dialects. See Language and languages
Dialing. See Sundials
Dialogue and drama. Reeves, J. and Culpan, N. $4 Plays
The dialogue of Christians and Jews. Schneider, P. pa $1.95 Seabury
Dialogue on education [by] Richard Kean [and others] 144p pa $1.25 '67 Bobbs
        LC 67-21396
Dialogue on poverty [by] Paul Jacobs [and others] 136p pa $1.25 '67 Bobbs LC 67-20450
A dialogue on science, psychology and God. Thompson, W. R. $3 Philosophical lib.
Dialogue on technology [by] Edward McIrvine. [and others] 109p pa $1.25 '67 Bobbs
        LC 67-20451
Dialogue with death. Koestler, A. $5.95 Macmillan (N Y); 30s Hutchinson
Dialogues on mathematics. Rényl, A. $4.95; pa $2.50 Holden-Day
Diamond, Aubrey Lionel
Introduction to hire-purchase law. xxiv,164p 17s 6d '67 Butterworth & co.
        LC 67-98820(GB)
The diamond necklace. Maupassant, G. de. $2.95 Watts, F.
Diamonds

        Juvenile literature
Switzer, G. Diamonds in pictures. $3.95 '67 Sterling
Diamonds in the salt. Woodard, B. A. $6.75 Pruett press
Diana is dead. Stand, M. 15s Hale, R.
Dianetics. See Mental hygiene; Psychotherapy
Diaries

Diaz-Plaja, Fernando
The Spaniard and the seven deadl from the Spanish by John Inderw 223p $4.50 '67 Scribner; Can$5.75 S.J.R.
DiBenedetto, Anthony T. 1933-
The structure and properties of 533p il $12.50 (£5) '67 McGraw L
Dible, James Henry, 1889-
The pathology of limb ischaemia. pl $8.25 '67 Warren, H. Green, Brentwood blvd, St. Louis, Mo, 6: Oliver; Can$12.25 Clarke, Irwin
        LC 67-27239;67
Dibner, Martin, 1911-
The admiral. 453p $5.95 '67 Dout
DiCerto, J. J.
Missile base beneath the sea; tł Polaris. 165p il $5.95 '67 St Martir Macmillan (Canada)
Dicey, Albert Venn, 1835-1922, at J. H. C.
The conflict of laws; 8th ed. unde eral editorship of J. H. C. Morris cialist editors. Q cxxv,1289p £7
        LC 6:
    The previous ed. was by A. V. Dicey
Dick, Philip Kindred
The penultimate truth. 254p 25s '
Dick Foote and the shark. Babbit Farrar, Straus
Dick Whittington and his [cat] i Howard. Q 15s '67 Faber
Dickason, Alfred
Sheet metal drawing and patter ment. 364p 45s '67 Pitman
Dickens, Arthur Geoffrey
Martin Luther and the reform: 12s 6d '67 English univs.
Dickens, Charles, 1812-1870
The adventures of Oliver Twis parish boy's progress; with t il. by George Cruikshank. 451 Ginn
Bleak house
—Charles Dickens: Bleak house. Rs hopadhyay
A Christmas carol; a facsim. of the Pierpont Morgan lib. with John Leech and the text from t tion. Q 142p $12.50 '67 Heinem

Coolidge, A. C. Charles Dickens as elist. $6 '67 Iowa state univ. prea
Hibbert, C. The making of Charle $5.95 '67 Harper; 45s (Can$9.95) ltd.
Price, M. ed. Dickens. $4.95; p Prentice-Hall
Dicker, E. C.
School certificate technical drawi il Aus$3.75 '66 Brooks, W.
Dickie-Clark, H. F.
The marginal situation; a sociolo of a coloured group. 226p $6.75 ' ties press;. 40s '66 Routledge
        LC 6(
Dickinson, Arthur William
Industrial relations in supervisor ment. 128p 17s 6d '67 Nelson
        LC 6'
Dickinson, David Ronald
Operators: an algebraic synthesis. '67 St Martins; 37s 6d Macmilla
        LC 6'
Dickinson, Edward, 1803-1874
Bingham, M. T. Emily Dickinson's pa $3 '67 Dover
Dickinson, Emily, 1830-1886
Bingham, M. T. Ancestors' broce '67 Dover
Bingham, M. T. Emily Dickinson's

F<small>IG</small>. 5. *Cumulative Book Index*. (Copyright: the H. W. Wilson Co.)

Association). Since 1962 this work, together with the *British Technology Index* and the *British Education Index*, has superseded the *Subject Index to Periodicals* (Library Association, 1915–61). The *Subject Index to Periodicals*, after some early experimenting, was, as its name implies, limited to indexing by subjects. From 1926 these were arranged in an alphabetical sequence. There was no index of authors of articles. The work was published annually.

The *British Humanities Index* (Fig. 6), which lists material relating to the arts and politics, provides a quarterly index of subjects in some 320 periodicals with an annual cumulation which also includes an author index. In 1954 *Regional Lists* were commenced indexing articles of local interest in a large number of periodicals not indexed in the main work. Except for Scotland, arrangement is by county. These lists provide invaluable information which does not appear in any other index.

The *International Index to Periodicals* (New York, Wilson, 1907–) is now concerned only with publications in the English language. In 1965 the work was retitled the *Social Sciences and Humanities Index*. This is an author and subject index in a single alphabetical sequence, covering some 180 periodicals. The same publisher's *Readers' Guide to Periodical Literature*, which commenced in 1900, indexes less scholarly and non-technical English language periodicals in all fields. Although generally less useful to the student it should certainly be checked.

Books and Periodical Articles

The most convenient guide to recent writings about the Victorian period, both in books and periodicals, is the annual "Victorian Bibliography" contributed since 1957 to *Victorian Studies* (Figs. 7–8). From 1932 to 1956 the bibliography was published in *Modern Philology*. Compiled by a committee of the Victorian Literature Group of the Modern Language Association of America, it offers extensive listing of writings about authors of the period (Section IV), but also includes more general sections of "Bibliographic material" (Section I), "Economic, political,

Public Record Office

Congestion in the Public Record Office: facts and figures. Archives, 8 (Oct 67) p.61-2

Documents in the Public Record Office. 4. Inventories of Church goods. A.A.H. Knightsbridge. Amateur Historian, 7 (1967) p.219-22. il.

Unlocked: the secrets of 20 years. Sunday Times, (31 Dec 67) p.17

Public Relations Consultants

The job behind the aid. [Public Relations Adviser, Overseas Containers Limited]. Times R. of Industry and Technology, 5 (Jul 67) p.24-5

See also:
Middlemen

Public Relations Consultants, Women

Who are the gentle persuaders? Rita Grosvenor. Times, (13 Apr 67) p.7

Public Schools

Burden of choice on public schools. David Gourlay. Guardian, (2 Oct 67) p.2

Loyalty in a closed society. Royston Lambert. Guardian, (6 Oct 67) p.6

State boarding and the future of public schools. Ronald King. New Society, (13 Jul 67) p.46-8

That Public Schools Commission. Economist, 224 (26 Aug 67) p.708-9

Public Schools: History

Pugin, Augustus Welby Northmore

In search of Pugin's church plate. I. Pugin, Hardman and the Industrial Revolution. Shirley Bury. Connoisseur, 165 (May 67) p.29-35. il.

Pugin, Edward Welby

Carlton Towers, Yorkshire. Mark Girouard. Country Life, 141 (2 Feb 67) p.230-3; 141 (9 Feb 67) p.280-3. il.

Pugwash Conferences on Science and World Affairs

Perspective on Pugwash. Leonard E. Schwartz. International Affairs, 43 (Jul 67) p.498-515

Pulcher, P. Clodius. See Clodius, Publius

Pulpits

Historical notes on pulpits. Frederick Burgess. Commemorative Art, 34 (Mar 67) p.93-96. il.

Pulpits: the example of St. Paul's Cathedral commemorative pulpit. Commemorative Art, 34 (Mar 67) p.91-2. il.

Punishment

Justice and legal punishment. James F. Doyle. Philosophy, 42 (Jan 67) p.53-67

Punishment-a field for experiment. J.W. Palmer. British J. of Criminology, 7 (Oct 67) p.434-41

Punishment (Ethics)

Intention and punishment. H.L.A. Hart. Oxford R., No.4 (Hilary 67) p.5-22

Mr. Thompson on the distribution of punishment. C.L.

Fig. 6. *British Humanities Index.* (Copyright: the Library Association.)

I. BIBLIOGRAPHICAL MATERIAL

(For other bibliographical materials, see II, Clebsch, and for those pertaining to individuals listed in Section IV, see ARNOLD: Brooks; CLOUGH: Gollin; DARWIN: Freeman; DICKENS: *Dickensian* (Smith), Stevens, Stone; DOYLE: Wolff; ELIOT: Marshall; GILBERT: Jones; HARDY: Colby, Kramer; HOPKINS: Cohen; HOUSMAN: White; HUTTON: Tener; MEREDITH: *Modern Love*; MILL: *Mill Newsletter* (Robson); RUSKIN: "Intramuralia"; SHAW: *Shaw R* (Stokes); SWINBURNE: "A Rare Find"; TENNYSON: Thomson, Smith; THACKERAY: Flamm; WHITE: Davis; WILDE: Mason.)

Ayo, Nicholas. "A Checklist of the Principal Book-Length Studies in the Field of English and American Literature Devoted to a Single Author's Use of the Bible." *BB* 25:7-8.
Single references to works about Browning, Dickens, Hardy, C. Rossetti, Ruskin, and Tennyson.

Bill, E. G. W. (ed.). *Catalogue of the Papers of Roundell Palmer (1812-1895), First Earl of Selborne*. London: Lambeth Palace Lib. Pp. 56.
Noticed in *TLS* 21 Sept.:845.

Bostetter, Edward. "Recent Studies in the Nineteenth Century." *SEL* 7:741-66.
Victorian scholarship, pp. 750-66.

Boyle, Andrew. *An Index to the Annuals, I: 1820-1850*. London: Andrew Boyle. Pp. 349.
Rev. in *TLS* 5 Oct.:948.

Bradner, Leicester. "*Musae Anglicanae*: A Supplemental List." *Library* 22:93-103.
Supplements a *History of Anglo-Latin Poetry, 1500-1925*.

Brown, R. D. "The Bodley Head Press: Some Bibliographical Extrapolations." *PBSA* 61: 39-50.
The importance of John Lane, publisher, in helping form the Decadent Movement.

Carter, John, and Graham Pollard. *The Forgeries of Tennyson's Plays*. Oxford: Blackwell. Pp. 21. "Working Paper No. 2."
Rev. by Laurence S. Thompson in *PBSA* 61:134-35.
Preliminary study for revised ed. of *An Enquiry into the Nature of Certain Nineteenth Century Pamphlets*; includes detailed information on Tennyson forgeries not to be included in revised book. — E.S.L.

Carter, John, and Graham Pollard. *Précis of Paden or The Sources of "The New Timon."* Oxford: Blackwell. Pp. 24. "Working Paper No. 1."
Rev. by Laurence S. Thompson in *PBSA* 61:134-35.

A Catalogue of Printed Books in the Wellcome Historical Medical Library. II. Books Printed from 1641 to 1850 A-E. . . . See VB 1966, 459.
Rev. by R. Hunter in *Library* 22:270-72.

Chilston, Viscount. *W. H. Smith.* . . . See VB 1966, 459.
Rev. by F. M. L. Thompson in *History* 52:359-61.

Clarke, Marian G. M. *David Watkinson's Library: One Hundred Years in Hartford, Connecticut, 1866-1966*. Hartford, Conn.: Trinity College P., 1966. Pp. xi + 177.
Rev. by David W. Davies in *LQ* 37:234-5.
History of a major special collection in history and literature, now a part of Trinity College Library.

Davies, Alun F. "Paper-Mills and Paper Makers in Wales, 1700-1900." *Natl Lib Wales J* 15:1-30.
Lists locations and proprietors, with statistics. Traces changes which took place with developing technology.

Day, Kenneth (ed.). *Book Typography 1815-1965 in Europe and the United States*. London: Benn.
Rev. by Stanley Hickson in *Publisher* 180 (September): 20,25.
Series of essays on 150 years of printing in various countries, including England, some references to Morris.

Dorsch, T. S., and C. G. Harlow. *The Year's Work in English Studies*. Vol. 46 (1965). London: John Murray. Pp. 416.
The 19th century section is annotated by P. M. Yarker and Brian Lee, pp. 253-93.

Ewing, Douglas C. "The Three-Volume Novel." *PBSA* 61:201-07.
General outline of development of three-vol. publication. Should be compared with C. E. & E. S. Lauterbach, "The Nineteenth Century Three-Volume Novel." *PBSA* 51:263-302.

Freeman, Ronald E. (ed.). "Victorian Bibliography for 1966." *VS* 10:457-517.

Harrison, Brian. "Drink and Sobriety in England 1815-1872: A Critical Bibliography." *International R of Social Hist* 12: 204-76.

Hartzog, Martha. "Nineteenth-Century Cloth Bindings." *PBSA* 61:114-19.

FIG. 7. *Victorian Studies* ("Victorian Bibliography", Section I). (Copyright: the Editors.)

15

and *Deportment from the Thirteénth to the Nineteenth Century.* London: Oxford U.P., 1965. Pp. xiv + 291.

Rev. by Clifford John Williams in *Theatre Notebook* 21:193-94.

Williams, Raymond. "Literature and the City." *Listener* 78:653-56.

Williams, Raymond. *The Long Revolution.* London: Chatto & Windus, 1965. Pp. xiv + 360.

Rev. by M. L. Cazamian in *EA* 20:101-02.

Wolff, Michael. "Charting the Golden Stream: Thoughts on a Directory of Victorian Periodicals" in *Editing Nineteenth-Century Texts,* 37-59. (See III, Robson.)

Woodhouse, A. S. P. *The Poet and His Faith.* . . . See VB 1966, 485.

Rev. by R. Gordon Cox in *N&Q* 14:79-80.

Woolf, Virginia. *Collected Essays,* III-IV. . . . See VB 1966, 485.

Rev. by Donald Hall in *NYTBR* 24 Dec:1; by Patrick Anderson in S 8 Sept:273.

Young, Percy M. (ed.). *Letters to Nimrod: Edward Elgar to August Jaeger, 1897-1908.* . . . See VB 1966, 485.

Rev. by Philip Radcliffe in *VS* 10:339-41.

Youngson, A. J. *The Making of Classical Edinburgh, 1750-1840.* N.Y.: Aldine. Pp. 338.

Rev. by P. Gellantly in *LJ* 92:1931.

Zeitler, Rudolf. *Die Kunst des 19. Jahrhunderts.* Berlin: Propyläen Verlag. Pp. 412 + 628 plates.

Rev. in *TLS* 24 Aug:756.

Zimmermann, George-Denis. *Irish Political Street Ballads and Rebel Songs, 1780-1900.* Genève: Imprimeria La Sirene, 1966. Pp. 342.

Rev. by Colm O Lochlainn in *StI* 56:331-35.

IV. INDIVIDUAL AUTHORS

ACTON (see also II, Milne; IV, NEWMAN: MacDougall).

Conzemius, Victor (ed.). *Ignaz von Döllinger: Briefwechsel, 1820-1890.* Vol. II: *Briefwechsel mit Lord Acton, 1869-70.* . . . See VB 1966, 486.

Rev. by Damian McElrath in *Hist J* 10: 318-21; by Owen Chadwick in *J of Eccl Hist* 18:124-25.

Schoeck, R. J. S. "Lord Acton as a Literary

Critic." *Rivista di letterature moderne e comparate* (Florence) 20:53-61.

Acton deserves to be compared "with the best minds of his age"—Newman, Arnold, and George Henry Lewes.

ADAMS.

Jones, Edgar. "Francis Adams, 1862-1893: A Forgotten Child of His Age." *Essays & Studies by Members of Engl Assoc* 20: 76-103.

On Adams's *A Child of the Age* (1894).

AINSWORTH (see also I, Smith).

ALLINGHAM.

Grigson, Geoffrey (ed.). *William Allingham's Diary.* London: Centaur P. Pp. xii + 404.

Rev. by Richard Church in *Country Life* 142:1438.

Warner, Alan. "The Diary of William Allingham." *Dublin Magazine* 6,ii:20-28.

ARCHER.

Schmidt, Hans. *The Dramatic Criticism of William Archer.* . . . See VB 1966, 486.

Rev. by J. C. Amalric in *EA* 20:99.

ARNOLD (see also III, Casey, Cook; IV, ACTON: Schoeck; HARDY: DeLaura; WILDE: DeLaura).

Alaya, Flavia M. "Arnold and Renan on the Popular Uses of History." *JHI* 28:551-74.

Finds similarities between the two as students of culture and "popularizers" of ideas.

Alaya, Flavia M. " 'Two Worlds' Revisited: Arnold, Renan, The Monastic Life, and the 'Stanzas from the Grande Chartreuse.' " *VP* 5:237-54.

Alexander, Edward. "Matthew Arnold and John Stuart Mill." *DA* 27:4213A (Minnesota).

Alexander, Edward. *Matthew Arnold and John Stuart Mill.* . . . See VB 1966, 486.

Rev. by R. H. Super in *MLQ* 27:347-49 (and see letter by Edward Alexander, 28: 126-28); by James Steintrager in *R of Politics* 28(1966):537-40; by David DeLaura in *Southwestern Social Science Q* 46 (1966):460-61; in *TLS* 2 Feb:90.

Alexander, Edward. "Roles of the Victorian Critic: Matthew Arnold and John Ruskin," *English Institute Essays,* pp. 53-84.

Comments on an article in the *Westminster Review* of Oct. 1863 contrasting Arnold and Ruskin as critics, considering Arnold "a model of the critical temper."

Allott, Kenneth (ed.). *The Poems of Matthew Arnold.* . . . See VB 1966, 455.

Rev. by Arnold B. Fox in *Amer Bk Coll*

FIG. 8. *Victorian Studies* ("Victorian Bibliography", Sections III–IV). (Copyright: the Editors.)

GENERAL GUIDES TO THE LITERATURE

religious, and social environment" (Secton II), and "The arts, movements of ideas, and literary forms" (Section III). Entries for books include references to reviews which they received. The early bibliographies have been collected in 3 volumes under the title *Bibliographies of Studies in Victorian Literature* (Urbana, Univ. of Illinois Pr., 1945, 1956, 1967), edited by W. D. Templeman (1932–44), A. Wright (1945–54), and R. C. Slack (1955–64).

The volume by R. C. Slack contains an introductory survey in which he notes that, although the policy of the bibliography has always been to list the noteworthy publications which have a bearing on Victorian literature, the work has aimed at greater inclusiveness since the bibliography was transferred from *Modern Philology* to *Victorian Studies*. In particular, the number of entries in the section devoted to "Economic, political, religious, and social environment" has increased markedly. To balance this the review comment has been reduced. The character of the bibliography has thus changed from a selective guide with at times lengthy review comment to a more inclusive list of new contributions to the study of the period. In his introduction Slack offers a most valuable and interesting analysis of some recent trends in Victorian scholarship as revealed by a study of successive bibliographies.

A shorter regular general list of recent works on the Victorian period in books and periodicals is included under the title "Recent publications: a selected list" in the *Victorian Newsletter* (New York, Univ. Pr., for the English X Group of the Modern Language Association).

Theses

The extensive research currently in progress on the Victorian period makes it essential for the student to check regularly lists of completed theses in order to avoid duplicating work already undertaken. The major British guide to thesis material is the *Index to British Theses* (Aslib, 1950/1–). This provides an annual list of postgraduate theses in classified order with author and subject indexes (Fig. 9).

American theses are similarly listed in subject groups with author and subject indexes in the monthly *Dissertation Abstracts* (Ann Arbor, University Microfilms, 1952–). Earlier volumes, covering the period 1935–51, were entitled *Microfilm Abstracts*. The list is confined to successful doctoral dissertations. Unlike the British *Index to Theses* this includes notes on the content and scope of each dissertation. Photographic copies of all works included are available for purchase.

Theses entered in *Dissertation Abstracts* are also listed in the *Index to American Doctoral Dissertations* which, since 1956, has constituted an extra annual issue of *Dissertation Abstracts*. The *Index*, which is compiled for the Association of Research Libraries, includes all successful doctoral dissertations in the United States and Canada whether or not these have been made available to University Microfilms for copying. From 1933/4 to 1954/5 this work appeared as *Doctoral Dissertations Accepted by American Universities* (New York, Wilson).

An older guide to theses is the *List of American Doctoral Dissertations Printed in 1912–38*, compiled by the Library of Congress (26 vols., Washington, Government Printing Office, 1913–40).

Abstracts of American Masters' theses, of which copies are available, are collected in the quarterly *Masters Abstracts* (Ann Arbor, University Microfilms, 1962–).

It should be noted that many individual universities publish regular lists or abstracts of their own successful theses.

Anonymous and Pseudonymous Authors

The identification of authors of books published anonymously or pseudonymously is a frequent problem in the Victorian period, though the problem is certainly even more acute in the study of periodical literature than in the examination of separately published works. For books and pamphlets the standard guide is S. Halkett and J. Laing, *Dictionary of Anonymous and Pseudonymous*

EDUCATION

811. HENDRIKZ, E. (LBkC). A cross-cultural investigation of the number concepts and level of number development in five-year-old urban Shona and European children in Southern Rhodesia. M.A.

812. HEIGHTON, C. (M). Some enquiries into visual imagery in primary school children. M.ED.

813. MATTHEWS, S. H. (No). The development of concepts in physics at the secondary stage of education. M.ED.

814. HARRHY, B. C. (W, *Swansea*). An investigation of substance, weight, volume, density, and related concepts in 10- to 12-year-old children. M.Sc.

History of Education in Gt. Britain and Ireland

815. MONAGHAN, J. L. (B). Some influences and attitudes which affected the provision and development of industrial education in England between 1850 and 1889. M.ED.

816. TURNER, E. E. (B). A history of education in Dudley, 1850–1903. M.ED.

817. SANDERSON, J. M. (C). The basic education of labour in Lancashire, 1780–1839. PH.D.

818. BASSETT, F. C. (D). The development of higher education in Leeds, 1800–1907. M.ED.

819. JENNINGS, E. (D). The development of education in the North Riding of Yorkshire, 1902–1939. M.ED.

820. PALLISTER, R. (D). An economic study of elementary education in County Durham in the early part of the nineteenth century. M.ED.

821. HANNAWAY, O. (G). Early university courses of chemistry. PH.D.

822. PEERS, F. G. (H). The development of Roman Catholic popular education in some midland counties in the nineteenth century. M.ED.

823. DOCKING, J. W. (Le). The development of Church of England schools in Coventry, 1811–1944. M.ED.

824. ROGERS, C. D. (Le). The history of charity schools in Bowdon, Cheshire. M.ED.

825. ZOLA, M. (Le). A critical survey of the testing of oral and written French free composition in English schools, from 1857 to the present day. M.ED.

826. FLUDE, W. E. (Lei). The development of science teaching in English "senior" and secondary modern schools. M.ED.

827. JONES, J. C. (Lei). The Labour Movement in relation to state secondary education, 1902–1924. M.ED.

828. TURNER, C. M. (Lei). The development of Mechanics' Institutes in Warwickshire, Worcestershire and Staffordshire, 1825–1890: a regional survey. M.ED.

829. PARTON, J. G. (Li). The development of the teaching of history in schools in England during the nineteenth and twentieth centuries. M.ED.

830. FACER, P. (LQMC). A history of Hipperholme School from 1660 to 1914, with a biography of its founder, Matthew Brodley (1586–1648). M.A.

41

FIG. 9. *Index to British Theses.* (Copyright: Aslib.)

ANNALS of the Peninsular campaigns from 1808 to 1814. By the author of *Cyril Thornton* [Captain Thomas Hamilton]. 3 vols. Fcap 8vo. [*Camb. Univ. Cat.*]   Edinburgh, 1829

ANNALS of the rescued. By the author of *Haste to the rescue* [Mrs Charles E. L. Wightman]. Fcap 8vo. [*Brit. Mus.*]   London, 1860

ANNALS of the road, or notes on mail and stage coaching in Great Britain. [By Captain Malet, 18th Hussars.] To which are added Essays on the road, by Nimrod [Charles James Apperley]. 8vo. Pp. xiii., 404.   London, 1876

ANNALS of the [Edinburgh] Round Table Club. Edited by J. G. M. [John G— M'Kendrick, M.D., Professor in Glasgow University]. 8vo. Pp. 161.
          Private print [Stonehaven], 1908

ANNALS of the Founders' Company. [By —— Williams.] 8vo.
          London, private print, 1867

ANNALS of the Skinners' Craft in Glasgow, from its incorporation in 1516 to the year 1616. [By William H. Hill.] 4to. [*Mitchell Lib.*]
          Glasgow, 1875

ANNALS of the twenty-ninth century; or, the autobiography of the Tenth President of the World Republic. [By Andrew Blair, M.D., Tayport.] 3 vols. 8vo.   London, 1874
Editorial note signed : "Stephenson Watt."

ANNALS of the virgin saints. By a priest of the Church of England [John Mason Neale, D.D.] Fcap 8vo. [*D.N.B.*, vol. 40, p. 145.] London, 1846

ANNALS of Thornlea [in Westruther]. [By A— Thomson, F.S.A.] 8vo.
          Galashiels, 1899

ANNANDALE ; a story of the times of the Covenanters. By Martha Farquharson [Mrs Martha Finley]. Fcap 8vo. [Cushing's *Init. and Pseud.*, i., p. 99.]   Philadelphia, N.D. [1856]

ANNE, and other tales. By Johnny Ludlow [Ellen Price, later Mrs Wood]. 8vo. [Cushing's *Init. and Pseud.*, i., p. 176.]   London, 1885

ANNE and Pierre ; or, our father's letter. By K. M. [Katharine M'Clellan]. 8vo. [Cushing's *Init. and Pseud.*, i., p. 179.]
          New York, 1865

ANNE Cave ; a tale, in three volumes. By Kenner Deene, author of *The dull stone house*, etc. [Charlotte Smith]. Fcap 8vo. [*Bodl.*]   London, 1864

ANNE Dysart ; a tale of every-day life. [By Christiana Jane Douglas, later Mrs Davies.] 3 vols. 8vo. [*Bodl.*]
          London, 1850

ANNE Furness [a novel]. By the author of *Aunt Margaret's trouble* [Frances Milton, later Mrs T. Anthony Trollope]. 3 vols. 8vo. [*Brit. Mus.*]
          London, 1871

ANNE Gray [a novel]. [By Lady Harriet Cradock, *née* Lister.] Edited by the author of *Granby* [her brother, Thomas Henry Lister]. 3 vols. Fcap 8vo. [Simm's *Bibl. Staff.*, p. 284].
          London, 1834

ANNE Mauleverer [a novel]. By "Iota" [Mrs Mannington Caffyn]. Cr 8vo. [*Lit. Year Book.*]   London, 1899

ANNE of Geierstein ; or, the maiden of the mist. By the author of *Waverley*, etc. [Sir Walter Scott, Bart.]. 3 vols. Post 8vo.   Edinburgh, 1829

ANNE Severin. By the author of *Le récit d'une Sœur* [Mrs Pauline Craven. Translated from the French by Lady Georgiana C. Fullerton]. 3 vols. 8vo. [*Camb. Univ. Lib.*]
          London, 1869

ANNE Sherwood ; or, social institutions of England. By Berkley Aikin [Frances Aikin Kortwright]. 3 vols. 8vo. [Cushing's *Init. and Pseud.*, i., p. 8.]   London, 1857

ANNESLEY Court ; or, Isabel Grant's story. By Adeline [Emily Frances Adeline Sergeant]. 8vo. [*D. N. B.*, *Second Supp.*, iii., p. 291.]
          London, 1872

ANNETTE ; or, ears to hear. By the author of *St Olave's* [Eliza Tabor, later Mrs Stephenson]. Fcap 8vo. [*Brit. Mus.*]   London, 1863

ANNEXATION (the) of Texas. By G. [John M. Galt]. 8vo. [Cushing's *Init. and Pseud.*, ii., p. 62.]
          Williamsburg, Virginia, 1852

ANNIE Balfour and her friends ; or, influence and how to use it. By "Theta" [Julia Putnam Henderson]. 12mo. [Kirk's *Supp.*]
          New York, 1870

FIG. 10. S. Halkett and J. Laing, *Dictionary of Anonymous and Pseudonymous English Literature*. (Copyright: Oliver & Boyd Ltd.)

English Literature (Fig. 10), the revised edition of which was published in 7 volumes between 1926 and 1934, with 2 further supplements in 1956 and 1962 (Edinburgh, Oliver & Boyd). Coverage of nineteenth-century works is good.

Two works by W. Cushing are also useful: *Anonyms: a dictionary of revealed authorship* (Cambridge, Mass., Cushing, 1889) and the 2-volume *Initials and Pseudonyms: a dictionary of literary disguises* (New York, Crowell, 1885–8).

CHAPTER 3

Victorian Periodicals and Newspapers

THE increasing recognition of the importance of Victorian periodicals and newspapers for the study of the period has been forcibly emphasized in recent years by the publication in 1966 of the first volume of *The Wellesley Index to Victorian Periodicals, 1824–1900*, edited by W. E. Houghton (Toronto, Univ. Pr.), and the commencement in January 1968 of the *Victorian Periodicals Newsletter*, published in Bloomington by the *Victorian Studies* Office.* The problems of studying Victorian periodicals are, however, enormous. The vast number of periodicals, together with the difficulties raised by the widespread practice of anonymous authorship, make the field very difficult to examine. W. E. Houghton has noted in the *Victorian Periodicals Newsletter* (no. 1, January 1968, p. 13) that "The great Victorian journals have been neglected because, in good part, the maps which the scholar needs in order to explore such a large, uncharted territory have not been available". Houghton estimates that during the period 1824–1900, 85–90 per cent of all articles were anonymous or pseudonymous.

M. Wolff has contributed an extremely valuable paper, "Charting the golden stream: thoughts on a directory of Victorian periodicals", in *Editing Nineteenth-century Texts*, edited by J. M. Robson (Toronto, Univ. Pr., 1967). In this paper Wolff suggests several reasons why "full and free use" of Victorian newspapers and periodicals is difficult. He notes the enormous scale of the material, estimated at thousands of serials and millions of articles, the scarcity of many titles, and the general inadequacy of bibliographies and finding-lists.

*Since this was written a Research Society for Victorian Periodicals has been established with *Victorian Periodicals Newsletter* as its official organ.

Lists of Periodicals

The basic problem of discovering what periodicals and news-papers were published during the period is partly solved by various existing lists. There is, however, no reliable comprehensive guide. The obvious need for such a work is now being met by the Victorian Periodicals Project under the supervision of M. Wolff at Indiana University. One of the aims of this project is to compile a list of all periodicals and newspapers published during the period. The project also seeks to examine how far copies of these serials still exist and to help in making them available by modern copying techniques.

The publication of the *Victorian Periodicals Newsletter* (Fig. 11) is a direct outcome of this work. The editor has stated that "The *Newsletter* should be thought of both as a publication in its own right and as a way of multiplying almost indefinitely the Project's correspondence with individual scholars".

The basic nineteenth-century guide to this material is the *Newspaper Press Directory*, published by C. Mitchell & Co. from 1846. At first irregular—no volumes were published during 1848–50, 1852–3, and 1855—this became established as an annual directory of newspapers and periodicals. It provides notes on date of commencement, frequency of publication and area of circulation, and indicates religious and political allegiance. The *Directory* includes, in addition to an alphabetical list, a geo-graphical list, a list arranged by broad subject groups, and lists of religious papers by denomination and of trade papers by trades. The large number of advertisements also give additional infor-mation about contents, circulation, and policy. Volumes published between 1846 and 1907 were issued on microfilm in 1968 by Microcard Editions of Washington.

Willing's Press Guide, which commenced publication in 1874, constitutes another useful annual guide to British newspapers and periodicals. This work provides basic information about the publication of serials listed but does not attempt such extensive classification as the *Newspaper Press Directory*.

56. THE VICTORIAN PERIODICALS PROJECT

Michael Wolff

In the first number of VPN I said that I would describe my work, both for the sake of the information and because this Newsletter itself is an important by-product of it. Since it wasn't clear to me how I could include enough detail without seeming pretentious, I thought I would risk the latter and present a slightly emended version of my report to the foundations (Chapelbrook and Council on Library Resources) who made the work possible.

My current interest in periodicals began in the course of my research in the British Museum in the fall of 1964 in the speculation that any general study of Victorian England that was to be sufficiently rich in detail required careful attention to Victorian journalism. However, when I tried to discover the currency or relevance of newspapers and periodicals, I was constantly stymied by lack of directories and other reference materials. In order to focus on both this problem and my research interests, I decided to see how difficult it was to find out what newspapers and periodicals were published in London during a given week. I chose at random the last week in October 1864 and by working with the British Museum Catalogue and other sources I came up with a surprising but probably incomplete total of nearly 750. Since this was obviously too large a number to investigate in detail I tried to do two things: first, to compile a simple record of this cross-section, and, second, to take a smaller sample and study it. The result was, "The Victorian Week that Was: Pearls from the Golden Stream," delivered at the Anglo-American Conference of Historians (London, July 1965) and further developed in "Pearls from the Golden Stream: Cultural History and Victorian Periodicals," given at the Midwest Conference of British Studies (Madison, Wis., November 1965). The response to these two papers was especially interesting in this regard: almost everyone who commented on the paper apparently learned something about his own area of specialization.

The inherent fascination of the material, the great difficulty in using it, the likelihood that, once made available, it would be extremely useful to a great range of scholars prompted me to commit myself to the Victorian Periodicals Project. I felt that my position as an editor of Victorian Studies and the presence of the Victorian Studies office as a sort of profession-wide headquarters gave me an unrivalled opportunity to do pioneer work in an area too complex for most individual scholars. The nature of the Project called for research assistants and materials and I therefore developed a research proposal for a feasibility study in the bibliography of Victorian journalism. This proposal was submitted to a number of foundations and received favorable replies from two -- The Chapelbrook Foundation and the Council on Library Resources -- who awarded me funds for research in Victorian periodicals through the summer of 1968.

FIG. 11. *Victorian Periodicals Newsletter*. (Copyright: the Editor.)

The most extensive collection of British newspapers and periodicals published at fortnightly or more frequent intervals is housed in the British Museum Newspaper Library at Colindale. Other periodicals, published at less frequent intervals, such as monthlies and quarterlies, are housed in the main collections. It should be noted that the Newspaper Library contains partial indexes to a number of its Victorian periodicals. In 1905 the British Museum issued a catalogue of *Newspapers Published in Great Britain and Ireland, 1801–1900,* providing lists of newspapers in an alphabetical sequence and by place of publication.

In 1920 *The Times* issued a *Tercentenary Handlist of English and Welsh Newspapers, Magazines and Reviews* (reprinted Dawsons, 1966). This is a chronological bibliography, together with title indexes, from 1620 to 1919 (Fig. 12). Works published in London and the provinces are listed separately. The *Handlist* is based initially on the British Museum collections.

H. and S. Rosenberg have compiled an extensive selection of nineteenth-century newspapers and magazines and writings about them for the *New Cambridge Bibliography of English Literature,* edited by G. Watson. The nineteenth-century volume of the *Bibliography* was published during 1969. The initial list, compiled by H. G. Pollard for the first edition of the *Cambridge Bibliography of English Literature* (CUP, 1940) has been completely revised and expanded. Despite the great difficulties of selection and presentation, the list contains an enormous amount of information. As the new edition continues the practice of adopting a broad definition of literature, it is also useful to students in a wide range of subject fields outside English literature.

The two major guides to locations of periodicals are the *British Union-Catalogue of Periodicals* (Butterworths) and the *Union List of Serials in Libraries of the United States and Canada* (New York, Wilson). The *British Union-Catalogue* (Fig. 13) records holdings in British libraries of periodicals in all languages. Details are entered under the earliest form of the title. Changes of title are noted and there are adequate cross-references from later to earlier titles. The titles form a single alphabetical sequence. Against

South African. No. 1.-156. Nov. 4, 1880
—Oct. 25, 1883.
Agricultural Engineer. No. 1-4. Dec. 1880—March 1881.
Coventry's Weekly Advertiser. No. 1. Dec. 3, 1880—June 24, 1881.
Mid-Surrey Standard. No. 233. Dec. 11, 1880—Sept. 24, 1881. Continued as Surrey Independent.
Radical. No. 1. Dec. 14, 1880—July, 1882.
War Cry and Official Gazette of the Salvation Army. No. 1. Dec. 27, 1880 —In progress.

1881.

Seeking and Saving, &c. 1881-90
The Scholastic Gazette. 1881-83
Household Words. (Ed. Chas. Dickens, the Younger.) 1881—In progress.
The Actor and Elocutionist, &c. 1881
The Family Doctor. 1881-83
English Etchings. (Ed. W.H.M.) Set 1-97. 1881-91
The English Stationer. &c. 1881-86.
Lobb's Theological Quarterly, with which is incorporated Dickenson's Theological Quarterly. Vol. 1. 1881.
The Legal Advertiser. No. 1-36. 1881-84.
The Little Papers and the M(ission) P(arcel) S(ociety). 1881-91. Continued as Monthly Papers of Mission News. 1892. And as Short Papers of Mission News. Quarterly. 1892-94.
The Charity Record and Philanthropic News. 1881—In progress.
Bible Light, &c. 1881-1892.
The Bell News and Ringers Record, &c. 1881—In progress.
The Preachers Monthly, &c. (Ed. W. Hope Davison.) 1881-85.
Art and Letters, &c. 1881-83.
The Antiquarian Magazine and Bibliographer. Vol. 1-10 (Ed. by E. Walford.) Vol. 11-12. (Ed. G. W. Redway.) Vol. 1-12. 1881-87.
The Christian Church. Vol. 1-4. 1881-84.
Celebrities of the Day, British and Foreign (Ed. S. E. Thomas.) Vol. 1-3. 1881-82.
The Catholic Literary Circular, &c. 1881-82.
The Burlington ; a high class monthly magazine. (Ed. H. B. Mathers.) 1881-82.
The Lantern. No. 1-12. 1881.
The Kneph. Official journal of the ancient and primitive rite of masonry, &c. (Ed. K. R. H. Mackenzie.) 1881-95.
The Practical Teacher, &c. (Ed. J. Hughes.) 1881—In progress.
The National Temperance Mirror. 1881-1907.
The Ophthalmic Review, a monthly record

Something to Read. (Ed. E. 1881—In progress.
The Sons of Temperance (Org Sons of Temperance). 188 gress.
The Rosebud. A monthly m: nursery nature and amuseme 1914.
Weldon's Bazaar of Children's 1881—In progress.
The Zoophilist, &c. 1881—In
The Voice of Warning. (Protes Society.) 1881-94. Continue Voice of Truth. 1895-99.
The Wheel World, &c. (Ed. I 1881-86. Continued as Olymp
The Whitefield Magazine. (E Wray.) 1881-84.
The Food Reform Magazine.
The Craftsman. 'A constitution dustrial review. Vol: 5-6. N 1881-86.
East and West. A quarterly literary, philosophical and sc 1. 1881.
The Drawing Room, Concert a 1881-83.
The Yachting Record, Remembr Advertiser. 1881-82.
The Metal World, a weekly jc engineers, &c. 1881-82.
Medical News and Collegiate 1881. Continued as the Medi 1882-83.
The Sporting Mirror. (Ed. " I 1881-85.
The Spottiswoode Magazine. 1881.
The Sugar-Plum ; a literary s for all. No. 1. 1881.
Our Little Ones, &c. (Ed. W. T 1881-83.
Our Times. No. 1-2. 1881.
The Orchid Album, &c. (Ed. R B. S. Williams, and others. figures by J. N. Fitch. 1881-
The Monthly Military Budget Army and Auxiliary Forces. :
Caterer and Hotel Keeper's Gaz 33. Jan. 1881—In progres
The Baptist Visitor. Jan., 1881—I
Lewisham and West Kent News Jan. 1, 1881—Oct. 2, 1885.
Educational Chronicle. No. 53- 1—June 25, 1881.
Wool and Textile Fabrics. N Jan. 1, 1881—Nov. 7, 1890.
Official Prices Current. Jan. 4 April 2, 1886. Incorporated w Recorder of Commerce.
Light. No. 1. Jan. 7, 1881—In
Journal of the Vigilance Associat

FIG. 12. *Tercentenary Handlist of English and Welsh Newspapers, Magazines and Reviews.* (Copyright: *The Times* (The Times Newpapers Ltd.))

VICTORIA

Victoria university of Manchester=**Owens college.**

Victoria university occasional papers. Victoria college. University. **Toronto.**

Victorian, The. A journal for the past and present members of Victoria college [Jersey]. 1-?, 2s 1-?, 3s 1-?, 4s 1-17[5]. 18..?-April 1940. *then b* Victoria college news. 1. Nov. 1940. *then* News letter ⟨O.V. news letter⟩. ⟨Victoria college at Bedford.⟩ 2-11. Summer 1941-Feb. 1946. *then* The Victorian. 18- . May 1946- . L a iv 7- (July 1905-); O b.

Victorian, The. 1-2[92]. Melbourne. 5 July 1862-2 April 1864. L.

Victorian, The. 1-2[2]. ⟨1897-98.⟩ L 1[1], 2[1-2].

Victorian, The. ⟨Queen Victoria school, Dunblane.⟩ Stirling. 1923- . L.

Victorian, The. ⟨Victoria institution.⟩ 1- . Selangor. 1925?- . L 2- (March 1926-).

"Victorian", C.P.O.S. *see* **North Atlantic times.**

Victorian agricultural and **horticultural gazette,** The. 1-4. Geelong. 1858-60. L (*w* 1[2]).

Victorian artists society. **Australian artist.**

Victorian Baptist magazine, The. 1-8. Melbourne. 1868-69. L.

Victorian diocesan association. **Outpost,** 1919[?]- .

Victorian engineers' association ⟨Victorian institute of engineers⟩.
— Proceedings ⟨Papers and discussions⟩. 1- . 1883/85- . Melbourne. 1917- . BlU 3 (1899/1902); GE *1912-13, 1915, 1923-38;* NwA 9-14, 16; *1925-28.*

Victorian golf association research section. Bulletin. 1-4. 1935-38. ByG 2-4 (1936-38).

Victorian geographical journal=Transactions. Victorian branch. R. **Geographical society** of **Australasia.**

Victorian Hansard, The. Containing the debates and proceedings of the Legislative council and assembly of the colony of Victoria. 1-11. Melbourne. 1857-65. L.

Victorian historical magazine, The. ⟨Historical society of Victoria.⟩ 1- . Melbourne. 1911- . [*Absorbed the* Proceedings of the Geographical society of Australasia New South Wales and Victorian branches.] L; ORH.

Victorian institute for the **advancement** of **science.** Transactions. 1854-June 1855. Melbourne. 1855. [*Then merged in the* Transactions of the Philosophical society of Victoria.] L.

Victorian institute of **architects,** R.
— Journal ⟨of proceedings⟩. 1- . Melbourne. 1903- . LIA 1-39 (1903-42); LVA *1912-42.*
— Quarterly bulletin. LIA July 1948-
— Architectural students' society.
——Journal ⟨Lines⟩. LIA 1939-40.

Victorian monthly magazi ⟨1859.⟩ L.

Victorian naturalist, The. the Field naturalists' club c 1885- . C; KB; L; LSC 54

Victorian poultry journal, bourne. [*Absorbed* Utility.]

Victorian pulpit, The. 1-7.

Victorian ruff or pocket racing 1861-63. L (*w* 1862).

Victorian year book. Statist's

Victories illustrated, The. exhibition gazette. 1. Man

Victory. ⟨1920.⟩ L.

Victory ⟨now and after⟩. Th 1-5[4]. ⟨1939⟩-⟨45⟩. *then* Vi 1946-Spring 1948. *then* Hun 1948- . [*Absorbed* World c O 2-10[2].

Victory ⟨bulletin⟩, 1941-43=**D**

Victory now and after=**Victo**

Victory for peace=**Victory,** 1

"Victory for **Socialism"** ca 1- . 1934- . L.

Victualling trades review=**Sco trade review.**

Vida hispánica. A bi-mont students of Spanish and Port Brazilian councils.⟩ 1-6[2]. I *then b* The New vida hispánic Spanish and Portuguese.⟩ 1

Vida marítima &*c.* Madrid.

Vida médica. Rio de Janeiro

Vida municipal. 1[1]. Ciudac

Vida nueva. 1- . Habana. 1 LMA *1944-* ; LMD 19-23*,

Vida e o pensamento na Gr: **thought.**

Vida y pensamiento británicos=

Vida portuguesa, A. Boletir 1[1-20]. Pôrto. 31 Oct. 1912-

Vida sobrenatural. Salamar

Vidar. Et ugeskrift, udgivet a 1-4. Christiania. 5 Aug. 18

Видавництво "Час" у Київі [1-4[40]. [Kiev. 1910.] L.

Видавництво "Кубанський кр krai"] Риппипа Ритлвии·

each title library holdings are noted, each library being indicated by a letter or group of letters. The work was published in 4 volumes during 1955–8 with a supplement to 1960 in 1962. Since 1964 it has been issued as a quarterly periodical which constitutes a continuing supplement to the previous volumes and also to the *World List of Scientific Periodicals*.

The *Union List* follows a similar pattern to the *British Union-Catalogue* except that periodicals are entered under the latest form of title. The third edition in 1965 comprised 5 volumes, listing the holdings of 956 libraries and covering the period to 1949. Holdings of periodicals published from 1950 are recorded in *New Serial Titles* (Washington, Library of Congress).

Both the *British Union-Catalogue* and the *Union List* are invaluable to students of the Victorian period. They provide a finding list for the location of copies of periodicals and also act as bibliographies, clarifying the often confusing changes of title and variations in numbering with the commencement of new series. For periodicals they constitute the most comprehensive guides at present available.

Indexes

The basis of all study of nineteenth-century periodical literature is the pioneer work of the American librarian, W. F. Poole (Fig. 14). *Poole's Index to Periodical Literature* (Boston, Houghton; reprinted Gloucester, Mass., P. Smith, 1963) consists, in its final form, of the basic work covering the period 1802–81 and 5 quinquennial supplements carrying the index to 1906. Four hundred and seventy-nine American and British periodicals are indexed by subject, but there is no attempt to compile an author index or to identify the authorship of articles. There are, of course, notable omissions among the periodicals included. The selection of subject headings is at times misleading and inconsistent. The treatment of book reviews is inadequate. Nevertheless, despite its inevitable deficiencies, the *Index* remains as a work of major importance, combining remarkable industry and appreciation of scholarly requirements with considerable technical expertise. In

IMAGES 625

Images, Generic, and Automatic Representation, Galton on. (G. C. Robertson) Mind, 4: 551. — 19th Cent. 6: 157. Same art. Pop. Sci. Mo, 15: 532.
— in Churches, Use of. U. S. Cath. M. 4: 491.
— Veneration of. Brownson, 7: 39.
Image Worship in the Church, Early. Chr. Obs. 77: 30.
— History of. Ecl. R. 86: 720.
Imagery, Mental, Galton on Statistics of. (A. Bain) Mind, 5: 564.
Imaginary Conversation, An. (F. B. Perkins) Putnam, 13: 358.
Imaginary Conversations. (W. S. Landor) Fraser, 52: 560. 53: 443.
Imaginary Quantities, Buëe on. (H. Brougham) Ed. R. 12: 306.
— Geometrical Interpretation of. (M. Argand) Ecl. Engin. 24: 16-313.
— Woodhouse on. (H. Brougham) Ed. R. 1: 407.
Imagination. (O. A. Brownson) Dem. R. 12: 48. — (E. Coues) Pop. Sci. Mo. 11: 455. — So. Lit. Mess. 21: 226.
— and Fact. Am. Whig R. 14: 392.
-- and Fancy, Hunt's. Dub. Univ. 25: 649. Same art. Ecl. M. 5: 500.
— and Language. (M. C. Putnam) Putnam, 11: 301.
— as a national Characteristic. St. Paul's, 4: 61.
— as the plastic Principle of Nature, Frohschammer on.

IMMORTALITY 625

Immaturity; Discourse on Veal. (A. K. H. Boyd) Fraser. 64: 199. Same art. Ecl. M. 54: 193. Same art. Liv. Age, 70: 643.
Immeritus Redivivus; a Romanesque. Sharpe, 17: 1-160.
Immermann, Karl. New Münchhausen. For. Q. 31: 1.
Immigrant, The. (J. Sill) Godey, 25: 180, 217.
— in Canada. (T. White) Canad. Mo. 2: 2.
Immigrant's Progress. (W. H. Rideing) Scrib. 14: 577.
Immigrants, Protection to. Republic, 1: 577.
Immigration. (F. Kapp) Am. Soc. Sci. J. 2: 1. — (T. White) Canad. Mo. 1: 193. — Bank. M. (N. Y.) 30: 173. — De Bow, 18: 699.
— Evils and Dangers of. (W. Barrows) New Eng. 13: 262.
— Juvenile Pauper. Canad. Mo. 12: 292.
— Labor, and Prices. (H. Clarke) Bank. M. (L.) 13: 731.
— Philosophy of. (W. Brown) Canad. Mo. 15: 696. — (J. G. McGee) Cath. World, 9: 399.
— to the United States. (E. Jarvis) Atlan. 29: 454. — (W. J. Mann) Mercersb. 2: 620. — (A. H. Everett) No. Am. 40: 457. — (O. C. Gardiner) Am. Whig R. 6: 455, 633. 7: 419. — Niles's Reg. 14: 380. 18: 157. — De Bow, 5: 243. 21: 574.
— German. (E. Everett) No. Am. 11: 1.
— in 1790-1852. (L. Schade) Hunt, 33: 509.
See Emigration.
Immorality in Authorship. (R. Buchanan) Fortn. 6: 289.

FIG. 14. Poole's Index to Periodical Literature. (Copyright: Peter Smith.)

all it succeeds in indexing more than 12,000 separate periodical volumes and provides more than 590,000 references.

In 1957 M. V. Bell and J. C. Bacon compiled *Poole's Index: date and volume key* (Chicago, Association of College and Reference Libraries). This identifies the actual years in which volumes indexed by Poole were published. The *Key* greatly facilitates the use of Poole's work. It is also valuable for its introduction which traces the growth of the *Index* and for an essay entitled "Muted voices from the past" by J. C. Hepler, which outlines the history and significance of nineteenth-century periodicals.

In 1944 H. G. Cushing and A. V. Morris edited the first 2 volumes of an ambitious project to compile a modern index to nineteenth-century periodicals. In the event, however, no further volumes appeared and the work remains in its incomplete state as the *Nineteenth Century Readers' Guide to Periodical Literature, 1890–1899, with Supplementary Indexing 1900–1922* (New York, Wilson). Only 51 periodicals are indexed, and of these only 13 are British. Authors, subjects and illustrations are indexed. Book reviews are entered under authors' names. An attempt is made to identify anonymous authors, mostly from publishers' lists. Some supplementary indexing of periodicals which continued after 1899 is included down to 1922.

From 1890 to 1902 contents of selected periodicals were noted in the *Annual Index to Periodicals* which formed a supplement and an index to the *Review of Reviews*. This index was largely the outcome of the initiative of the editor W. T. Stead, who wrote perceptively, if pompously, in his preface to the first volume: "An index can never pretend to be light reading for an idle hour, but it is the indispensable key which opens the storehouse of knowledge." This is primarily a subject index, but some author entries are also included. In each entry the reference is given not only for the article itself, but also for a summary or notice of it if one has appeared in the monthly numbers of the survey periodical, *Review of Reviews*. The index is particularly useful in covering many periodicals not indexed by Poole.

The most important recent attempt to index the contents of Victorian periodicals is *The Wellesley Index to Victorian Periodicals, 1824–1900*, edited by W. E. Houghton. The first volume of this work (Toronto, Univ. Pr., 1966) indexes 8 major monthly and quarterly serials: *Blackwood's Edinburgh Magazine, The Contemporary Review, The Cornhill Magazine, The Edinburgh Review, The Home and Foreign Review, Macmillan's Magazine, The North British Review*, and *The Quarterly Review*. The contents of each issue of the periodicals are arranged in tabular form (Fig. 15). Poetry, however, is not included in the listing. If the title of an article is not self-explanatory, the subject is indicated in square brackets. Similarly, books reviewed within articles are noted in square brackets after the title of the article. Authors are identified wherever possible, and the evidence for the attribution of anonymous and psuedonymous articles is cited. Identification is based on external evidence rather than on stylistic characteristics. Of the 27,000 entries for the contents of the 8 periodicals indexed in the first volume, the authorship of 97 per cent has been either established or suggested. Uncertain identification is clearly indicated by the use of the coding "prob." or "?", according to the degree of doubt which remains.

The second section of the volume lists articles and stories under the names of authors (Fig. 16); 4780 authors are listed. This section serves as a contribution to the bibliography of these authors, and also provides a convenient guide to the location of the original date and place of periodical publication of a novel or of an article or story later published elsewhere either in separate form or in the collected writings of the author. The third section of the volume comprises an index of pseudonyms and initials, supplementing that compiled by S. Halkett and J. Laing for books and pamphlets in the *Dictionary of Anonymous and Pseudonymous English Literature*.

A further volume of *The Wellesley Index* is projected to cover 30 more periodicals, and there may be additional volumes later. The second volume will be arranged on the same plan as the first. When this is published, the contributions of some 7000

250   *Contemporary Review*, 33 (Aug. 1878)—34 (Feb. 1879)

1316 Contemporary life and thought (No. I): in Italy, 155–165. **Angelo de Gubernatis**. Signed.
1317 Contemporary life and thought (No. II): in Russia, 165–179. Signed: T.S. **Elizaveta D. Bezobrazova**. Cf. no. 1235.
1318 Contemporary essays and comments, 180–189.
1319 Contemporary literature, 190–212.

VOLUME 33, SEPTEMBER, 1878

1320 Mr. Froude's "Life and Times of Thomas Becket" (Part IV), 213–241. **Edward A. Freeman**. Signed.
1321 Progress of Indian religious thought (Part I), 242–271. **Monier Williams**. Signed.
1322 The legal position of the Catholic Church in France, 286–309. **Edmond de Pressensé**. Signature.
1323 Selling the soul, 310–321. **R. H. Horne**. Signed.
1324 The sun's corona and his spots, 322–338. **Richard A. Proctor**. Signed; repr. *Mysteries of Time and Space*, 1883.
1325 The life of Jesus and modern criticism, 339–360. **Bernhard Weiss**. Signed.
1326 Cavendish College: an experiment in university extension, 361–375. **Joseph Lloyd Brereton**. Signed.
1327 Antiquities at the Paris Exhibition, 376–401. **François Lenormant**. Signed.
1328 Contemporary essays and comments, 402–411.
1329 Contemporary literature, 412–423.

VOLUME 33, OCTOBER, 1878

1330 The sixteenth century arraigned before the nineteenth: a study on the Reformation [reply to no. 1314], 425–457. **W. E. Gladstone**. Signed; repr. *Gleanings*, III. (See no. 1363.)
1331 England and America as manufacturing competitors, 458–469. **James Henderson**. Signed.
1332 The atheistic controversy, 470–497. **F. W. Newman**. Signed.
1333 Methods of social reform (No. I): amusements of the people, 498–513. **W. Stanley Jevons**. Signed; repr. *Methods*.

John Tulloch. Signed. (See nos. 1355, 1356.)
1337 Contemporary life and thought (No. I): in France, 588–599. **Gabriel Monod**. Signature.
1338 Contemporary life and thought (No. II): in Russia, 599–614. Signed: T.S. **Elizaveta D. Bezobrazova**. Cf. no. 1235.
1339 Contemporary literary chronicles (No. I): church history, &c., 615–626. **Samuel Cheetham**. Written under his direction, p. 615.
1340 Contemporary literary chronicles (No. II): modern history, 626–629. **S. Rawson Gardiner**. Written under his direction, p. 626.
1341 Contemporary literary chronicles (No. III): literature of the middle ages, 630–636. **J. Bass Mullinger**. Written under his direction, p. 630.
1342 Contemporary literary chronicles (No. IV): essays, novels, poetry, &c., 636–645. **W. B. Rands**. Written "under the direction of Matthew Browne", p. 636; see *DNB* for this pseudonym.
1343 Contemporary literary chronicles (No. V): political economy, 645–652. **Bonamy Price**. Written under his direction, p. 645.
1344 Contemporary literary chronicles (No. VI): physical science, mathematics, &c., 652–659. **Richard A. Proctor**. Written under his direction, p. 652.
1345 Contemporary literary chronicles (No. VII): geography, geology, &c., 659–664. **T. G. Bonney**. Written under his direction, p. 659.

VOLUME 33, NOVEMBER, 1878

1346 What is going on at the Vatican: a voice from Rome, 665–682.
1347 The alcohol question (No. I), 683–691. **James Paget**. Signed.
1348 The alcohol question (No. II), 691–700. **T. Lauder Brunton**. Signed.
1349 The alcohol question (No. III), 700–706. **Albert J. Bernays**. Signed.
1350 On henotheism, polytheism, monotheism, and atheism, 707–733. **Friedrich Max Müller**. Signature.
1351 The text of Wordsworth's poems, 734–757. **Edward Dowden**. Signed; repr. *Transcripts*.
1352 Originality of the character of Christ,

FIG. 15. W. E. Houghton, *The Wellesley Index to Victorian Periodicals* (Tabular Listing). (Copyright: Routledge and Kegan Paul Ltd.)

Gissing, George Robert, 1857–1903, novelist. *DNB.*

A victim of circumstances, **Bk** 6855

A life's morning, in 12 installments from **CM** 2458 to 2533

Gladstone, John Hall, 1827–1902, chemist. *DNB.*

History of lighthouse illumination, **Mac** 238

Gladstone, Mary: see Drew, Mary Gladstone

Gladstone, William Ewart, 1809–1898, statesman. *DNB.*

Letter: **Bk** 6155

The shield of Achilles, **CR** 796
Reply of Achilles to Agamemnon, 826
Homer's place in history, 835, 844
Ritualism and ritual, 870
Life of the Prince Consort, 937
Is the Church of England worth preserving? 946
Homerology, 1022, 1032, 1054
The courses of religious thought, 1041
Russian policy in Turkistan, 1082
Hellenic factor in the Eastern problem, 1090
Piracy in Borneo, 1154
The Iris of Homer: her relation to Genesis IX, 1257
A study on the Reformation, 1330
The great Olympian sedition, 2520
The Homeric Herê, 2602
The Irish demand [for Home Rule], 2612
Triple Alliance and Italy, 2801
Letter: 764, 1029
Note: 3712

Farini's *Stato Romano*, **ER** 2150
The session and its sequel, 2753
Germany, France and England, 2868

The dominions of Odysseus, **Mac** 1726

Ward's *Ideal of a Christian Church*, **QR** 798
Life of Mr. Blanco White, 816
Scotch ecclesiastical affairs, 835
From Oxford to Rome, 886
Lachmann's *Essays on Homer*, 893
Duke of Argyll on Presbytery, 941
Clergy Relief Bill, 972
Giacomo Leopardi, 978
Montalembert on Catholic interests, 1084

Homeric characters, 1233
Bill for divorce, 1234
France and the late ministry, 1258
Past and present administrations, 1273
Foreign affairs—war in Italy, 1290
Tennyson's *Poems*, 1303
Phoenicia and Greece, 1588
Life of Bishop Patteson, 1840
Speeches of Pope Pius IX, 1852
Lord Macaulay, 1898
See: 1824

Glascock, William Nugent, 1787?–1847, naval officer. *DNB.*

Dibdin's sea songs, **Bk** 753

Glass, Henry Alexander, religious historian. *LCCat.*

Gospel State Church of the Commonwealth, **CR** 3360

Glehn, Mary Emilie (known as Mimi) von, musician. Graves, *Grove*, index.

Translations: **Mac** 1131? 1358, 1367, 1376, 1384, 1392

Gleig, Charles Edward Stuart, army officer; son of Rev. G. R. Gleig. Blackwood, *Army List.*

Dred [Harriet Beecher Stowe], **Bk** 3536

Gleig, George Robert, 1796–1888, chaplain-general of the forces. *DNB.*

Letters from the vicarage, **Bk** 128, 141, 156
Subaltern, 162, 181, 190, 202, 212, 225, 230
Letters on India, 191, 201, 224, 233, 241
The country curate, 251, 273, 285, 316
The Book of Common Prayer, 256
The Church of England, 276
Military policy, 353, 381
Political History of India, 390
Snodgrass's *Burmese War*, 413
Subaltern in America, 421, 433, 440, 452, 475, 489
The Indian army, 442
The Duke of Wellington, 483
The siege of Bhurtpore, 554
Londonderry's *Narrative of War in Spain and Portugal*, 572
Our beginning of the last war, 3417
Military education, 3601, 3619

FIG. 16. W. E. Houghton, *The Wellesley Index to Victorian Periodicals* (Bibliographies of Contributors). (Copyright: Routledge and Kegan Paul Ltd.)

authors to almost 40 major periodicals will have been indexed. This work is clearly of the greatest importance for the student of the period. It provides both direct bibliographical information about Victorian authors and a convenient survey of the contents of major periodicals which may not be held in the library in which the student is working. It is now a simple matter to analyse the range of subjects discussed in, for example, *The Contemporary Review* during the period of its publication, or to survey the extent to which important issues are discussed in a specific period. In its layout, the work is exemplary, making the *Index* both a convenient reference tool and a stimulating guide to further research.

In 1967 Andrew Boyle Ltd., of Worcester, published the first volume of *An Index to the Annuals* by A. Boyle (Fig. 17). This volume is an index to the authors of contributions to English annuals during the period 1820–50. A second volume, indexing the artists during the same period, is announced as possibly for publication at some future date.

In addition to these guides to the contents of several serials, some Victorian periodicals and newspapers are supplied with their own indexes, though these are often intermittent or cover only short periods. The most frequently consulted is *Palmer's Index to The Times Newspaper* which covers the period 1790–1941, the official index only commencing outside our period in 1906. *Palmer's Index*, though often confusing to use, is an invaluable guide to the contents of *The Times*. The obituary notices alone provide an enormous fund of biographical information about Victorian figures.

A useful list of indexes has been compiled by D. C. Haskell in *A Check List of Cumulative Indexes to Individual Periodicals in the New York Public Library* (New York, Public Library, 1942). This lists thousands of indexes to periodicals, mostly of the nineteenth and twentieth centuries.

DOUBLEDAY—DOWNING]   AUTHORS (NAMED OR IDENTIFIED)

Anniversary.
    The Fisher's Call, " The thorn is in the bud," 29, 63 ;
    Lines to an Old Bagpipe, " You're rough and rusty, old compeer,"
       29, 256;
    The Poet, " Say, who is independent. He enrolled," 29, 249 ;

Aurora Borealis.
    Stanzas of the Sea, " The night was on the deep," 33, 208.

Douglas (Mrs. James).
    Christmas Box.
       The Minnow Fisher, 29, 128.

Douglas (R. K.).
    Amulet.
       The Caldron Linn, 29, 274.

Dover (Lord), George James Welbore Agar Ellis, first Baron Dover, (1797–
    1833). Politician and miscellaneous writer. Edited Walpole's
    Letters.

Keepsake.
    Stanzas, " A hallow'd fane," 30, 69 ;
    A Tragedy of Other Times," 30, 129 ;
    Chesterfield and Fanny, 31, 1 ;
    Human Life, " Search all the paths of human life, examine ev'ry
       way," 32, 39 ;
    Vicissitudes in the Life of a Princess of the House of Brunswick,
       33, 1. ;
    My Native Spot, " My native spot, my native spot," 34, 188.

Downes (Rev. George). Author of several travel books on Germany and
    the North.

Forget-me-not.
    To the New Year, " Beautiful art thou in thy coming forth," 29, 92.
    Hulseburg, " They have pass'd away—and the innocent flower,"
       31, 192 ;

Amulet.
    A Psalm of Wieland, " Praised be our Lord ! Let everything which
       hath," 26, 112 ;
    The Tablet of Lauterbrunnen, " Here—in the face of yon eternal
       snows," 28, 175 ;
    Faustus—The Brocken—Goethe, 28, 361.

Downing (Mrs. Harriet).

FIG. 17. A. Boyle, *Index to the Annuals*. (Copyright: Andrew Boyle Ltd.)

Studies of Periodicals and Newspapers

The basic narrative introduction to English periodicals is W. Graham, *English Literary Periodicals* (New York, Nelson, 1930; reprinted New York, Octagon Books, 1966). For newspapers H. R. Fox Bourne, *English Newspapers: chapters in the history of journalism* (2 vols., Chatto & Windus, 1887), has not been superseded. Both these works provide broad surveys of the material.

E. E. Kellett's survey of "The press" in the second volume of *Early Victorian England, 1830–65*, edited by G. M. Young (OUP, 1934), includes accounts of the history, policy, contents, and readership of a variety of notable newspapers and periodicals. Useful examinations of the readership of periodicals are found in R. D. Altick, *The English Common Reader: a social history of the mass reading public, 1800–1900* (Chicago, Univ. Pr., 1957), and in A. Ellegård, *The Readership of the Periodical Press in Mid-Victorian Britain* (Göteborg, Univ. Pr., 1957). A. Ellegård has also surveyed the reception of Darwin's evolutionary theory in the British periodical press between 1859 and 1872 in *Darwin and the General Reader* (Göteborg, Univ. Pr., 1958). E. L. Casford, *The Magazines of the 1890s* (Eugene, Univ. Pr., 1929), studies the last decade of the nineteenth century with special reference to *The Albemarle*, *The Yellow Book*, and *The Savoy*.

The influence exercised by periodicals and the way in which it was used has been studied in essays by several writers. M. Wolff has discussed "Victorian reviewers and cultural responsibility" in *1859: entering an age of crisis*, edited by P. Appleman, W. A. Madden, and M. Wolff (Bloomington, Indiana Univ. Pr., 1959). R. G. Cox contributed two articles on "The great reviews" in *Scrutiny* (vol. 6, 1937, pp. 2–20 and 155–75) and an essay on "The reviews and magazines" in *From Dickens to Hardy*, edited by B. Ford (Harmondsworth, Penguin Books, 1958). D. Thompson surveyed "A hundred years of the higher journalism" in *Scrutiny* (vol. 4, 1935, pp. 25–34).

Some nineteenth-century periodicals and newspapers have been studied individually. The following varied examples of histories and analyses illustrate many of the better features of this type of study:

Academy. D. Roll-Hansen, *The Academy, 1869–79: Victorian intellectuals in revolt* (Copenhagen, Rosenkilde & Bagger, 1957).

Athenaeum. L. A. Marchand, *The Athenaeum: a mirror of Victorian culture* (Chapel Hill, Univ. of North Carolina Pr., 1940).

Birmingham Post. H. R.G. Whates, *The Birmingham Post, 1857–1957: a centenary retrospect* (Birmingham, *Birmingham Post*, 1957).

Edinburgh Review. W. Bagehot, "The first Edinburgh Reviewers" in the first volume of his *Literary Studies* (Longmans, 1879). L. Stephen, "The first Edinburgh reviewers" in the second volume of his *Hours in a Library* (Smith, Elder, 1874–9).

Fortnightly Review. E. M. Everett, *The Party of Humanity: the Fortnightly Review and its contributors, 1865–74* (Chapel Hill, Univ. of North Carolina Pr., 1939).

Fraser's Magazine. M. M. H. Thrall, *Rebellious Fraser's: Nol Yorke's magazine in the days of Maginn, Thackeray and Carlyle* (New York, Columbia Univ. Pr., 1934).

London Magazine. J. Bauer, *The London Magazine, 1820–29* (Copenhagen, Rosenkilde & Bagger, 1953).

Manchester Guardian. Sir. W. Haley and others, *C. P. Scott, 1846–1932: the making of the Manchester Guardian* (Muller, 1946).

Monthly Repository. F. E. Mineka, *The Dissidence of Dissent: the Monthly Repository, 1806–1838* (Chapel Hill, Univ. of North Carolina Pr., 1944).

Pall Mall Gazette. J. W. R. Scott, *The Story of the Pall Mall Gazette* (OUP, 1950).

Punch. M. H. Spielmann, *The History of Punch* (Cassell, 1895).

Quarterly Review. H. and H.C. Shine, *The Quarterly Review under Gifford: identification of contributors, 1809–1824* (Chapel Hill, Univ. of North Carolina Pr., 1949).

Rambler. J. L. Altholz, *The Liberal Catholic Movement in England: the Rambler and its contributors, 1848–1864* (Burns & Oates, 1962).

Saturday Review. M. M. Bevington, *The Saturday Review, 1855–1868: representative educated opinion in Victorian England* (New York, Columbia Univ. Pr., 1941, reprinted New York, AMS Pr., 1966).

Savoy. S. Weintraub, *The Savoy: nineties experiment* (University Park, Pennsylvania State Univ. Pr., 1966).

Westminster Review. G. L. Nesbitt, *Benthamite Reviewing: the first twelve years of the Westminster Review, 1824–1836* (New York, Columbia Univ. Pr., 1934).

F. W. Fetter has supplied a very useful series of discussions of the economic articles which appeared in certain major periodicals. In *Economica* (new series, vol. 32, November 1965, pp. 424–37) he surveyed "Economic controversy in the British reviews, 1802–1850". He has also contributed to the *Journal of Political Economy* essays on the authorship of economic articles in *The Edinburgh Review*, 1802–47 (vol. 61, June 1953, pp. 232–59), *The Quarterly Review*, 1809–52 (vol. 66, February 1958, pp. 47–64, and April 1958, pp. 154–70), and *The Westminster Review* (vol. 70, December 1962, pp. 570–96).

It is not possible here to indicate more than a few such articles. Much useful information is hidden in theses and periodical articles which have not been reprinted. It is clear that there is a considerable need for a comprehensive bibliography of writings about nineteenth-century periodicals and newspapers. Such a bibliography is currently projected jointly by the Victorian Studies Centre in the University of Leicester and by H. and S. Rosenberg, compilers of the bibliography of nineteenth-century serials for the *New Cambridge Bibliography of English Literature*. Information about the progress of this and similar projects is communicated regularly to the *Victorian Periodicals Newsletter*.

CHAPTER 4

Guides to Special Collections
and Source Materials

Guides to Collections of Books and Manuscripts

The best general guide to special collections of material held in British libraries and institutions is the *Aslib Directory: a guide to sources of information in Great Britain and Ireland.* This was edited by M. Alman and was published in 2 volumes by Aslib in 1957. This edition provides an alphabetical list by location, indicating, among other details, the size of each institution's holdings and the subject of its special collections. The comprehensive index volume provides a classified arrangement with its own subject index. It is thus possible to trace the classification number for a specific subject or person and then, by reference to the classified arrangement, to discover those British libraries and institutions which possess special collections in the field.

A new edition of the *Aslib Directory* is now in progress (Aslib, 1968–). Coverage is very much wider and many organizations are included as sources of information.

A useful 1-volume guide is the *Libraries, Museums and Art Galleries Year Book* (Clarke). This provides brief information about the scope of collections. Despite its title this is not a regular annual publication.

An older work which is still occasionally useful is A. J. Philip, *An Index to the Special Collections in Libraries, Museums and Art Galleries (Public, Private and Official) in Great Britain and Ireland* (Brown, 1949). This directory is chiefly notable for its attempt to locate special collections in small libraries.

Special Library and Information Services in the United Kingdom, edited by J. Burkett (2nd edn., Library Association, 1965), comprises a collection of essays on various types of specialized information sources, including the following sections of particular interest to the student of the Victorian period: national libraries; government departmental libraries; public authorities; libraries of learned and professional societies; and medical and law libraries.

The Libraries of London, edited by R. Irwin and R. Staveley (2nd edn., Library Association, 1961), similarly includes essays on a wide variety of libraries. This is a most important and wide-ranging survey of the history, collections, and services of these libraries, and the work possesses great value for the student of the Victorian period. Among others it includes chapters on the libraries of the British Museum, Victoria and Albert Museum, Patent Office, National Central Library, House of Lords, House of Commons, Government departments, London boroughs, Guildhall, London County Council, University of London, British Library of Political and Economic Science, London Library, and the specialized learned society, technical and professional, industrial, ecclesiastical and theological, law, medical, and music libraries. Although this work supplements and corrects an earlier book by R. A. Rye, *The Students' Guide to the Libraries of London* (3rd edn., Univ. of London Pr., 1927), it does not entirely replace it.

A. N. L. Munby, *Cambridge College Libraries: aids for research students* (2nd edn., Cambridge, Heffer, 1962), describes research collections of books and manuscripts in college libraries and in the Fitzwilliam Museum and the University Archives.

Much of the research material for the study of Victorian Britain is now held by American libraries. It is therefore necessary for the student to be aware of similar guides to American collections. L. Ash and D. Lorenz, *Subject Collections: a guide to special book collections and subject emphases as reported by university, college, public, and special libraries in the United States and Canada* (3rd edn., New York, Bowker, 1967), is a basic work of reference.

The *American Library Directory* (New York, Bowker) includes brief details of special collections in libraries in the United States and Canada. A. T. Kruzas, *Directory of Special Libraries and Information Centers* (2nd edn., Detroit, Gale, 1968), gives details of subject coverage and includes a subject index. *Special Library Resources* (4 vols., New York, Special Libraries Association, 1941-7) lists collections in special, public, and university libraries.

R. B. Downs, *American Library Resources: a bibliographical guide* (Chicago, American Library Association), was published in 1951 with a supplement in 1962 for the years 1950-61. This is not strictly a directory of sources but a guide to bibliographies of libraries and their special collections. It must be noted that where collections have not been bibliographically listed they are not included. R. B. Downs also compiled *Resources of New York City Libraries* (Chicago, American Library Association, 1942) and *Resources of Southern Libraries* (Chicago, American Library Association, 1938).

Although they do not list details of collections, there is often considerable value in guides to specialist societies which may themselves be able to provide an information service within their own field of interest. The annual directory, *Scientific and Learned Societies of Great Britain* (Allen & Unwin), lists societies by subject groups.

Government Libraries and their Collections

The value of the chapters on British government libraries in J. Burkett, *Special Library and Information Services in the United Kingdom*, and in *The Libraries of London*, edited by R. Irwin and R. Staveley, has already been noted. A convenient introduction to the subject is *Government Information and the Research Worker*, edited by R. Staveley and M. Piggott (2nd edn., Library Association, 1965). This work contains a collection of essays on the resources and publications of various government libraries and information centres, indicating their value for students.

Further information in the form of a directory is given in *A Guide to Government Libraries*, which is compiled by the Treasury (2nd edn., HMSO, 1958). This work lists some 80 libraries and includes a brief history of each, details of the facilities offered and notes on special collections. The *Guide* was compiled primarily for the use of readers outside government departments.

Guides to Government Publications

Few research workers in nineteenth-century studies will not at some time require information from government publications. The most convenient and reliable short introduction to parliamentary papers is P. and G. Ford, *A Guide to Parliamentary Papers: what they are; how to find them; how to use them* (new edn., Oxford, Blackwell, 1956). This work places particular emphasis on the sessional papers. J. G. Ollé has provided a very useful short guide to the publications of Parliament and of government departments in *An Introduction to British Government Publications* (Association of Assistant Librarians, 1965). Although designed primarily for use by librarians this book will also be of great value as an introductory guide for research students. P. R. Lewis, *The Literature of the Social Sciences* (Library Association, 1960), also includes a useful outline of government publications.

P. and G. Ford have compiled a *Select List of British Parliamentary Papers, 1833–1899* (Oxford, Blackwell, 1953). This is to be reprinted by the Irish University Press. The list is arranged by subject with alphabetical index (Fig. 18). The same authors have also compiled breviates of parliamentary papers covering the period 1900–54 (3 vols., Oxford, Blackwell, 1952–61). These breviates contain abstracts of papers listed. For the period before the Victorian age there is *Hansard's Catalogue and Breviate of Parliamentary Papers, 1696–1834* (reprinted Oxford, Blackwell, 1953).

The best guide to Acts of Parliament is the *Index to Statutes in Force, 1234–1954* (HMSO, 1955). For private Acts the *Index to Local and Personal Acts, 1801–1947* (HMSO, 1949) is valuable. A

V. TRADE AND INDUSTRY

1. **General Trade Conditions and Policy.**
2. **Particular Trades and Manufactures.**
3. **Overseas Trade and Commercial Relations.**
4. **Insurance, Friendly Societies.**

5. **Co-operative Trading.**
6. **Exhibitions, Commercial Intelligence.**
7. **Bankruptcy, Company Law.**
8. **Commercial Law and Practice.**
9. **Weights and Measures.**

1. **General Trade Conditions and Policy**

1833	(690)	vi	Manufactures, Commerce and Shipping. Sel. Cttee. Rep., mins. of ev., etc.
1835	(598)	v	Arts and Manufactures (Extending a Knowledge of the Arts and of the Principles of Design among the Manufacturing Population). Sel. Cttee. Rep., mins. of ev., etc.
1836	(568)	ix	—— Sel. Cttee. Rep., mins. of ev., etc.
1847	(232)	x	Navigation Laws. Sel. Cttee. 1st Rep., mins. of ev.
	(246)	,,	—— 2nd Rep., mins. of ev.
	(392)	,,	—— 3rd Rep., mins. of ev., etc.
	(556)	,,	—— 4th Rep., mins. of ev.
	(678)	,,	—— 5th Rep., mins. of ev., etc. (Reprint of 1st–4th Reps.: 1847–8 (7) xx. Pt. I)
1847–8	(340)	xx Pt. II	Navigation Laws. Sel. Cttee. HL. 1st Rep., mins. of ev.
	(431)	,,	—— 2nd Rep., mins. of ev.
	(754)	,,	—— 3rd Rep., mins. of ev., etc.
1847–8	(395)	viii Pt. I	Commercial Distress (How far it has been affected by the Issue of Bank-notes payable on Demand). Secret Cttee. 1st Rep., mins. of ev.
	(584)	,,	—— 2nd Rep., mins. of ev.
	(395,584)	viii Pt. II	—— App., index, etc.
1847–8	(565)	viii Pt. III	Commercial Distress (How far it has been affected by the Issue of Bank-notes payable on Demand). Secret Cttee. HL. Rep., mins. of ev., etc.
	(565–II)	,,	—— Index. (Reprint: 1857 Sess. 1 (0.50) ii.)
1857–8	(381)	v	The Operation of the Bank Act of 1844 and of the Bank Acts for Ireland and Scotland of 1845, and the Causes of the Recent Commercial Distress. How far it has been affected by the Laws for regulating the Issue of Bank-notes payable on Demand. Sel. Cttee. Rep., mins. of ev., etc.
1884–5	(348)	lxxi	Depression of Trade and Industry. R. Com. Memo.

FIG. 18. P. and G. Ford, *Select List of British Parliamentary Papers, 1833–1899.* (Copyright: Basil Blackwell (Publishing) and Irish University Press.)

useful guide to the *Acts of Parliament Concerning Wales, 1714–1901* is edited by T. I. Jeffreys-Jones (Cardiff, Univ. of Wales Pr., 1959).

During the late nineteenth century, HMSO published sale catalogues of its publications. Originally a *List of Yearly Papers for Sale* was published as a sessional paper. This was superseded from 1894 to 1896 by a *Quarterly List of Official and Parliamentary Publications* and thereafter from 1897 to 1921 by a *Quarterly List of Official Publications* and a *Quarterly List of Parliamentary Publications*. These are, however, inadequate in coverage and indexing.

A very useful index for the Victorian period is *A Century of Diplomatic Blue Books, 1814–1914*, edited by H. Temperley and L. M. Penson (CUP, 1938; reprinted Cass, 1966). This gives lists of the Blue Books relating to foreign policy published during the period of office of each Secretary of State for Foreign Affairs (Fig. 19). Each entry is annotated to indicate the date on which the paper was laid before Parliament and the reason for its presentation. Each list is preceded by a narrative historical introduction discussing the Blue Book policy of each Foreign Minister. The range of selection is very wide. The editors note that "Generally, the list aims at completeness for papers whose bearing on foreign affairs is direct, and contains also a selection of others, in which students of diplomatic history may find material of special interest". Another useful guide is M. I. Adams, *Guide to the Principal Parliamentary Papers Relating to the Dominions, 1812–1911* (Edinburgh, Oliver & Boyd, 1913).

Archives and Manuscripts

It is not possible here to do more than indicate briefly some useful general guides to archives and manuscripts and their locations which may be useful for the student of the Victorian period. Fuller accounts may be found in two works by P. Hepworth: *Archives and Manuscripts in Libraries* (2nd edn., Library Association, 1964) and *How to Find Out in History* (Oxford,

160   3 DECEMBER 1857 TO 2 AUGUST 1858

549*c*   Papers respecting the Excavations at Budrum.   PAGE 671
         [2359]   L/C. 26 Mar. 1858.

549*d*   Further Papers [Ap. 1858].*   PAGE 745
         [2378]   L/C. 14 May 1858.

VOLUME LXI (1857–8)

Slave Trade

550   Class B. Correspondence with British Ministers and Agents in
        Foreign Countries, and with Foreign Ministers in England,
        relating to the Slave Trade [1 Ap. 1857–31 Mar. 1858].
                                                    PAGE 175

        [2443–I]   L/C. 2 Aug. 1858.

1ST SESSION 3 FEBRUARY TO 19 APRIL 1859

VOLUME XXVII (1859)

Slave Trade; State Papers

551   Correspondence relating to the Slave Trade (Zanzibar).
                                                    PAGE 1
        111   R–A. (HC. 22 Feb.), HC. 4 Mar., O.T.B.P. 7 Mar.
                  1859.

551*a* Correspondence respecting the French Emigration Scheme.
                                                    PAGE 17
        [2481]   L/C. HC. 8 Mar., HL. 10 Mar. 1859.

552   Treaties (Austria): Copy of Treaties, Political and Territorial,
        1815–48.   PAGE 21
        [2497]   R–A. (HC. 25 Mar.), 18 Ap. 1859.

* Papers laid on this subject in later sessions are omitted, as they are not diplomatic
in character.

FIG. 19. H. Temperley and L. M. Penson, *A Century of Diplomatic
Blue Books, 1814–1914.* (Copyright: Cambridge University Press.)

Pergamon Pr., 1966). The former includes a valuable comprehensive list of published guides and catalogues to collections in British libraries. V. H. Galbraith, *Introduction to the Use of the Public Records* (OUP, 1952) is also valuable. A good brief introduction is F. G. Emmison, *Introduction to Archives* (British Broadcasting Corporation, 1964). The same author's *Archives and Local History* (Methuen, 1966) is an invaluable guide to local source materials.

The holdings of the Public Record Office, which is the national repository for the records of the British Government, are listed in the *Guide to the Contents of the Public Record Office* (2 vols., HMSO, 1963) (Fig. 20). This work is a "revised and extended" edition of an earlier *Guide* by M. S. Giuseppi. It covers holdings to 1960. Important new accessions are noted in the annual *Report of the Keeper of Public Records* (HMSO). The Public Record Office issues a guide to *Record Publications* (HMSO). This lists public records and guides which have been published.

Catalogues of the considerable manuscript holdings of the British Museum are listed in *The Catalogues of the Manuscript Collections* (rev. edn., British Museum, 1962). It should be noted that this work is not itself a catalogue of the collections but a guide to the separate catalogues which exist.

It is, of course, impossible to list all the published and unpublished guides to collections of materials in libraries and archive centres. Some information may be obtained from the basic general guides such as the *Aslib Directory* and the *Libraries, Museums and Art Galleries Year Book* noted above. For American holdings, *A Guide to Archives and Manuscripts in the United States*, edited by P. M. Hamer (New Haven, Yale Univ. Pr., 1961), is useful.

The information centre for the location of archives in Britain is the National Register of Archives in London. This office collects reports or lists of holdings. These are compiled either by the staff of the National Register of Archives or by the local record office or library which holds the collection. The reports are indexed by short title and by county. Their contents are recorded in three

MATERIAL DEPARTMENTS

The following classes include records of the Surveyor and (from 1860) of the Controller of the Navy.

IN-LETTERS

Admiralty to the Surveyor (Adm. 83). 1815 to 1850. 64 volumes.

Admiralty to the Steam Department

Series I (Adm. 84). 1850 to 1859. 20 volumes.

Series II (Adm. 85). 1850 to 1859. 58 volumes.

Register of Series I and II (Adm. 86). 1850 to 1859. 6 volumes.

A numerical register with an index, references to Series I being shown in red ink. Many of the letters in Series II have been weeded out.

Letters relating to Ships (Adm. 87). 1806 to 1860. 77 volumes, etc.

Letters relating to Ships: Register (Adm. 88). 1832 to 1860. 16 volumes.

Letters relating to Yards (Adm. 89). 1854 to 1859. 4 bundles.

Letters relating to Yards: Register (Adm. 90). 1854 to 1859. 2 volumes.

OUT-LETTERS

General Letter Books (Adm. 91). 1688 to 1860. 24 volumes.

Minutes and entries of letters, indexed from 1833 onwards.

Submission Letter Books (Adm. 92). 1813 to 1860. 21 volumes.

The minutes and recommendations of the Committee of Surveyors. The second series beginning in 1832 is indexed.

Steam Department Letter Books (Adm. 93). 1847 to 1858. 17 volumes.

Submission books similar to the foregoing.

Steam Department Letter Books: Index (Adm. 94). 1847 to 1854. 1 volume.

An index to volumes 1 to 10 of the foregoing class, each of the remaining volumes of which contains its own index.

SHIPS' BOOKS

Series I (Adm. 135). 1807 to 1873. 520 volumes.

Series II (Adm. 136). 1854 to 1947. 19 volumes.

These consist of reports and other papers giving the history of the maintenance of a ship (hull, machinery and armament) from construction to disposal; in some cases details of complements are also given.

The earliest Ships' Books consist of bound volumes and Series I contains the surviving Books of this type. Later Ships' Books take the form of loose-leaf albums, and Series II contains a selection of Ships' Books in this form.

SHIPS' COVERS

FIG. 20. *Guide to the Contents of the Public Record Office.* (Copyright: the Controller of Her Majesty's Stationery Office.)

indexes: a selective index of persons mentioned, which aims to note persons who are included in the *Dictionary of National Biography* or who are of similar importance; a subject index; and a topographical index.

The National Register of Archives forms part of the Historical Manuscripts Commission, which publishes an annual *List of Accessions to Repositories* (HMSO, 1955–) covering manuscript accessions to repositories in Great Britain, and a periodical *Bulletin* (HMSO, 1948–), which consists primarily of descriptions of collections of manuscripts. The Historical Manuscripts Commission and the British Records Association have published a guide to *Record Repositories in Great Britain* (2nd edn., HMSO, 1966). New information about collections is also included in the periodicals *Archives* and *Journal of the Society of Archivists*.

A convenient guide to the type of material to be found in the counties is F. G. Emmison and I. Gray, *County Records* (2nd edn., Historical Association, 1961). J. S. Purvis, *An Introduction to Ecclesiastical Records* (St. Anthony's Pr., 1953), and F. J. C. Hearnshaw, *Municipal Records* (SPCK, 1918), are also useful guides. Notes on ecclesiastical records are contained in the *Survey of Ecclesiastical Archives* (Pilgrim Trust, 1952), which is concerned with Anglican material; *Archives in Religious and Ecclesiastical Bodies and Organisations other than the Church of England* (British Records Association, 1936); and an article by C. E. Welch on "Archives and manuscripts in Nonconformist libraries" in *Archives* (vol. 6, 1964, pp. 235–8). Information about archive material of interest to business historians is included in the periodical, *Business Archives* (Business Archives Council, 1957–).

CHAPTER 5

Philosophy

Guides and Bibliographies

The most important attempt at a large-scale bibliography of philosophy is B. Rand, *Bibliography of Philosophy, Psychology, and Cognate Subjects* (new edn., 2 vols., New York, Macmillan, 1928). This was originally published in 1905 as part of an encyclopedic work by J. M. Baldwin, *Dictionary of Philosophy and Psychology*. The first volume of Rand's work provides a guide to general studies and works by and about individual figures. The second volume arranges works by major subject fields. The bibliography documents a large selection of important writing and is particularly strong on nineteenth-century contributions.

A new attempt at a detailed bibliography of writings since the end of the First World War has been commenced by W. Totok under the title *Handbuch der Geschichte der Philosophie* (Frankfurt, Klostermann, 1964–). This lists writings with occasional annotations. Narrative comments between the different sections indicate the progress of philosophical thought.

Totok's *Handbuch* is a logical successor both to Rand's *Bibliography* and to F. Ueberweg, *Grundriss der Geschichte der Philosophie* (12th edn., 5 vols., Berlin, Mittler, 1923–8; reprinted Basel, Schwabe, 1957). Although this is a narrative history it offers very full documentation of the literature and provides a valuable guide to the bibliography of philosophy. Despite an evident bias towards German works, this is an impressive compilation covering a wide range of literature in various languages.

G. Varet, *Manuel de Bibliographie philosophique* (2 vols., Paris, Presses Universitaires, 1956), is an excellent selective guide to the whole field of philosophy, listing books and periodical articles. The first volume is arranged chronologically while the second lists works on the different branches of the subject.

Useful single-volume guides to basic works include D. H. Borchardt, *How to Find Out in Philosophy and Psychology* (Oxford, Pergamon Pr., 1968). This provides information about dictionaries and encyclopedias, retrospective bibliographies and handbooks, current bibliographies and reviewing journals, national bibliographies, and bibliographies of specialized fields. There are also notes on some societies and associations devoted to the promotion of study in these subjects.

J. Hoffmans, *La Philosophie et les Philosophes: ouvrages généraux* (Brussels, Van Oest, 1920) lists dictionaries, general treatises, histories, periodicals, and bibliographies, and offers good coverage of works of the seventeenth to nineteenth centuries. L. de Raeymaker, *Introduction à la Philosophie* (4th edn., Louvain, Institut Supérieur de Philosophie, 1956), surveys books, periodical articles, and publications of academic societies and congresses. J. Passmore, *A Hundred Years of Philosophy* (Duckworth, 1957), surveys philosophic thought in the last century and includes extensive references to the literature in notes and a good bibliography at the end of the volume.

Bibliographische Einführungen in das Studium der Philosophie, edited by I. M. Bochenski (Bern, Francke, 1948–), is a series of pamphlets on various aspects of philosophy and on individual philosophers. These short bibliographies concentrate on twentieth-century materials, and there is an emphasis on German language works. The first volume of the series, by I. M. Bochenski and F. Monteleone, is a general guide, *Allgemeine philosophische Bibliographie*.

Other bibliographical works tend to list writings on the subject within a limited period. Thus *Bibliographica Philosophica, 1934–1945*, edited by G. A. de Brie (2 vols., Utrecht, Editiones Spectrum, 1950–4), is an international survey of writings in 12 languages. Bibliographies contributed as supplements to the *Journal of Philosophy* were published as *Bibliography of Philosophy, 1933–36*

(4 vols., New York, *Journal of Philosophy*, 1934–7). This is primarily a guide to material in English, French, German, and Italian.

A useful guide to the literature of a specific area of philosophic study is E. M. Albert and others, *A Selected Bibliography on Values, Ethics and Esthetics in the Behavioral Sciences and Philosophy, 1920–1958* (New York, Free Pr., 1959). This includes some 2000 books and periodical articles.

Current Work

From 1937 to 1953 books, periodical articles, and theses were listed in *Bibliographie de la Philosophie*, compiled by the Institut Internationale de la Philosophie (Paris, Vrin). In 1954, however, this became an abstracting journal for books only.

The *Répertoire bibliographique de la Philosophie* (Louvain, Institut Supérieur de Philosophie) has since 1934 provided a wide-ranging bibliography of books and periodical articles arranged by subject with author indexes.

The Centre Nationale de la Recherche Scientifique in Paris devotes section 19 of its *Bulletin signalétique* to "Sciences humaines", including philosophy. This provides a classified index to periodical articles from various countries with brief abstracts in French.

A selective guide, providing reviews of new books, is the quarterly *Philosophical Books* (Leicester, Univ. Pr., 1960–).

Encyclopedias and Dictionaries

The Encyclopedia of Philosophy, edited by P. Edwards (8 vols., New York, Macmillan and the Free Pr., 1967), attempts to cover "the whole of philosophy as well as many of the points of contact between philosophy and other disciplines". The editor states that articles aim to be "authoritative, clear, comprehensive, *and* interesting". Contributors were not asked to assume complete neutrality but were invited to express their personal views while keeping in mind the basic goal of any reference work to supply information in a clear and authoritative fashion. Articles are by specialists and are signed. Each article has a selective bibliography. The work includes some 900 biographical articles on individual thinkers.

J. M. Baldwin, *Dictionary of Philosophy and Psychology* (3 vols. in 4, New York, Macmillan, 1901–5; reprinted Gloucester, Mass., Peter Smith, 1960), has already been noted for Rand's *Bibliography* which is contained in the last 2 volumes of the work. The first 2 volumes constitute the *Dictionary* proper, providing concise signed articles by specialists and short bibliographies of philosophers, excluding those still living at the time of writing. The work is particularly useful for the nineteenth century.

R. Eisler, *Wörterbuch der philosophischen Begriffe* (4th edn., 3 vols., Berlin, Mittler, 1927–30), was originally published in 1 volume in 1889. It includes scholarly articles with bibliographies. Despite its title its treatment is encyclopedic, for it traces historically the use and meaning of philosophic concepts and terms. A similar plan is followed by A. Lalande, *Vocabulaire technique et critique de la Philosophie* (Paris, Presses Universitaires, 1956).

Other works offering historical explanations of the development of philosophic terms include W. Brugger, *Philosophisches Wörterbuch* (4th edn., Freiburg, Herder, 1951); J. Hoffmeister, *Wörterbuch der philosophischen Begriffe* (2nd edn., Hamburg, Meiner, 1955); and H. Schmidt, *Philosophisches Wörterbuch*, edited by J. Streller (13th edn., Leipzig, Kröner, 1955). Schmidt's work also includes notes on individual philosophers.

A comprehensive scholarly reference tool is provided by the *Enciclopedia Filosofica* (4 vols., Venice, Istituto per la Collaborazione Culturale, 1957). J. Ferrater Mora, *Diccionario de Filosofía* (4th edn., Buenos Aires, Sudamericana, 1958), is a reliable shorter work. Both these works include many biographical articles and good bibliographies.

J. O. Urmson, *The Concise Encyclopedia of Western Philosophy and Philosophers* (Hutchinson, 1960), is intended for the intelligent layman. It is useful to the non-specialist student of the Victorian period for its biographical articles.

Biographical Works

Considerable biographical information may be obtained from the encyclopedias noted above and from the general biographical dictionaries discussed in Chapter 14. Among works of collected biography of philosophers which include useful material for the student of the Victorian period only two are notable. R. Eisler, *Philosophen-Lexikon: Leben, Werke und Lehren der Denker* (Berlin, Mittler, 1912), contains articles on philosophers and their schools and includes short bibliographies.

A similar work containing longer articles and information on living persons is *Philosophen-Lexikon: Handwörterbuch der Philosophie nach Personen*, edited by W. Zeigenfuss and G. Jung (2 vols., Berlin, De Gruyter, 1949–50). Although it reveals a bias towards German figures, this work contains reliable information about a wide variety of philosophers with good bibliographies as a guide to further materials.

CHAPTER 6

The Christian Church

THE primary object of this chapter is to note guides for the historian both of the Victorian church in general and of specific denominations. It does not attempt systematically to list sources for the study of particular aspects of Christian thought and doctrinal development in the nineteenth century, though such information is included incidentally. It is, of course, impossible finally to separate the development of religious thought and the progress of the institutions through which such thought finds expression, and the bibliographies, histories, and encyclopedias noted generally include discussions of both these aspects of the Victorian church.

Guides and Bibliographies

General

J. G. Barrow, *A Bibliography of Bibliographies in Religion* (Ann Arbor, Edwards, 1955), is a general list which attempts to provide a comprehensive annotated guide to "all separately published bibliographies in the field of religion" from the fifteenth century to the present. The main emphasis is on Christianity.

Dr. Williams's Library in London, which specializes in theological works, has published various author catalogues of its collections. The annual *Bulletin* lists new accessions to the library.

Among bibliographies of writings about Christian history a very useful brief list is O. Chadwick, *The History of the Church: a select bibliography* (rev. edn., Historical Association, 1966). This contains a selection of works on Victorian religious history.

There is a valuable selective list of books in the first volume of O. Chadwick, *The Victorian Church* (Black, 1966). The second volume of this history has not yet been published. A. R. Vidler, *The Church in an Age of Revolution, 1789 to the Present Day* (Harmondsworth, Penguin, 1961), also includes a selective bibliography.

A Bibliographical Guide to the History of Christianity, edited by S. J. Case (Chicago, Univ. Pr., 1931; reprinted New York, P. Smith, 1951), provides an extensive listing for scholars. A more selective modern guide to books is R. P. Morris, *A Theological Book List* (Oxford, Blackwell, 1960). A supplement to this was published in 1963.

There is a good bibliography of Christian history in the American Historical Association's *Guide to Historical Literature* (New York, Macmillan, 1961). K. S. Latourette, *A History of the Expansion of Christianity* (7 vols., Eyre & Spottiswoode, 1938–45), includes extensive bibliographies. Volume 4, covering the period 1800–1914 in Europe and the United States of America, lists many useful items for the study of the Victorian church.

M. B. MacGregor, *The Sources and Literature of Scottish Church History* (Glasgow, McCallum, 1934), is a guide to sources and secondary material, including biography.

R. Rouse and S. C. Neill, *A History of the Ecumenical Movement, 1517–1948* (SPCK, 1954) includes a very good selective bibliography.

The last decade of the nineteenth century is covered by E. C. Richardson, *Periodical Articles on Religion: an alphabetical subject index and index encyclopaedia to periodical articles on religion, 1890–1899* (2 vols., New York, Scribner, 1907–11). This work indexes some 58,000 articles in 600 periodicals by authors and subjects. It is not limited in coverage to Christianity.

Denominations

Writings on Baptist history are listed in E. C. Starr, *A Baptist Bibliography: being a register of printed material by and about Baptists, including works written against the Baptists* (Rochester,

American Baptist Historical Society, 1947–). An older guide is W. T. Whitley, *A Baptist Bibliography: being a register of the chief materials for Baptist history, whether in manuscript or in print* (2 vols., Kingsgate Pr., 1916).

During the nineteenth century J. Smith compiled a series of catalogues of writings relating to the Society of Friends. These include *Descriptive Catalogue of Friends' Books, or Books Written by Members of the Society of Friends* (2 vols., Smith, 1867) with a supplement (Hicks, 1893); *Bibliotheca Quakeristica* (Smith, 1883), "a bibliography of miscellaneous literature relating to the Friends"; and *Bibliotheca Anti-Quakeriana* (Smith, 1873), "a catalogue of books adverse to the Society of Friends".

Current Work

The *Revue d'Histoire ecclésiastique* (Louvain, 1900–) includes in each issue an extensive survey of recent books and periodical articles. The American Theological Association published an *Index to Religious Periodical Literature* (Chicago, The Association, 1949/52–) indexing a large number of periodicals. *Religious and Theological Abstracts* (Youngstown, Theological Publishers, 1958–) is a quarterly journal providing abstracts in English of a selected number of periodicals. Coverage is not restricted to Christianity.

The *Journal of Ecclesiastical History* (CUP, 1950–) includes regular bibliographical surveys of particular areas of study. *Theologische Literaturzeitung* (Leipzig, Hinrichs, 1876–) is a comprehensive survey of books and periodical articles in many languages. An older guide, discontinued in 1916, should also be noted. This is *Theologischer Jahresbericht* (Tübingen, Mohr, 1882–1916).

For Roman Catholic literature the *Guide to Catholic Literature* (Detroit, Romig, 1940–) is an annual survey of books by Roman Catholics and of Catholic interest. The annual volumes were preceded by a volume covering books published between 1888 and 1940.

Much information about individual denominations may be obtained from the periodicals devoted to the study of their history. These frequently include bibliographical notes on current work and research in progress. Good examples of these are the Methodist *Proceedings of the Wesley Historical Society* (The Society, 1897–), the *Journal of the Friends Historical Society* (The Society, 1903–), and the *Baptist Quarterly* (Baptist Historical Society, 1908–).

It should be noted that the guides to current historical writing, listed in Chapter 13, also contain useful material for ecclesiastical history.

Theses

In addition to the general guides to theses noted in Chapter 2, the Council on Graduate Studies in Religion issued a list of *Doctoral Dissertations in the Field of Religion, 1940–52* (New York, Columbia Univ. Pr., 1954) and has supplemented this by annual volumes.

L. C. Little, *Bibliography of Doctoral Dissertations in Religious Education, 1885 to 1959* (Pittsburgh, Univ. Pr., 1962), lists over 6000 items in the fields of personality, character, and religious education.

Encyclopedias and Dictionaries

Encyclopedias and dictionaries of religion abound, and it is possible here to list only a selection. *The Oxford Dictionary of the Christian Church*, edited by F. L. Cross (OUP, 1957), is a very useful 1-volume work containing an enormous amount of information. Most articles include good selective bibliographies. *Dictionary of English Church History*, edited by S. L. Ollard, G. Crosse, and M. F. Bond (3rd edn., Mowbray, 1948), contains articles with brief bibliographies.

Among multi-volume works the standard encyclopedia is *Die Religion in Geschichte und Gegenwart*, edited by K. Galling (3rd edn., 7 vols., Tübingen, Mohr, 1957–65). This includes lengthy articles with extensive bibliographies. The work contains good biographical entries.

The New Schaff-Herzog Encyclopedia of Religious Knowledge (13 vols., New York, Funk & Wagnalls, 1908–12; reprinted Grand Rapids, Baker, 1949–50) is a useful reference work with good bibliographies.

J. Hastings compiled a series of encyclopedias which are still valuable both for their accurate information and as evidence of late Victorian and early twentieth-century attitudes and opinions. The *Encyclopaedia of Religion and Ethics* (12 vols., Edinburgh, Clark, 1908–27) includes signed articles with good bibliographies. Other works by Hastings include the *Dictionary of the Bible* (5 vols., Edinburgh, Clark, 1898–1904), *Dictionary of Christ and the Gospels* (2 vols., Edinburgh, Clark, 1906–8), and *Dictionary of the Apostolic Church* (2 vols., Edinburgh, Clark, 1916).

The *Dictionnaire d'Histoire et de Géographie ecclésiastique* (Paris, Letouzey, 1912–) is an extensive but slowly compiled encyclopedia of matters relating to the Roman Catholic church. It is particularly valuable for its biographies of little-known figures. Articles include good bibliographies. The *Dictionnaire de Théologie catholique* (Paris, Letouzey, 1909–) also contains authoritative articles with reliable bibliographies.

Among English language works the *New Catholic Encyclopedia* (15 vols., McGraw-Hill, 1967) aims to be "an international work of reference on the teachings, history, organization, and activities of the Catholic church, and on all institutions, religions, philosophies, and scientific and cultural developments affecting the Catholic church from its beginning to the present". Good bibliographies are included. There are many biographical entries. This replaces an older work, *The Catholic Encyclopedia* (17 vols., New York, Catholic Encyclopedia Pr., 1907–22).

W. E. Addis and T. Arnold, *A Catholic Dictionary*, revised by T. B. Scannell (16th edn., Routledge, 1957), is a 1-volume guide to Roman Catholic doctrines. The first edition was published in 1883 and this and other early editions are of interest for students of the Victorian period.

Biographical Works

Much biographical information may be obtained from the encyclopedias noted above and from the general biographical dictionaries discussed in Chapter 14.

A useful 1-volume dictionary is E. S. Moyer, *Who Was Who in Church History* (Chicago, Moody Pr., 1962). This includes biographies of some 1700 notable figures.

For the Church of England, *Crockford's Clerical Directory* (OUP, 1858–) is an annual guide to living figures. Volumes also include much statistical and general information about the Church of England and churches in communion with it.

J. J. Delaney and J. E. Tobin, *Dictionary of Catholic Biography* (Garden City, Doubleday, 1961), includes details of some 15,000 persons who have contributed to the development of the Roman Catholic church.

A very useful guide to members of the Society of Friends in the nineteenth century is *Quaker Records*, edited by J. J. Green (Hicks, 1894). This is an index to over 20,000 obituary notices of members of the Society which appeared in *The Annual Monitor* between 1813 and 1892.

H. Scott, *Fasti Ecclesiae Scotianae* (rev. edn., 8 vols., Oliver & Boyd, 1915–50), gives brief biographical sketches of ministers of the Church of Scotland from the Reformation onwards.

CHAPTER 7

Social and Economic Life and Thought

General Guides

The very extensive literature of the social sciences is well surveyed in P. R. Lewis, *The Literature of the Social Sciences: an introductory survey and guide* (Library Association, 1960). This provides information about basic works on the social sciences in general and on economics, economic history, statistics, commerce and industry, political science and public administration, law, international affairs, and sociology. Although the emphasis is particularly on twentieth-century materials, the book contains much information for the historian. The sections devoted to libraries and their problems are extremely useful both for students and for librarians.

C. M. White and others, *Sources of Information in the Social Sciences: a guide to the literature* (Totowa, Bedminster Pr., 1964), discusses sources of information in the major fields of study. Chapters are devoted to the social sciences in general, history, economics and business, sociology, anthropology, psychology, education, and political science. Each chapter contains a general narrative bibliographical survey followed by an annotated list of reference sources.

A Reader's Guide to the Social Sciences, edited by B. F. Hoselitz (New York, Free Pr., 1959), devotes separate chapters to history, geography, political science, economics, sociology, anthropology, and psychology. Each chapter notes developments within the subject and provides a narrative survey of the literature.

Bibliographies

The most important subject guide to the literature of the social sciences is the *London Bibliography of the Social Sciences* (London School of Economics, 1931–). The introduction to the first volume states: "Broadly, the aim has been to include all the principal collections in London which are likely to interest serious students of any branch of the Social Sciences and are open to such students without charge . . . " The first 5 volumes record the holdings as at 1929–31 of various London collections, including the British Library of Political and Economic Science, Goldsmiths' Library, National Institute of Industrial Psychology, Royal Anthropological Institute, Royal Institute of International Affairs and Royal Statistical Society. Volume 6 records additions during 1931–6 to the British Library of Political and Economic Science and to Goldsmiths' Library. From the seventh volume the work has become primarily a guide to the British Library of Political and Economic Science. It must be noted that this work is an alphabetical subject catalogue of books, pamphlets, and periodical articles (Fig. 21). Current additions to the British Library of Political and Economic Science are recorded in its *Monthly List of Additions*.

Two French compilations provide useful general bibliographies. A. Grandin, *Bibliographie générale des Sciences juridiques, politiques, économiques et sociales de 1800 à 1925/26* (Paris, Sirey, 1926), was published in 3 volumes. Annual supplements were published from 1928. This work is international in scope but with special emphasis on French-speaking countries. R. Maunier, *Manuel bibliographique des Sciences sociales et économiques* (Paris, Sirey, 1920), lists bibliographies and reference works in French, English, German, and Italian, and is particularly strong on eighteenth- and nineteenth-century materials.

Annals of the Social Sciences: a bibliographical survey, 1401–1918 (Tokyo, Dobunkan, 1957–) aims to provide a chronological listing of materials for a world bibliography of the social sciences.

EVIL EYE.
For related headings see
SUPERSTITION; WITCHCRAFT.

EVIL SPIRITS.
See DEMONOLOGY.

EVOLUTION.
[1888] 1904. Clodd (E.)
The story of creation.
pp. 128.

1899. Woltmann (L.) D.
Darwinsche Theorie u. d.
Sozialismus. pp. viii,
397. Düsseldorf.

1900. Pearson (K.) Mathemat.
contribs. to the theory of
e.: on the law of reversion.
pp. 140-164.

1903. Lombroso (C.) I
fenomeni regressivi dell'
evoluzione. (in h. Il
momento attuale)

1904. Romin (K.) Historya
ziemi i istot żyjących.
pp. 35. Kra.

[c. 1910] Small (L.)
Darwinism and socialism.
pp. 14.

[1948] Kempf (E.J.)
Holistic laws of life.
pp. 79-123. Z. N.Y.

1949. Engels (F.) The part
played by labour in the
trans. f. ape to man.
pp. 19. Mo.

[1952] Kern (F.) Gesch. u.
Entwicklung. pp. 72. Bern.

[1956] Teilhard de Chardin
(P.) Le phénomène humain.
pp. 348.

1957. Medawar (P.B.) The
uniqueness of the individual.
pp. 191. Z.

1958. Chapiro (M.) La révol.
originelle: essai sur la
gênèse de l'homme et de la
société. pp. 144. Z.

[1958] De Beer (Sir G.R.)
The Darwin-Wallace centenary.

1958. Waddington (C.H.)
Theories of e. (in
Barnett (S.A.) ed. A cent.
of Darwin)

1959. Darwin (C.R.) The
orig. of species...: a
variorum text. pp. 816.
Phila.

[1959] Glass (H.B.) and
others, eds. Forerunners
of Darwin, 1745-1859.
pp. (iv), 471. Balt.

[1959] Himmelfarb (G.)
Darwin and the Darwinian
revolution. pp. ix, 422.
Z.

1959. Teilhard de Chardin
(P.) The phenomenon of
man. pp. 320.

[1959] Willey (B.) Darwin
and cler. orthodoxy. (in
Appleman (P.) and others,
eds. 1859: entering an
age of crisis)

[1959] Zirkle (C.) E.,
marxian biology, and the
soc. scene. pp. 527. Z.
Phila.

1960. Boromé (J.A.) The e.
controversy. (in Sheehan
(D.H.) and Syrett (H.C.)
eds. Essays in American
historiography)

1960. Gurev (G.A.) Darwin-
isme et religion. pp. 229.
Mo.

1960. Tax (S.) ed. E.
after Darwin. 3 v. Z.
Chi.

1960. Willey (B.) Darwin
and Butler: two versions
of e. pp. 116.

1961. Ardrey (R.) African
genesis: a personal
investig. into the animal
origs. and nature of man.
pp. 380. Z.

1961. Banton (M.P.) ed.
Darwinism and the study

FIG. 21. *London Bibliography of the Social Sciences.* (Copyright: the British Library of Political and Economic Science.)

J. B. Williams, *A Guide to the Printed Materials for English Social and Economic History, 1750–1850* (2 vols., New York, Columbia Univ. Pr., 1926), is occasionally useful for materials relating to the early part of the Victorian period.

Periodicals are listed in *World List of Social Science Periodicals* (3rd edn., Paris, UNESCO, 1968).

Among selective lists of economic works H. E. Batson, *A Select Bibliography of Modern Economic Theory, 1870–1929* (Routledge, 1930), is an annotated guide to books and periodical articles. It is arranged by subject and author. Another useful annotated selection is *A Selected Bibliography of Economics Reference Works and Professional Journals*, compiled by the Department of Political Economy of Johns Hopkins University, (Baltimore, 1956). This lists 164 basic reference works and 87 periodicals.

Two short unannotated lists are worthy of notice. Oxford University has issued *A Bibliography for Students of Economics* (OUP, 1968), including both books and periodical articles. The *Reader's Guide to Economics* (Library Association, 1957) is a useful list of treatises, textbooks, and reference works.

Several standard histories of economic thought provide valuable bibliographies. Thus volumes of *The Cambridge Economic History of Europe* (CUP, 1941–) contain extensive lists of works. For the Victorian period, *The Industrial Revolution and After: incomes, population and technological change*, edited by H. J. Habakkuk and M. Poslan (2 vols., CUP, 1965), provides a useful selective list of references. W. Cunningham, *The Growth of English Industry and Commerce* (6th edn., 3 vols., CUP, 1915–19), and W. H. Marwick, *Economic Developments in Victorian Scotland* (Allen & Unwin, 1936), include good bibliographies.

The American Economic Association compiles an *Index of Economic Journals* (Homewood, Irwin, 1961–) listing articles in English published since 1886 in a large number of periodicals. Entries are arranged in classified order and each volume contains an author index. The first volume, covering the years 1886–1924, is especially useful for the Victorian student.

H. Schleiffer and R. Crandall, *Index to Economic History Essays in Festschriften, 1900–1950* (Cambridge, Harvard Univ. Pr., 1953), is a guide to material which often proves elusive. The work is arranged by broad subject groups with indexes of authors and names.

D. V. Glass, *Introduction to Malthus* (Watts, 1953), includes a list of books dealing with the population question, 1793–1880.

There are extensive bibliographies of labour history in G. D. H. Cole, *Short History of the British Working-Class Movement, 1789–1947* (new edn., Allen & Unwin, 1948), and in G. D. H. Cole and R. Postgate, *Common People, 1746–1946* (4th edn., Methuen, 1949). G. D. H. Cole, *Introduction to Trade Unionism* (Allen & Unwin, 1953), contains a useful bibliography. An *International Bibliography of Trade Unionism* by V. L. Allen has recently been announced for publication.

There is a strong financial bias to the *Bibliography of Economic Science*, compiled by Osaka University of Commerce (4 vols., Tokyo, Maruzen, 1934–39). The first volume covers public finance, volumes 2 and 3 deal with money and finance, and volume 4 is devoted to commerce and industry. M. Masui, *A Bibliography of Finance* (Kobe, University of Commerce, 1935), arranges material by language, topic, and period covered.

For studies of banking history there is a useful check-list of "U.K. banking history" in the Institute of Bankers' *Monthly List* (vol. 8, 1956, pp. 6–13). This notes over 150 items, including general works and histories of individual banks and companies. E. Coppetier, *English Banknote Circulation, 1694–1954* (The Hague, Louvain Institute, 1955), contains an excellent bibliography.

The sources of the study of business history are well surveyed in T. C. Barker and others, *Business History* (Historical Association, 1960). This pamphlet is one of the Historical Association's very useful series of Helps for Students of History.

The Study of Urban History, edited by H. J. Dyos (Arnold, 1968), includes an extremely valuable bibliographical survey by the editor, entitled "Agenda for urban historians".

Among guides to sources of information for transport history A. M. Milne, *Economics of Inland Transport* (2nd edn., Pitman, 1963), provides a useful basic bibliography. The standard guide to the literature of railways history is G. Ottley, *A Bibliography of British Railway History* (Allen & Unwin, 1965) (Fig. 22). The *Journal of Transport History* (Leicester, Univ. Pr., 1953–) includes a regular transport bibliography, reviews and a series of articles on the sources of transport history (Fig. 23). *Transport History* (Newton Abbot, David & Charles, 1968–) also includes useful reviews and notes.

Current Work

The UNESCO project on *Documentation in the Social Sciences* has instituted four periodicals listing new works. These form part of the programme devised by the International Committee for Social Sciences Documentation. The periodicals, published by UNESCO, are *International Bibliography of Sociology* (1951–), *International Bibliography of Economics* (1952–), *International Bibliography of Political Science* (1952–), and *International Bibliography of Social and Cultural Anthropology* (1955–). They contain extensive selective lists of books, pamphlets, periodical articles, and government publications. Entries are arranged in broad subject groups with English author and subject indexes. Each bibliography contains a list of periodicals indexed.

Another useful general bibliography of modern works is *Bibliographie der Sozialwissenschaften* (Vandenhoeck & Ruprecht) which was published as a periodical from 1905 to 1943. In 1950 it recommenced as part of the *Jahrbuch für Sozialwissenschaft*. This bibliography provides an extensive classified listing of books and periodical articles in various languages.

Many periodicals give information about new works on economic history. *Economic History Review* (CUP, 1926–) and *Journal of Economic History* (New York, Univ. Pr., 1940–) both include book reviews, book-lists, and bibliographical articles. The *American Economic Review* (Evanston, American Economic Association, 1911–) includes extensive literature surveys and

4342 REPORT of the public meeting of railway shareholders held in Liverpool, 16th of April, 1849, to consider the propriety of petitioning Parliament to amend the law in respect to the rating of railways. *Liverpool*, 1849. pp. 21.   BRE

4343 WEBB, C. L. A letter to . . . Henry Labouchere, M.P., President of the Board of Trade, etc., etc., on railways, their accounts and dividends, their progress, present position and future prospects, their effects on trade and commerce; with suggestions for Government assistance and the amendment of the General Railway Acts of 1845. *London*, [1849.] pp. 64, with fold. table.   BM

4344 WHITEHEAD, J. Railway prostration: causes and remedies: letter to . . . Sir Robert Peel. *London*, 1849. pp. 25.   BM
Warning against a too rapid expansion of railway development. Urges Government control.

4345 LARDNER, D. Railway economy: a treatise on the new art of transport, its management, prospects and relations, commercial, financial and social . . . *London*, 1850. pp. xxiii, 528.   BM
A very detailed work on railways in general and on specific aspects and problems.
—— another edn. *New York*, 1850. pp. xxiii, 442.

4346 RICHARDSON, J. A revised and complete report of the recent trial for libel, Richardson v[ersus] Wodson; with preliminary observations on the Railway Mania of 1845–6–7–8. Also, a biographical sketch of Mr. George Hudson . . . together with an appendix setting forth in detail the whole system of railway mismanagement and railway frauds pursued since the establishment of railways in the City of York. *London*, [1850.] pp. xvi, 27.   BM

4347 HODGSON, H. J. Summary of the law as applied to the rating of railways and other undertakings extending through several parishes, with notes of all the cases hitherto decided by the Court of Queen's Bench on the subject of railway rating, and some observations on the practical mode of assessing a railway. *London*, 1851. pp. xii, 108.   BM

4348 LAING, S. Audit of railway accounts: letter to the proprietors of the London, Brighton & South Coast Railway Company.

4350 PENFOLD, C. Rating of railways: the Great Western Railway and Tilehurst parish: observations upon Lord Campbell's declaration of the necessity of Parliament fixing a rule for the assessment of railways; in a letter addressed to Henry Chase, Jun., of Reading, Berks., solicitor to the parish. *London*, 1851. pp. 16.   LSE
Assessing railways for the relief of the poor.

4351 RIGHTWAY, L. Rail-ways, public-ways, and government-ways. *London*, 1851. pp. 11.   BM

4352 SMIRKE, E. A letter to Lord Campbell on the rating of railways. *London*, 1851. pp. 26.   BM
The inadequacies of railway law.

4353 BEAUMONT, G. D. B. Railway amalgamation by a scale. *London*, 1852. pp. 12.

4354 CRIPPS, H. W. How to rate a railway in accordance with the decisions of the Court of Queen's Bench. *London*, 1853. pp. vi, 85.   BM

4355 MARSHALL, W. Railway legislation and railway reform considered with special reference to Scottish lines. *Edinburgh & London*, 1852. pp. iv, 111.   BM
—— 2nd edn. *Edinburgh*, 1853. pp. 114. BM

4356 CASTLE, H. J. Contributive value a necessary element in the parochial principle of railway assessments; what it is and how it can be measured . . . with a brief history of railway rating. *London*, 1854. pp. 63. BM

4357 COATES, T. Notes on the present condition of railway legislation. *London*, 1854. pp. 28.   BM
Condemning as impracticable, Cardwell's Bill for the introduction of an interchange system between railways in place of amalgamations.

4358 PARLIAMENTARY repudiation. [1854?] pp. 71.   BM
No title page in BM copy.
A protest against *An Act to enable the Eastern Union Railway Company to redeem their preference shares, etc.* (16 & 17 Vict. cap. ccxxi) [20 August, 1853], and an exposure of corruption in the House of Commons with regard to Railway Bills generally.
Contains much detail on the affairs of the Eastern Union Rly., of Thomas Brassey the

FIG. 22. G. Ottley, *A Bibliography of British Railway History*. (Copyright: George Allen & Unwin Ltd.)

TRANSPORT BIBLIOGRAPHY

I. PUBLICATIONS ON THE HISTORY OF TRANSPORT IN BRITISH PERIODICALS, 1963

This list (in continuation of that for 1962, printed in Vol. VI, No. 1 of this JOURNAL, pp. 56–7) takes account of papers actually published in 1963, irrespective of the dates the journals bear on their title-pages. It does not, as a rule, include papers in journals specifically devoted to transport.

The Amateur Historian
  M. Bouquet. The Provincial Seaports of the Nineteenth Century. v (1962–), 177–82.
  B. F. Duckham. Inland Waterways: some Sources for their History. vi (1963–), 8–10.

Architectural Review
  D. Walters and A. F. Sealey. The first Iron Railway Bridge. cxxxiii (1963), 190–2.

The Banker
  A. Day. Modernising Britain's Railway System. cxiii (1963), 311–8.
  Cash in Transit. *Ibid.*, 614–20.

Design
  Special Issue on British Railways. No. 171, Mar. 1963.
  R. Carr. Design Analysis: Bicycle. No. 176 (Aug. 1963), 42–7.

Economic Journal
  A. Silberston. Hire Purchase Controls and the Demand for Cars. lxxiii (1963), 32–53.
  Comment and Reply: *ibid.*, 553–8.

Economica
  D. Usher. The Transport Bias in Comparisons of National Income. n.s. xxx (1963), 140–58.
  M. E. Beesley, A. J. Blackburn, and C. D. Foster. Urban Transport Models and Motorway Investment. *Ibid.*, 243–61.

Greece and Rome
  J. E. T. Brown. Hannibal's Route across the Alps. 2nd ser., x (1963), 38–46.

History Today
  T. C. Barker. The Centenary of London's Underground. xiii (1963), 115–22.

  A. Horne. By Balloon from Paris. *Ibid.*, 441–8.
  D. Sawers. The Rigid Airship. *Ibid.*, 757–66.

British Journal of Industrial Relations
  P. Duncan. Conflict and Co-operation among Trawlermen. 1 (1963), 331–47.

National Institute Economic Review
  G. F. Rag and R. E. Crum. Transport: Notes and Comments. No. 24 (May 1963), 23–41.

Nature
  C. H. Gibbs–Smith. The Wright Brothers and their Invention of the Practical Aeroplane. cxcviii (1963), 824–6.

Oxford Economic Papers
  A. D. Brownlie and M. F. Lloyd Prichard. Professor Fleeming Jenkin, 1833–85. xv (1963), 204–16.
  A. J. Harrison. Economies of Scale and the Structure of the Road Haulage Industry, *Ibid.*, 287–307.

Bulletin of the Oxford University Institute of Economics and Statistics
  A. J. Harrison, Road Transport and the Motorways. xxv (1963), 215–37.

Planning
  Transport in the Common Market. xxix (1963), 225–83.

Railway Steel Topics
  C. E. R. Sherrington. Some Milestones in Railway Engineering. vii (1963), 4–11.

189

FIG. 23. *Journal of Transport History.* (Copyright: Leicester University Press.)

annual lists of theses in American universities. *Economic Journal* (Macmillan, 1891–) includes annotated lists of periodical articles and new books.

Economic Abstracts (The Hague, Nijhoff, 1953–) contains abstracts of books and periodical articles. Each issue has a detailed subject index. *Journal of Economic Abstracts* (Cambridge, Harvard Univ. Pr., 1963–) is published under the auspices of the American Economic Association and contains lengthy abstracts of articles selected from about 35 periodicals. It has author and subject indexes.

Population Index (Princeton, Univ. Pr., and the Population Association of America, 1935–) is an unannotated bibliography of books and periodical articles on all aspects of the population question.

Urban History Newsletter (Leicester, 1963–) includes an annual bibliography of recent books and periodical articles (Fig. 24) and an annual register of research in progress. The editor, H. J. Dyos, has contributed a valuable list of "British university theses on the urban history of Great Britain, 1911–65" (no. 5, December 1965, pp. 9–43).

The International Institute of Social History publishes a *Bulletin* which includes annotated bibliographies. The *International Review of Social History* (Amsterdam, 1956–) also includes bibliographies.

Theses

General guides to theses are discussed in Chapter 2. A few lists which are included in periodicals are noted above.

In 1952 UNESCO published a list of *Theses in the Social Sciences, 1940–1950*. This is an international analytical catalogue of unpublished doctoral theses arranged by subject with author index.

Until 1956/7 the National Institute of Economic and Social Research compiled a *Register of Research in the Social Sciences*, published successively by CUP and Aslib. From 1968 the annual *Scientific Research in British Universities and Colleges* (HMSO) includes a volume dealing with the social sciences (Fig. 25). This

CURRENT BIBLIOGRAPHY OF URBAN HISTORY

(1) GENERAL

*   — , City and Nation in the Developing World /selected case studies of social change in Asia, Africa and Latin America/ American Univs. Field Staff, 196., pp.256 il.

*   — , The City in American History /Report of Yale Conference on the teaching of Social Studies/ Yale, 1967, pp.111, il.

*   — , 'Symposium on the Victorian city', Victorian Studies, 11 (Mar 68), pp.275-406.

*   — , 'The conscience of the city' /an attempt to analyse the inter-relatedness of already-defined urban problems and to produce practical policy solutions/ Daedalus, (Fall 68), pp. v-xi + 1091-1430 /issued as Vol. 97, No. 4, Proc. of Amer. Acad. Arts & Sciences/

*   — , 'Venice' /includes reference to its place in urban hist/ Urbanistica, 52 (Jan 68),

*   ARRIAGA, EE, 'Components of city growth in selected Latin American countries', Milbank Memorial Fund Qutly, 2(Apr 68), pp237-52

FIG. 24. Urban History Newsletter. (Copyright: the Editor.)

39. Leicester University (*continued*)

M.J. Pullen	Retail trade patterns in the East Midlands (1967–68; Department of Economic Affairs)
C.H. Sharp, Ph.D. with K.L. Usher	Passenger transport in the "Greater Leicester" area (1966–67; East Midlands Planning Council, Ministry of Transport)
K.L. Usher and M. Jewsbury (Miss)	Effect of construction and use regulations on the economics of goods vehicles, including a study of the net benefits likely to result from raising the maximum laden weight of vehicles from 32 to 38 tons (1967–68; Social Science Research Council)

40. Leicester Regional College of Technology (*Business and Management Studies*)

D.E. John (Head of Department)	
J.R. Knibbs	Productivity bargaining and its implications for management, with special reference to a specific agreement
D.C. Spencer	Development of ultra-stable production and stock control systems: examination of the role of stocks as a causal factor in generating economic instability

41. Liverpool University

Professor F.E. Hyde, Ph.D. with P.N. Davies and S. Marriner (Miss)	Six volume study of British shipping companies
P.N. Davies	British West African shipping companies 1910–66 (1966–continuing)
J.R. Harris, Ph.D.	Origins of the St. Helens glass industry
	Capital formation in Lancashire 1680–1710 (1966–continuing)
	Coal technology and economic progress 1680–1780 (1966–continuing)
H.R. Parker	Retailing: house values
R.C. Skinner	Income-asset ratios of quoted companies as a means of ascertaining relative profitability (1966–continuing)
	Analysis of overhead cost variances in standard costing (1967–68)
	Relevance or otherwise of book values in machine replacement decisions (1967–68)
M.J. Gates	Supply of gold in the event of a rise in its price (1966–continuing)
R. Bean	Labour organizations in Liverpool in the 1890's (1966–68)
M.H.J. Finch	Economic development of Uruguay since 1914 (1968–69)
	Economic maturity and the Canadian economy (1968)
W.A. Thomas	Provincial stock markets
P.L. Cottrell	British capital market, 1856–80, with special reference to the supply of domestic funds and to the position of the "crédit mobilier" type finance houses in this period
J.H. Porter	Wages and industrial conciliation and arbitration, 1860–1914
O.E. Obinna	Impact of rising crops on Nigerian economic growth
Professor G.H. Lawson	Corporate financial planning, with special reference to invest-

FIG. 25. *Scientific Research in British Universities and Colleges* (Part III: *Social Sciences*). (Copyright: the Controller of Her Majesty's Stationery Office.)

provides a note on research in progress by staff and students for doctoral degrees. The work is sponsored by the Department of Education and Science and the British Council.

Research Collections

The British Library of Political and Economic Science, which was established in 1896 on the initiative of Sidney Webb, acts both as the library of the London School of Economics and as the national collection of materials for research. Its scope includes the social sciences in the widest sense. It contains good collections in the history of local government, anthropology, and socialism. *A Guide to the Collections* was published in 1948. Although now out of date, this is still a useful guide to basic bibliographies and reference books.

The Goldsmiths' Library of Economic Literature, housed in the University of London Library, contains a notable collection of nineteenth-century works, especially of the first half of the century. Many of its holdings are included in the *London Bibliography of the Social Sciences*.

Many government departmental libraries have important collections for the student of the Victorian period. Guides to these have been discussed in Chapter 4.

The Institute of Bankers Library includes works on economics, banking, and finance, and the National Institute of Economic and Social Research has a specialized collection of works on economic theory and income and wealth. The Royal Statistical Society issued a *Catalogue of the Library* in 1921.

Many other libraries and institutions are noted in P. R. Lewis, *The Literature of the Social Sciences* (Library Association, 1960). Others may be traced in the *Aslib Directory* (new edn., Aslib, 1968–). A useful guide to economic collections is D. D. Reeves, *Resources for the Study of Economic History: a preliminary guide to pre-20th century printed materials in collections located in certain American and British Libraries* (Boston, Baker Library, 1961).

Encyclopedias

The social sciences are well served by the *International Encyclopedia of the Social Sciences*, edited by D. L. Sills (17 vols., New York, Macmillan and Free Pr., 1968). This work covers the fields of anthropology, economics, geography, history, law, political science, psychiatry, psychology, sociology, and statistics. Each article is followed by a selective bibliography. The work includes biographies of some 600 persons whose research and writings have had an impact on the social sciences. The introduction states that the *International Encyclopedia* is "designed to complement, not to supplant, its predecessor", the *Encyclopaedia of the Social Sciences*, edited by E. R. A. Seligman and A. Johnson (15 vols., New York, Macmillan, 1930–5). This older work includes some 4000 biographical articles, most of them shorter than the biographical entries in the later work.

A convenient 1-volume guide is *A Dictionary of the Social Sciences* (Tavistock, 1964).

Handwörterbuch der Sozialwissenschaften (7 vols., Stuttgart, Fischer, 1952–) is a new edition of *Handwörterbuch der Staatswissenschaften* (4th edn., 9 vols., Jena, Fischer, 1923–9). Both titles will prove occasionally useful, as will *Staatslexikon: Recht, Wirtschaft, Gesellschaft* (6th edn., 8 vols., Freiburg, Herder, 1957–).

Among encyclopedic works published during the Victorian period, the *Dictionary of Political Economy*, edited by R. H. I. Palgrave (3 vols., Macmillan, 1894), is still useful for its treatment of economic thought from a nineteenth-century viewpoint. The work includes biographies and brief bibliographies.

CHAPTER 8

Education

Guides and Bibliographies

The most useful basic general guide is S. K. Kimmance, *A Guide to the Literature of Education* (rev. edn., Institute of Education, Univ. of London, 1961), which was published as the first supplement to the *Education Libraries Bulletin*. The guide provides an annotated list of a wide variety of significant reference works (Fig. 26).

D. J. Foskett, *How to Find Out: educational research* (Oxford, Pergamon Pr., 1965), is a complementary work which aims to explain the various types of publication in this research field and to offer advice on their use. It is not itself a detailed guide to the literature of education.

Among other general guides, C. Alexander and A. J. Bourke, *How to Locate Educational Information and Data* (4th edn., New York, Teachers College, Columbia Univ., 1958), has a marked American bias but covers a large number of guides to the literature. S. K. Wigmore, *An Annotated Guide to Publications Related to Educational Research* (Toronto, Department of Educational Research, Ontario College of Education, Univ. of Toronto, 1960), has a strong emphasis on Canada but includes sections on general and British educational writings. Use of both these works will involve a selective approach, but both reveal valuable information.

The *International Guide to Educational Documentation, 1955–1960* (Paris, UNESCO, 1963) is a well-annotated guide to educational materials and sources in 95 countries and territories. The section for the United Kingdom lists basic reference works and

RESEARCH

The centre for educational research in Britain is the
National Foundation for Educational Research - their
annual reports and other publications (mentioned elsewhere) are some of the means of keeping up-to-date with
current problems in the field. In the United States the
publications of the American Educational Research Association perform much the same function as the NFER over
here; note their journal Review of Educational Research
(described on page 51).

Various guides on methods of procedure in conducting
educational research are often useful aids to the literature of the subject also. A very helpful book is:

Alexander, Carter and Burke, Arvid, J. - How to locate
educational information and data. Fourth edition revised.
New York, Bureau of Publications, Teachers College,
Columbia University. 1958.

This looks at research from the bibliographical angle,
and includes chapters on such topics as - official
publications; publications of educational associations;
statistics; and there is one on 'Making the most of the
Education Index'. It is American in outlook, but as this
covers quite a large amount of literature in use in
British libraries, it is important.

A directory of educational research agencies and studies -
compiled by Raymond J. Young. Indiana, Phi Delta Kappa.
1957.

Again completely American, amongst other information it
gives names and address of research organisations, and
states whether their reports are printed or duplicated.

Other American books on this topic are:

Best, John W. - Research in education. New Jersey,
Prentice Hall. 1959.

FIG. 26. S. K. Kimmance, *A Guide to the Literature of Education*. (Copyright: the Librarian, University of London Institute of Education.)

guides to research publications and educational bodies and their publications. The work also includes much general information about administration and policy.

W. S. Monroe and L. Shores, *Bibliographies and Summaries in Education to July 1935* (New York, Wilson, 1936), lists more than 4000 annotated bibliographies and summaries, mainly published in the period 1910–35, although a selection of bibliographies published before 1910 is also included. Arrangement is by author and subject with brief annotations.

A very valuable guide for the student of English education is G. Baron, *A Bibliographical Guide to the English Educational System* (3rd edn., Athlone Pr., 1965). This concise narrative summary of selected literature contains many useful references to works on historical aspects of education.

The most important list of materials and British locations for the student of Victorian educational history is *Sources for the History of Education: a list of materials (including school books) contained in the libraries of the institutes and schools of education, together with works from the libraries of the universities of Nottingham and Reading*, edited by C. W. J. Higson (Library Association, 1967) (Fig. 27). Three of the five sections of this work are of interest for the Victorian period. These list "Books on education published, or first published, 1801–1870", "Textbooks and children's books published, or first published, 1801–1870", and "Government publications up to and including 1918". For each entry bibliographical details are given together with a list of locations which contain copies of the work. Although some foreign publications are included, the emphasis is naturally on British books and pamphlets. As is noted in the preface, some of the titles and many of the editions listed are not in the catalogue of the British Museum. Duplicated supplementary lists have been produced in the University of Leicester School of Education Library.

The government publications listed in *Sources for the History of Education* will often supplement information derived from the general lists noted in Chapter 4. A good brief introduction for the historian of education is M. Argles and J. E. Vaughan, *British*

SECTION C

Books on education published, or first published, 1801-1870

C1 ABBOTT, Jacob, 1803–1879. (1833) The teacher; or, moral influences employed in the in-. struction and government of the young. Darton, [1833]. LEE; Revised by the Rev. Charles Mayo. Seeley, etc., 1834. LEI NE; Darton, [c. 1836]. HU

C2 ABBOTT, John Stevens Cabot, 1805–1877. The mother at home; or, the principles of maternal duty familiarly illustrated. Revised. R.T.S., [1833?]. LEI

C3 ABERCROMBIE, John, 1780–1844. (1830) Inquiries concerning the intellectual powers and the investigation of truth. 15th ed., Murray, 1857. LEI

ABERDARE, Henry Austin Bruce, 1st baron. See Bruce, Henry Austin

C4 ABERDEEN. Public meeting on national education, 1851. Report of the proceedings at a public meeting, held in the Mechanics' Hall, Aberdeen, 25th April 1851 on . . . national education. [From the 'Aberdeen Herald'.] Aberdeen, L. Smith, 1851. HU

C5 ABERDEENSHIRE. Prison board. Aberdeenshire reports on juvenile delinquency, 1845, 1848, 1851. HU

C6 ABRAHAM, J. H., ed. Juvenile essays: comprising . . . the first and second half-yearly prize compositions of the pupils belonging to the Milk Street Academy, Sheffield, to which is prefixed a brief history of education and a table of the system pursued in the above academy. W. Todd, 1805. SH

Academic errors. See Gilly, William Stephen

Account of public charities in England and Wales. See Wade, John

Account of the progress of Joseph Lancaster's plan for the education of poor children. See Lancaster, Joseph

C7 An ACCOUNT of the visit of his royal highness the Prince Regent and their imperial and royal majesties the Emperor of Russia and the King of Prussia to the University of Oxford in June MDCCCXIV. Oxford, Clarendon Pr., 1815. ReU

C10 ACLAND, Sir T. D. (1858) S of the origin and objects of the new C nations for the title of Associate in ; ed., Ridgway, 1858. ReU

C11 ADAM, A. Mercer. ed. (1857) album. Dumfries, Dumfries & Mechanics Institution, 1857. LEI

C12 ADAM, James. The knowledge . a plan for the reciprocal extension of e the franchise. Edinburgh, Tait, 1837.

C13 ADAMS, Francis, ed. The Eleme tion act, 1870; with analysis, index a Simpkin, Marshall, 1870. BR

C14 ADAMS, John. (1850) Summary A charge to the Grand Jury of the qu. of the county of Middlesex . . . at the 1850. J. T. Norris, 1850. HU

C15 ADDERLEY, Charles Bowyer, 1st i 1814–1905, and GRIFFITHS, William. (spondence between Mr. Adderley and Griffiths of Tutbury on the principles Graham's scheme for national educati 1843. LEE

Address on national education . . . by of Magdalene Hall. See Macbride, J

Admonitions for Sunday schools. Peter

Adèle et Théodore. See Genlis, comt

C16 ADSHEAD, Joseph. On juveni reformatories and the means of r perishing and dangerous classes servi state. Manchester, Harrison, 1856. from the Transactions of the Manches society.] BR

C17 AETAS, pseud. The reform of connection with that of our public universities. A letter addressed to Honourable Lord Viscount Palmerst Daldy, 1855. LO

C18 AIMÉ-MARTIN, Louis. (Fr. 183· cation of mothers of families; or, the c the human race by women . . . Trai the 3rd Paris edition, with remarks on t methods of education . . . by E. Lee.

FIG. 27. C. W. J. Higson, *Sources for the History of Education*. (Copyright: the Library Association.)

Government Publications Concerning Education: an introductory guide (Liverpool, Institute of Education, Univ. of Liverpool, 1966). A selection of official documents with introduction and brief notes which includes much nineteenth-century material is J. S. Maclure, *Educational Documents, England and Wales, 1816–1967* (Chapman & Hall, 1968).

Adult education is well served by *A Select Bibliography of Adult Education in Great Britain, Including Works Published to the End of the Year 1961*, edited by T. Kelly (2nd edn., National Institute of Adult Education, 1962). The preface states that this bibliography attempts to include "all books of substantial merit, together with a selection of pamphlets and articles presenting information or points of view not adequately represented in book form". Entries are annotated. This work is supplemented by annual lists in the *Year Book* of the National Institute of Adult Education.

M. Argles, *South Kensington to Robbins: an account of English technical and scientific education since 1851* (Longmans, 1964), contains an excellent selected bibliography of works in this field. P. H. J. H. Gosden, *Educational Administration in England and Wales: a bibliographical guide* (Leeds, Institute of Education, Univ. of Leeds, 1967), lists several nineteenth-century works and also includes a selective list of the more important statutes dealing with educational administration during the last 100 years.

The *British Journal of Educational Studies* (Faber, 1952–) has published a series of important bibliographical articles on sources for the history of various fields of education. A convenient list, with much other valuable information, is provided in an informative article by C. W. J. Higson, "Some bibliographical tools for students of the history of education" in the *History of Education Society Bulletin* (no. 1, Spring 1968, pp. 30–40).

Theses

The most important guide to British theses in education is A. M. Blackwell, *A List of Researches in Education and Educational*

Psychology, Presented for Higher Degrees in the Universities of the United Kingdom, Northern Ireland and the Irish Republic (Newnes, for the National Foundation for Educational Research in England and Wales, 1950–). The first volume covered the period 1918–48 and later volumes have continued the listing to 1957. Theses are arranged in classified order with subject and author indexes.

Because of the lack of documentation for the period after 1957, the Scottish Council for Research in Education published *A List of Researches in Education and Educational Psychology Presented for Degrees in Scottish Universities from 1958 to 1961*. This is supplemented by regular lists in the Council's Annual Report.

The National Foundation for Educational Research in England and Wales publishes at intervals a list of *Current Researches in Education and Educational Psychology*. This gives details of research in progress in universities, colleges of education, and other similar institutions and by private individuals. The lists are based on answers to questionnaires. Although incomplete, these provide a useful guide to work in progress. The Foundation has also published in a single volume *Technical Education and Training in the United Kingdom: research in progress, 1962–64* and a *Supplement, 1963–1964, of Reported Researches*. Although the projects listed in these volumes are concerned primarily with contemporary educational practice, a few are devoted to historical aspects of technical education.

Paedagogica Historica (Ghent, 1961–) includes regular lists of recent theses on the history of education. Occasional retrospective lists are also included and there are notes on research in progress.

For American theses, two useful cumulated lists have been published by Phi Delta Kappa under the title *Research Studies in Education*. These, covering the years 1941–51 (Bloomington, 1952) and 1952–63 (Bloomington, 1965), index doctoral dissertations, reports, and field studies. Other American lists include W. C. Eells, *American Dissertations on Foreign Education 1884–1958* (Washington, Committee on International Relations, 1959), and the United States office of Education Library's annual

Bibliography of Research Studies in Education (Washington, Government Printing Office, 1926/7–1939/40).

Current Work

The *British Education Index* (Library Association, 1954–) is compiled by Librarians of Institutes and Schools of Education and is published 3 times a year and cumulated every 2 years (Fig. 28). It indexes articles in more than 60 British periodicals. Arrangement is by author and subject. It should be noted that entries are not limited to subjects of British interest.

Education Index (New York, Wilson, 1929–) is published monthly except for July and August. Until June 1961 it included author and subject entries for books and periodical articles. From September 1961, however, it has become a subject index to more than 200 periodicals, proceedings, year books, bulletin and monograph series published in the United States, Canada, and Britain. Most of the titles covered by the *British Education Index* are not indexed by the *Education Index*, and the 2 works are complementary.

Among abstracting journals, *Sociology of Education Abstracts* (Liverpool, School of Education, Univ. of Liverpool, 1965–) and *Technical Education Abstracts* (National Foundation for Educational Research in England and Wales, 1961–) are especially useful. *Education Abstracts* (Paris, UNESCO, 1949–1964/5) was not, in fact, an abstracting journal but a collection of bibliographical articles. Each issue usually covered the bibliography of one aspect of education.

Encyclopedias

There is a useful bibliography of "Encyclopaedias and dictionaries of education" in *Education Abstracts* (vol. 9, no. 9, November 1957). Among English-language works, *The Encyclopaedia and Dictionary of Education*, edited by F. Watson (4 vols., Pitman, 1921–2), includes many signed articles with brief bibliographical

Education: Aims & Philosophy—cont:
Vertical translation and the philosophy of education. S. B. Wynburne. Ed. for Teaching, 66 (Feb 65) p.56-9
What is a good teacher? consensus of world opinion. Times Ednl. Supp., no.2578 (16 Oct 64) p.661

Education: Classification Schemes
Classification in training colleges. N. Roberts. Ed. Lib. Bulletin, 19 (Spring 64) p.25-9
Les étapes principales de l'enseignement: une classification des systèmes scolaires. Franz Hilker. Paedagogica Europaea, (1965) p.35-43, 45 [The main stages of education: a classification of educational systems. English abstract on p.44]

Education: History. See under the names of specific persons, topics and countries

Education: Policy
Education: programmes and men. Quinton Hoare. New Left R., no.32 (Jul-Aug 65) p.40-52
Education: wrong direction? A. B. Clegg. New Society, (11 Feb 65) p.20-2
Education and change. Alexander King. Nature, 206 (12 Jun 65) p.1078-83 [Annual Guinness Awards Lecture (27 Apr 65)]
Education as a political exercise. Brian Chapman. Nature, 201 (14 Mar 64) p.1065-70 [Lecture at Bangor]
Educational policy for regional groups. A. Biedermann.

Educationally Subnormal Children. See Subnormal Children
Electrical Engineering Education. See Vocational Education: Electrical Engineering
Electricity Teaching. See Physics Teaching: Electricity
Electronics Engineering Education. See Vocational Education: Electronics Engineering

Emdrupborg Experimental School
An experiment with gradual modification of the school organisation at the post-primary stage. Wilhelm Marckmann. International R. Ed., 10. (1964) p.464-8

Emotionally Disturbed Children. See Maladjustment

Employment of Youth
First jobs. Catherine Avent and Ann Bryden. Technical Ed., 7 (May 65) p.212-3
Studying the employment and training of a national sample of 17-year-olds. David M. Nelson. Occup. Psych., 38 (Jul/Oct 64) p.183-90
What happens to classics graduates? Michael Kendall. Didaskalos, 1 .(1964) p.142-7
Young workers in their first jobs: an investigation of attitudes to work and their correlates. Virginia C. Palmer. Occup. Psych., 38 (Apr 64) p.99-113

Engineering Drawing. See Vocational Education: Engineering Drawing
Engineering Education. See Vocational Education: Engineering

FIG. 28. *British Education Index*. (Copyright: the Library Association.)

references. Although rather popular in treatment, it contains considerable valuable biographical and bibliographical information.

Sonnenschein's Cyclopaedia of Education, edited by A. W. Fletcher (2nd edn., Sonnenschein, 1889), is extremely valuable and an indication of the educational outlook in the Victorian period. *The Teacher's Encyclopaedia of the Theory, Practice, History and Development of Education at Home and Abroad*, edited by A. P. Laurie (7 vols., Caxton, 1911) is similarly useful. A 2nd edition was published in 4 volumes in 1922. *A Cyclopedia of Education*, edited by P. Monroe (5 vols., New York, Macmillan, 1911–13), although showing American bias, is useful for the historian.

More modern encyclopedias include the *Lexicon der Pädagogik* (3 vols., Berne, Francke, 1950–2). The first 2 volumes contain articles, while the third includes a valuable biography section listing details of educators of all periods and countries. *The Encyclopedia of Modern Education*, edited by H. N. Rivlin and H. Schueler (New York, Philosophical Library, 1943), has some useful articles with bibliographies.

The *Encyclopedia of Educational Research*, edited by W. C. Harris (3rd edn., New York, Macmillan, 1960), is not a conventional encyclopedia but a summary of research on educational topics. Topics are arranged alphabetically and each entry comprises a descriptive and evaluative narrative survey followed by a bibliography of books and articles.

Biographical Works

Considerable biographical information is contained in the encyclopedias noted above and in the general biographical works discussed in Chapter 14. A most valuable bibliographical guide is A. Christophers, *An Index to Nineteenth Century British Educational Biography* (Institute of Education, Univ. of London, 1965), which was published as the 10th supplement to *Education Libraries Bulletin*. This includes a section listing works of collected biography followed by a list of biographies of individuals active

6. ADAMS, Sir John, 1857-1934.
Head of Scottish grammar schools and training colleges;
later first Professor of Education in University of
London.

SADLER, Sir Michael
John Adams; a lecture in his memory. ... London,
Humphrey Milford, O.U.P., for the Institute of
Education, 1935.
18 p., 25 cm. (University of London Institute of
Education studies and reports, no. 6.)

7. ALLEN, William, 1770-1843.
Treasurer of the British and Foreign School Society.

ALLEN, William
Life of William Allen, with selections from his
correspondence. London, Charles Gilpin, 1846-1847.
3 v., 21½ cm.

SHERMAN, James
Memoir of William Allen, F.R.S. London, Charles
Gilpin; Edinburgh, Adam and Charles Black; Dublin,
J.B. Gilpin, 1851.
viii, 463 p., 19½ cm.

8. ALMOND, Hely Hutchinson, 1832-1903.

MACKENZIE, Robert Jameson
Almond of Loretto, being the life and a selection
from the letters of Hely Hutchinson Almond; M.A.,
Glasgow; M.A., Oxon.; LL.D., Glasgow; headmaster of
Loretto School (1862-1903). 2nd impression. London,
Archibald Constable and co., 1906.
x, 408 p., port., 22½ cm.
First published 1905.

9. ANDERSON, Elizabeth Garrett, 1836-1917.

ANDERSON, Louisa Garrett
Elizabeth Garrett Anderson, 1836-1917. London,
Faber and Faber, 1939.
338 p., 8 ports., 20½ cm.

10. ANDREW, James, 1774?-1833.
Headmaster of East India Company's Military Seminary
at Addiscombe, Surrey.

D.N.B., Vol. 1; p. 400.

11. ANDREWS, Frederick, 1850-1922.
Headmaster of the Quaker school at Ackworth, 1877-1920.

FIG. 29. A. Christophers, *An Index to Nineteenth Century British Educational Biography.* (Copyright: the Librarian, University of London Institute of Education.)

82

in education between 1800 and 1900. The list is arranged alphabetically by biographees (Fig. 29). Periodical articles are not included.

J. E. Roscoe, *The Dictionary of Educationists* (4th edn., Pitman, 1914), is concerned primarily with British figures. It is a useful guide to several little-known educationists. F. P. Graves, *Great Educators of Three Centuries: their work and its influence on modern education* (New York, Macmillan, 1912), includes short bibliographies of each person listed.

There is a useful guide to *Welsh Political and Educational Leaders in the Victorian Era*, edited by J. V. Morgan (Nisbet, 1908). This includes over 50 biographical sketches by various authors. A. Morgan, *Makers of Scottish Education* (Longmans, 1929), includes a useful bibliography.

CHAPTER 9

Science

GENERAL

Guides and Bibliographies

The basic introductory guide to the history of science is G. Sarton, *Horus: a guide to the history of science* (Waltham, Chronica Botanica, 1952). This contains 3 general essays followed by extensive bibliographies of books and articles on all aspects of the subject, including details of general reference works, studies of science in various countries, studies of the history of special sciences, periodicals, libraries, societies, and international congresses. Each section of the bibliography is preceded by a short narrative introduction.

For the Victorian period the major bibliographical tool is the *Catalogue of Scientific Papers, 1800–1900*, compiled by the Royal Society of London, which was published during 1867–1925 by Clay and later by CUP. Volumes of this work have been reprinted by the Johnson Reprint Corporation of New York. The author catalogue, comprising 19 volumes, indexes articles in various languages in 1555 periodicals. It should be noted that, although the listing is extensive, it is by no means complete. Thus papers by a scientist which were published in "non-scientific" periodicals are not indexed. A subject index to the author catalogue was commenced and was intended to comprise 17 volumes covering the 17 sciences recognized in the catalogue. Volumes indexing entries in the fields of pure mathematics, mechanics and physics (2 parts) were published during 1908–14 but, unfortunately, no further volumes have appeared.

From 1902 to 1919 the Royal Society of London published for the International Council an *International Catalogue of Scientific Literature*. This was planned as a sequel to the Society's nineteenth-century catalogue and was to comprise an annual bibliography of books and periodical articles. Each annual issue was to contain 17 volumes devoted to the main subject groupings as in the subject index to the Society's *Catalogue of Scientific Papers, 1800–1900*. In fact, volumes for the 14 years 1901–14 were published before the work fell a casualty to the First World War. Each volume includes author and subject entries. The Johnson Reprint Corporation of New York has undertaken a reprint of this work.

During 1903–40 the British Museum (Natural History) issued a *Catalogue of the Books, Manuscripts, Maps and Drawings in the British Museum (Natural History)*. This was published in 5 volumes with 3 supplementary volumes and comprises an author index to the collections.

A Bibliography of the History of Technology, edited by E. S. Ferguson (Cambridge, Massachusetts Institute of Technology Pr., 1968), is a guide to the literature of this field. *Technology in Western Civilization*, edited by M. Kranzberg and C. W. Pursell (2 vols., OUP, 1967), includes comprehensive bibliographies. The first volume covers the period to 1900.

A History of Technology, edited by C. Singer, E. J. Holmyard, A. R. Hall, and T. I. Williams (5 vols., Oxford, Clarendon Pr., 1954–8), includes selective bibliographies at the end of each chapter. The final 2 volumes cover the nineteenth century.

F. Russo, *Histoire des Sciences et des Techniques: bibliographie* (Paris, Hermann, 1954), is a bibliography of works on the history of science and technology. Some entries are annotated. A short supplement was published in 1955.

A concise bibliography in the Library Association's series of Special Subject Lists is K. J. Rider, *The History of Science and Technology: a select bibliography for students* (Library Association, 1967).

C. C. Gillispie, *The Edge of Objectivity: an essay in the history of scientific ideas* (Princeton, Univ. Pr., 1960), includes a "Bibliographical essay" which provides a useful selective listing of books and periodical articles on many aspects of the history of science, including the nineteenth century.

J. L. Thornton and R. I. J. Tully, *Scientific Books, Libraries and Collectors: a study of bibliography and the book trade in relation to science* (2nd edn., Library Association, 1962), is a history of scientific books to the end of the nineteenth century with a chapter on the bibliography of science.

Current Work

The periodical *Isis* (1913–), the journal of the History of Science Society, includes an annual bibliography of recent books and periodical articles on the history of science (Fig. 30). Many entries are annotated and include references to reviews of books listed. Since 1955 this has been a "Critical bibliography of the history of science". Entries in this bibliography during the years 1913–65 are now being edited and rearranged to provide a cumulative bibliography of the history of science. As the annual bibliography includes references to the contents of *Isis* itself, the cumulative bibliography will also constitute a comprehensive index to the periodical. The work is to be published in several parts. The first part will index all entries relating to persons and to institutions and societies. Subsequent parts will be arranged by periods and subjects. The work is being edited by Mrs. M. Whitrow and is supported by grants from the United States Steel Foundation and the National Science Foundation. It is to be published by Mansell Information/Publishing.

Technology and Culture, the quarterly periodical of the Society for the History of Technology (Chicago, Univ. Pr., 1960–), has from 1962 included an annual specialized bibliography of recent books and periodical articles under the title "Current bibliography in the history of technology" (Fig. 31).

Both these periodicals include book reviews. The quarterly *Bulletin signalétique: histoire des sciences et des techniques* (Centre

1804–1859. 440 pp., plts., map, bibl. Wiesbaden: Franz Steiner, 1961.
Rev. by G. R. Crone in *Geogr. J.*, 1964, *130*:304.

BELL, WHITFIELD J., JR. The American Philosophical Society as a national academy of sciences. *Proc. 10th int. Cong. Hist Sci.*, 1962 (pub. 1964), *1*:165–177.
With comments by J. C. Greene.

CAFIERO, L. (ed.). Cinque lettere di Giovanni Varlati a E. Mach. *Riv. crit. Stor. Fil.*, 1962, *17*:68–74.

CANNON, WALTER F. History in depth: The early Victorian period. *Hist. Sci.*, 1964, *3*:20–38.

CANNON, WALTER F. The normative role of science in early Victorian thought. *J. Hist. Ideas*, 1964, *25*:487–502.

CANNON, WALTER F. The role of the Cambridge movement in early 19th-century science. *Proc. 10th int. Cong. Hist. Sci.*, 1962 (pub. 1964), *1*:317–320.

CANNON, WALTER F. William Whewell, F.R.S. (1794–1866). Contributions to science and learning. *Notes Rec. R. Soc. Lond.*, 1964, *19*:176–191.

CHECKLAND, S. G. The rise of industrial society in England, 1815–1885. xiv + 471 pp., bibl., index. New York: St Martin's, 1964. $7.00.

DAVIS, RICHARD BEALE. Intellectual life in Jefferson's Virginia, 1790–1830. x + 507 pp., illus., bibl., notes, index. Chapel Hill: Univ. North Carolina Press, 1964. $8.75.
Rev. by Charles A. Barker in *J. Am. Hist.*, 1964, *51*:491–492.

DINGLE, HERBERT. Reason and experiment in relation to the special relativity theory. *Br. J. Phil. Sci.*, 1964, *15*:41–61.

DOUGLAS, A. VIBERT. Early scientific writing in Canada. *Proc. 10th int. Cong. Hist. Sci.*, 1962 (pub. 1964), *1*:321–323.

EISEN, SYDNEY. [Thomas Henry] Huxley

FLORIAN, A. Dr. Julius Barash (in Hebrew). *Koroth*, 1964, *3*:331–337.

FULLMER, JUNE Z. Humphry Davy's Weltanschauung. *Proc. 10th int. Cong. Hist. Sci.*, 1962 (pub. 1964), *1*:325–328.

GOETHE, J. W. Die Schriften zur Naturwissenschaft. I Abt., Bd. 8: Naturwissenschaftliche Hefte. Ed. by D. Kuhn. 434 pp. Weimar: Hermann Böhlaus Nachfolger, 1962. DM 23.20.
Rev. by Bruno Endlich in *Naturw. Rdsch.*, 1964, *17*:39.

GORKI, MAXIM. Gorkii i nauka. stat'i, rechi, pis'ma, vospominaniya. (Gorki and science. Articles, speeches, letters, recollections.) 282 pp. Moscow: Izd-vo "Nauka," 1964. 1r. 23k.

HARIG, GERHARD. Alexander von Humboldt—der Naturforscher des deutschen Humanismus. *Z. Gesch. Naturw. Tech. Med.*, 1960, *1*, Heft 1:50–61.

HENNEMANN, G. Hans Christian Oersted als Naturphilosoph. *Philosophia nat.*, 1959, *5*:348–353.

JOJA, CRIZANTEMA. Science et histoire de la philosophie chez Hegel. *Proc. 10th int. Cong. Hist. Sci.*, 1962 (pub. 1964), *1*:303–305.

JONES, HOWARD MUMFORD; I. BERNARD COHEN (eds.). Science before Darwin; an anthology of British scientific writing in the early nineteenth century. vi + 372 pp. London: André Deutsch, 1963. 30s. Boston: Little, Brown, 1963, edition is titled A treasury of scientific prose. $6.75.
Rev. by C. A. Russell in *Archs. int. Hist. Sci.*, 1964, *17*:316–317; by G. S. Fraser in *Vict. Stud.*, 1964, *7*:317–318.

KELLNER, CHARLOTTE. Alexander von Humboldt. viii + 247 pp., illus. London/New York: Oxford Univ. Press, 1963. $5.75; 25s.
Rev. by Hanno Beck in *Hisp. Am. hist. Rev.*, 1964, *44*:294–295; by Norman Feather in *Physics Today*, 1964, *17*, No. 1:78–80.

KONARSKA, BARBARA. Materials for the

FIG. 30. *Isis* ("Critical bibliography of the history of science"). (Copyright: the Editor.)

XVIII (December 1962, published July 1964), 195–215. A great deal of detailed information about a minor but versatile millwright, instrument maker, president of Smeatonian Society, etc.; useful descriptions of things made by Yeoman and others. (ESF),

RONCHI, VASCO. "Galileo, Maestro di Tecnica," *Luce e Immagini,* XVIII (1964), 35–42. (SAB)

SPARROW, W. J. *Knight of the White Eagle: a Biography of Sir Benjamin Thompson, Count Rumford (1753–1814).* London: Hutchinson, 1964. Pp. 302. A major work, based upon researches in England, Germany, France, and the United States. (ESF)

THOMPSON, KATHERINE S. "Dr. Manning's Mill," *Old-Time New England,* LV (Summer 1964), 11–22. Account of John Manning and his building (in 1794) of a horizontal windmill in Ipswich, Massachusetts, as a source of power for textile machinery. The power being insufficient, the mill was forced to close in 1800.

USEMANN, K. W. "Zum 50. Todestag von Hermann Rietschel—Ein Lebensbild," *Gesundheits-Ingenieur,* (February 1964), pp. 33–36. Rietschel (1847–1914) was the founder of the Institute for Heating and Ventilation in the Technische Hochschule, Berlin-Charlottenburg. Article includes a complete list of his publications.

VRILLON, H. "Denis Papin," *Bibliothèque de Travail,* No. 591 (October 1, 1964), pp. 5–37. In French. Listed in the *Newcomen Bulletin,* No. 75, March 1965. Papin (1647–1712) contributed to the development of the steam engine. (ESF)

WILLAM, HORST ALEXANDER. "Carl Zeiss, Mensch und Werk," *Tradition, Zeitschrift für Firmen Geschichte und Unternehmer Biographie,* IX (April 1964), 58–69. Based on previously unpublished archival material in the possession of the Zeiss family.

WILLIAMS, L. PEARCE. *Michael Faraday.* London: Chapman & Hall, 1964. Pp. 531. The description of Faraday's im-

ZEKERT, OTTO. *Carl Wilhelm Scheele, Apotheker-Chemiker-Entdecker.* Stuttgart: Wissenschaftliche Verlagsgesellschaft, 1963. Pp. 149 and 32 plates. Reviewed in *Blätter für Technikgeschichte,* XXVI (1964), 172–73.

See also: 1–Gille, Institution of Mechanical Engineers; 2–Barr; 7–Hammond; 8–Sloan, Strandh, Tsiolkovsky, Westlake; 9–Johnson, Lysholm; 10–Gillis; 13–Bunting.

4. TECHNICAL SOCIETIES, TECHNICAL EDUCATION

ADAMSEN, P. "En Restaureringsopgave," Danmarks Tekniske Museum, *Arbog.,* XII (1963 [published 1964]), 31–35. Describes the restoration of several locomotives preserved in the Museum. In Danish.

ARGLES, MICHAEL. *South Kensington to Robbins: an Account of English Technical and Scientific Education since 1851.* London: Longmans, 1964. Pp. 178. A straightforward account of a complex story which includes schools of design, mechanics' institutes, colleges, and universities. "Robbins" refers to the controversial Robbins Report on Higher Education (1963), a study made for the British government. A sensible bibliography (pp. 151–61) provides an entry to the field of English technical education. Reviewed briefly in the *Times Literary Supplement,* September 10, 1964, p. 844. (ESF)

ATKINSON, FRANK. "An Open-Air Museum for the North-East," *Journal of Industrial Archaeology,* I (May 1964), 3–8 and plates 1–4. Description of a new museum being planned for erection at Aykley Heads (near the city of Durham) which will typify the industrial development, as well as portray the social and cultural history, of the northeast of England.

BOWEN, J. H. "Chemical Engineering Education in Australia," *Chemical Engineer,* No. 177 (1964), CE55–CE57. Reviews developments from 1915 to date.

CROSS, D. A. E. "The Industries of Wit-

FIG. 31. *Technolagy and Culture* ("Current bibliography in the history of technology"). (Copyright: the Editor and University of Chicago Press.)

National de la Recherche Scientifique, 1961–) is also useful for its inclusion of reviews of new books which are not usually listed in the other bibliographies.

Encyclopedias

The importance for the historian of Victorian science of nineteenth-century editions of general encyclopedias should be emphasized. The rapid development of scientific ideas makes older editions of such works as *Encyclopaedia Britannica* of special value in this field. As G. Sarton notes in *Horus: a guide to the history of science*: "Historians of science need not only the latest encyclopaedias but also the old ones, as such offer one of the simplest means of recapturing the educated opinion of earlier times".

The *Lexikon der Geschichte der Naturwissenschaften: Biographien, Sachwörter und Bibliographen* (Vienna, Hollinek, 1959–) covers the history of science to the end of the nineteenth century. It includes articles on scientific subjects, geographical areas, and individual scientists. Articles are supplied with extensive bibliographies. For the biographical articles these list works by and about the person discussed.

Biographical Works

Much biographical information will be obtained from the encyclopedias noted above and from the general biographical works discussed in Chapter 14.

J. C. Poggendorff, *Biographisch-literarisches Handwörterbuch zur Geschichte der exacten Wissenschaften*, is the standard work of universal collected biography of scientists. It was published in Leipzig by Barth and later by Verlag Chemie in 6 volumes bound in 11. A reprint by Edwards of Ann Arbor was published in 10 volumes in 1945. The first 2 volumes cover the period to 1857. Later volumes cover the period to 1931. For each scientist there is a short descriptive sketch followed by a detailed bibliography of his writings, including periodical articles. From 1955 the Akademie-Verlag of Berlin has been publishing a continuation of this work under the title *Biographisch-literarisches Handwörter-buch der exacten Naturwissenschaften*. Volumes include supplementary material for names mentioned in earlier volumes and entries for new names.

Until the commencement of the annual *Obituary Notices of Fellows of the Royal Society* (Royal Society of London, 1932/5–1954), which was succeeded by the *Biographical Memoirs of Fellows of the Royal Society* (The Society, 1955–), such notices were published in the *Proceedings of the Royal Society*. Volume 75 of the *Proceedings* (1905) contained obituaries of Fellows who died during the period 1898–1904 together with a general index to previous obituary notices, covering the period 1860–99.

A Biographical Dictionary of Scientists, edited by T. I. Williams (Black, 1969), contains biographies of over 1000 notable scientists and technologists. The work covers all periods and countries. Entries include bibliographies of books and articles.

A major biographical dictionary, announced for publication shortly, is the *Dictionary of Scientific Biography* (New York, Scribner). This is to comprise 8 or more volumes and will include a general subject index. The work is to be modelled on the *Dictionary of National Biography*.

Among bibliographical guides to individual scientists, R. B. Freeman, *The Works of Charles Darwin: an annotated bibliographical handlist* (Dawsons, 1965), and W. R. Dawson, *The Huxley Papers* (Macmillan, 1946), should be noted. Dawson's work is a descriptive catalogue of Thomas Henry Huxley's correspondence, manuscripts, and miscellaneous papers.

N. O. Ireland, *Index to Scientists of the World from Ancient to Modern Times: biographies and portraits* (Boston, Faxon, 1962), indexes 338 English language collections of biography. Entries include full names and dates of birth and death with a brief distinguishing identification and reference to collections in which biographies and portraits may be found.

E. S. Barr has contributed useful bibliographical surveys of biographical material to the periodical *Isis*. These include "Biographical material in the *Philosophical Magazine* to 1900" (vol. 55, 1964, pp. 88–90); "*Nature*'s 'Scientific worthies' " (vol. 56, 1965, pp. 354–6), and "Biographical material in the first series of the *Physical Review*" (vol. 58, 1967, pp. 254–6).

MEDICINE
Guides and Bibliographies

The history of medicine is well documented. Among general guides to the literature the American Medical Library Association's *Handbook of Medical Library Practice: with a bibliography of the reference works and histories in medicine and the allied sciences*, edited by G. L. Annan (3rd edn., Chicago, Medical Library Association, 1969), is very useful. W. D. Postell, *Applied Medical Bibliography for Students* (Springfield, Thomas, 1955), has useful sections on historical materials. L. T. Morton, *How to Use a Medical Library* (4th edn., Heinemann, 1964), has notes on bibliographical sources and an annotated list of the principal medical libraries in Britain. Another useful guide to British medical libraries is the *Directory of Medical Libraries in the British Isles*, compiled by the Medical Section of the Library Association (Library Association, 1957).

F. H. Garrison, *Introduction to the History of Medicine* (4th edn., Philadelphia, Saunders, 1929), covers the whole history of medicine and includes useful bibliographies. A valuable complementary guide is A. Castiglioni, *A History of Medicine*, translated and edited by E. B. Krumbhaar (2nd edn., New York, Knopf, 1947).

The great *Index-Catalogue of the Library of the Surgeon-General's Office* (61 vols., Washington, Government Printing Office, 1880–1961) includes author and subject listing of the collection of the National Library of Medicine, formerly the Surgeon-General's Library and the Army Medical Library. Books, pamphlets, and a large number of periodical articles are listed, including many obituary and biographical notices. Because of its enormous coverage the work is useful not only for medicine but also for many other subjects, including various aspects of the history of science and social conditions.

Garrison and Morton's Medical Bibliography: an annotated checklist of texts illustrating the history of medicine by F. H. Garrison and L. T. Morton (2nd edn., Deutsch, 1965) is a convenient basic bibliography of books and periodical articles.

Among catalogues of great private collections W. Osler, *Bibliotheca Osleriana: a catalogue of books illustrating the history of medicine and science* (Oxford, Clarendon Pr., 1929), is an annotated catalogue of the collection which was bequeathed to McGill University.

E. Brodman, *The Development of Medical Bibliography* (Baltimore, Medical Library Association, 1954), surveys medical bibliography since 1500 and includes histories and descriptions of older bibliographies. An appendix lists 250 medical bibliographies since 1500.

B. W. Weinberger, *Dental Bibliography* (2nd edn., 2 vols., New York, First District Dental Society, *c.* 1929–32), lists literature on dentistry in the library of the New York Academy of Medicine. The same author's *An Introduction to the History of Dentistry* (2 vols., St. Louis, Mosby, 1948) includes bibliographical references.

A Bibliography of Nursing Literature, 1859–1960, edited and compiled by A. M. C. Thompson (Library Association, 1969), is a survey of the principal publications with an historical introduction. I. M. Stewart and A. L. Austin, *A History of Nursing from Ancient to Modern Times* (5th edn., New York, Putman, 1962), includes valuable bibliographies.

W. J. Bishop and S. Goldie, *A Bio-Bibliography of Florence Nightingale* (Dawsons, 1962), is an essential source of information for the study of a major figure in Victorian nursing.

Current Work

The most convenient guide to recent periodical articles is the quarterly *Current Work in the History of Medicine: an inter-*

national bibliography (Fig. 32), compiled by the Wellcome Historical Medical Library in London (Wellcome Institute of the History of Medicine, 1954–). This library is extremely important for its very rich collection of works on the history of medicine, formed initially by Sir Henry Wellcome. Current accessions to the library include a large number of periodicals in this subject field.

The major comprehensive index of current literature on all aspects of medicine is *Index Medicus*, published since 1960 by the National Library of Medicine in Washington. In its first form this periodical dates back to 1879 and the early volumes provide contemporary listing of materials now useful for the historian of medicine.

The United States National Library of Medicine compiles an annual *Bibliography of the History of Medicine* (Washington, Government Printing Office, 1965–). This lists monographs and periodical articles relating to all aspects and periods of medical history. The work is divided into 3 parts, comprising biographical and subject entries and an author index. The *Bibliography* is to be cumulated every 5 years.

Biographical Works

J. L. Thornton, A. J. Monk, and E. S. Brooke, *A Select Bibliography of Medical Biography* (Library Association, 1961), lists English-language books published in the nineteenth and twentieth centuries. Collective and individual biographies are included.

The *Catalogue of Biographies* of the Library of the New York Academy of Medicine has been photographically printed (Boston, Hall, 1960). This lists biographies of physicians and scientists with some autobiographies and family histories.

Among general biographical dictionaries the most extensive is *Biographisches Lexikon der hervorragenden Ärzte aller Zeiten und Völker* (2nd edn., 5 vols., Berlin, Urban, 1929–35; reprinted 1962). This includes physicians who had reached maturity before 1880. Entries include bibliographies of works by the physicians and

NOTTINGHAM: Medical School Merskey, H. The first Nottingham Medical School:
967   1833-1835? Med. Hist., 1968, **12**, 84-9, refs.
NOVELS and NOVELISTS, Medical Amat, Enrique and Leal, Carmen. Muerte y
968   enfermedad en los personajes Galdosianos. Asclepio, 1965, **17**, 181-206.
— — Barrucand, D. A propos des médecins et de la médecine dans 'Les Thibault'
969   de Roger Martin Du Gard. Ann. méd. psychol., 1966, **124**, 409-46, refs.
— — DeBakey, Lois. The fictional physician-scientist of nineteenth-century
970   America. Anesth. Analg. curr. Res., 1967, **46**, 725-733, refs.
— — Théodoridès, Jean. Un modèle probable d'Octave de Malivert. Communi-
971   cations présentées au Congrès Stendhalien de Civitavecchia et réunies par
V. del Litto. (Publ. Inst. Français de Florence, Ser. 1, No. 16) Forence:
Sansoni. Paris: Didier. 1966. pp. 267-284, refs.
— — Théodoridès, J. Deux curieux personnages de Stendhal: les docteurs Du
972   Poirier et Sansfin. Presse méd., 1966, **74**, 2706.
— — Whitmore, P. J. S. Rita-Christina [a bi-cephalous monster]: a reference to
973   a real person in the 'Comédie humaine'. French Stud., 1967, 319-22, 10 refs.
NÓVOA SANTOS, Roberto [b. 1885] Cabaleiro Goás, M. Un medico humanista: Roberto
974   Nóvoa Santos. Asclepio, 1965, **17**, 69-94, refs.
NUMISMATICS Hein, W.-H. Leonhard Posch's Medaille auf Carl Ludwig Willdenow.
975   Pharm. Ztg, 1967, **112**, 1519-1520, ports., refs.
— — Lydman, Åke. Medals struck in honour of pharmacists and pharmaceutical
976   jubilees in Finland. Farm. Notisblad., 1963, Nr. 3, 119-128. Med.-hist. Årsb.,
1967, 149-58 [Swedish]; 262 [Engl. abstr.]; illus.
— — Sokołowska-Grzeszczyk, Kazimiera. Portraits of physicians on Polish
977   medals. Arch. Hist. Med. (Warszawa), 1967, **30**, 209-96, illus., 264 refs.
— — Tricou, Jean. Jetons et armoiries du Collège des Chirurgiens de Lyon.
978   Cah. lyon. Hist. Méd., 1966-7, **10**(4), 9-15, refs.
NURSING Medicine in the 1896 Rebellion. [Drawing by Baden-Powell of a Dominican
979   nursing sister in his 'Album, Matabeleland', 1896.] Cent. Afr. J. Med., 1967, **13**,
216, illus.
— — Cooper, S. S. Activating the inactive nurse: a historical review. Nurs. Out-
980   look, 1967, **15**, Oct., 62-5.
— — Fricke, A. Agnes Karll. Int. Nurs. Rev., 1967, **14**, June, 43-4.
981
— — Gowan, M. O. Influence of graduate nurses on the formative years of a Uni-
982   versity School of Nursing. A memoir. Nurs. Res., 1967, **16**, 261-6.
— — Wyklicky, Helmut. Zur Geschichte der Krankenpflege. Öst. Ärzteztg, 1967,
983   No. 20, front cover, illus.
NUTRITION Aylward, F. Food habits in western tropical Africa. Chem. Industr.,
984   1966, **39**, 1624-7.
— — Carlson, A. J. Some obstacles in the path towards an optimum diet. Tex.
985   Rep. Biol. Med., 1967, **25**, Spring, 7-26.
OBSTETRICS see also MATERNAL WELFARE; MATERNITY HOSPITALS; MIDWIVES
OBSTETRICS Bitkowski, Jósef. Midwifery at Gdansk from the XVI to the XIX century.
986   [Polish.] Arch. Hist. Med. (Warszawa), 1967, **30**, 161-99, illus., ports., 84 refs.
— — Bitkowski, J. Development of obstetrics in Gdansk from 16th to 20th century.
986a   [Polish.] Ginek. pol., 1966, **37**, 909-15.
— — Gómez Robledo, Roberto. Historia de la ginecologia y la obstetricia en
987   Honduras. Rev. Soc. Geogr. Hist. Honduras, 1965, **42**(10-12), 4-14.
— — Grasby, E. D. Epochs in obstetrics. Nurs. Times, 1967, **63**, 1207-9.
988
— — Kremling, H. Geburtshilfe und Gynäkologie in den letzten 100 Jahren. Med.
989   Klin., 1966, **61**, 1932-4.
— — Ritter, G. Die Anfänge des geburtshilflichen Unterrichtes an der Georg-
991   August-Universität zu Göttingen. Zbl. Gynäk., 1966, **88**, 1-9.

304

FIG. 32. *Current Work in the History of Medicine.* (Copyright: the
Wellcome Institute of the History of Medicine.)

occasionally add bibliographical references about them. The work is often useful for scientists in other fields who practised medicine or possessed a medical degree. The work was continued by *Biographisches Lexikon der hervorrangenden Ärzte der letzten 50 Jahre* (2 vols., Berlin, Urban, 1932–3; reprinted 1962).

Occasional help may be obtained from H. Bailey and W. J. Bishop, *Notable Names in Medicine and Surgery* (3rd edn., Lewis, 1959). G. H. Brown, *Lives of the Fellows of the Royal College of Physicians in London, 1826–1925* (Royal College of Physicians, 1955), contains short biographies of 874 Fellows elected between 1826 and 1925. This forms the fourth volume of William Munk's *Roll* of Physicians of the College. V. G. Plarr, *Lives of the Fellows of the Royal College of Surgeons of England* (2 vols., Simpkin, Marshall, 1930), includes biographies of the Fellows from the foundation in 1843.

SOME OTHER SPECIALITIES

Much information about useful works for the historian of specific sciences will be found in G. Sarton, *Horus: a guide to the history of science* (Waltham, Chronica Botanica, 1952). It is possible here to note only a few of the more important guides to the material.

Mathematics

There is a chapter on mathematical history and biography in J. E. Pemberton, *How to Find Out in Mathematics* (Oxford, Pergamon Pr., 1964). N. G. Parke, *Guide to the Literature of Mathematics and Physics, Including Related Works on Engineering Science* (2nd edn., New York, Dover, 1958), is a useful handbook with an annotated bibliography.

F. Müller, *Führer durch die mathematische Literatur, mit besonderer Berücksichtigung der historisch wichtigen Schriften* (Leipzig, Teubner, 1909), and G. Lorca, *Guido allo Studio dell*

Matematiche (2nd edn., Milan, Hoepli, 1946), are guides to the literature of the history of mathematics in all periods and countries.

Astronomy

The basic bibliographical guide is J. C. Houzeau and A. Lancaster, *Bibliographie générale de l'Astronomie jusqu'en 1880*. This work, which originally appeared in 1880–9, has recently been published in a new edition with an introduction and author index by D. W. Dewhirst (2 vols. in 3, Holland Pr., 1964). The work comprises an extensive list of separately printed works, manuscripts, and memoirs, and papers in academy publications and periodicals.

Physics

B. Yates, *How to Find Out About Physics* (Oxford, Pergamon Pr., 1965), discusses sources of information for historical and biographical studies. Additional information may be found in J. Burkett and P. Plumb, *How to Find Out in Electrical Engineering* (Oxford, Pergamon Pr., 1967). N. G. Parke, *Guide to the Literature of Mathematics and Physics*, noted above, is useful.

Nineteenth-century American theses may be traced in M. L. Marchworth, *Dissertations in Physics: an indexed bibliography of all doctoral theses accepted by American universities, 1861–1959* (Stanford, Univ. Pr., 1961).

Chemistry

H. C. Bolton, *Select Bibliography of Chemistry* (4 vols., Washington, Smithsonian Institution, 1893–1904), comprises a basic list for the period 1492–1892 with supplements for 1492–1897 and 1492–1902. The fourth volume lists academic dissertations. C. R. Burman, *How to Find Out in Chemistry* (2nd edn., Oxford, Pergamon Pr., 1967), includes useful information.

A. J. Ihde, *The Development of Modern Chemistry* (New York Harper, 1964), contains an extremely valuable section of "Bibliographic notes" covering books and periodical articles. J. R. Partington, *A History of Chemistry* (3 vols., Macmillan, 1961–4), is another well-documented survey.

The collection of D. I. Duveen, now in the University of Wisconsin Library, is catalogued in *Bibliotheca Alchemica et Chemica* (Weil, 1949) and includes many nineteenth-century works. J. Ferguson, *Bibliotheca Chemica* (2 vols., Glasgow, Maclehose, 1906), is a catalogue of the historical collection of James Young.

E. Farber, *Great Chemists* (New York, Interscience, 1961), is a collection of over 100 biographies with bibliographies. H. M. Smith, *Torchbearers of Chemistry* (Academic Pr., 1949), gives portraits and brief biographies. This work has a useful "Bibliography of biographies" by R. E. Oesper giving fuller references.

Geology

H. Hölder, *Geologie und Paläontologie in Texten und ihrer Geschichte* (Freiburg, Alber, 1960), R. M. Pearl, *Guide to Geological Literature* (McGraw-Hill, 1951), and B. Mason, *The Literature of Geology* (New York, the Author, 1953) are useful introductory guides.

For the nineteenth century, E. de Margerie, *Catalogue des Bibliographies géologiques* (Paris, Gauthier-Villars, 1896), lists bibliographies published during the period 1726–1895. The work contains much useful information on the bibliography of individual geologists. This is continued by E. B. Mathews, *Catalogue of Published Bibliographies in Geology, 1896–1920* (Washington, National Research Council, 1923).

From 1894 to 1934 the Geological Society of London published annual lists of *Geological Literature Added to the Geological Society's Library*.

A. La Rocque, *Contributions to the History of Geology* (3 vols., Columbus, Department of Geology, Ohio Univ., 1964), includes biographies of geologists and a bibliography of the history of geology. C. C. Gillispie, *Genesis and Geology: a study in the relations of scientific thought, natural theology, and social opinion in Great Britain, 1790–1850* (Cambridge, Harvard Univ. Pr., 1951; reprinted New York, Harper, 1959), includes a very extensive "Bibliographical essay", surveying secondary material, biographical sources, contemporary literature, and periodicals.

Biology

A. E. Kerker and E. M. Schlundt, *Literature Sources in the Biological Sciences* (Lafayette, Purdue Univ. Libraries, 1961), is a basic guide. B. Dawes, *A Hundred Years of Biology* (Duckworth, 1952), includes a useful bibliography. M. R. Murray and K. Kopech, *A Bibliography of the Research in Tissue Culture, 1884–1950* (2 vols., Academic Pr., 1953), indexes 15,000 periodical articles.

Botany

J. C. Bens, "Bibliographies of botany", published in *Progressus Rei Botanicae* (vol. 3, pt. 2, 1909, pp. 331–456), is an annotated bibliography of bibliographies. G. A. Pritzel, *Thesaurus Literaturae Botanicae Omnium Gentium* (rev. edn., Leipzig, Brockhaus, 1872–77; reprinted Milan, Görlizh, 1950), lists separately published books. It is supplemented by B. D. Jackson, *Guide to the Literature of Botany* (Longmans, 1881), which lists 9000 works of which nearly 6000 are stated to be not in Pritzel's *Thesaurus*.

J. Britten and G. S. Boulger, *Biographical Index of Deceased British and Irish Botanists* (2nd edn., Taylor & Francis, 1931), gives brief biographical facts and references to further information.

Zoology

R. C. Smith, *Guide to the Literature of the Zoological Sciences* (6th edn., Minneapolis, Burgess, 1962), is a useful general guide.

The literature of zoology from 1700 to 1880 is well indexed in three classified works: W. Engelmann, *Bibliotheca Historico-Naturalis* (Leipzig, Engelmann, 1846), covers the period 1700–1846; the period 1846–80 is covered in *Bibliotheca Zoologica*, edited by V. Carus and W. Engelmann (2 vols., Leipzig, Engelmann, 1861); and *Bibliotheca Zoologica II*, edited by O. Taschenberg (8 vols., Leipzig, Engelmann, 1887–1923).

Among periodicals, the annual *Zoological Record* (Zoological Society of London, 1865–) is an index to the zoological literature of the world. The first 6 volumes were entitled *Record of Zoological Literature*. *Bibliographia Zoologica* (Zürich, 1896–1934) and *Zoologischer Jahresbericht* (Leipzig, 1879–1913) contain useful bibliographical information.

More specialized bibliographies include R. M. Strong, *A Bibliography of Birds* (4 vols., Chicago, Natural History Museum, 1939–59), and B. Dean, *Bibliography of Fishes* (rev. edn., 3 vols., New York, American Museum of Natural History, 1916–23).

CHAPTER 10

The Visual Arts

FINE ARTS

The works discussed in this section are chiefly devoted to the fine arts in general and to painting, drawing, prints and engravings, and sculpture in particular. Many of them, however, also include information about architecture and the applied arts, more specific guides to which are noted in later sections of this chapter.

Guides and Bibliographies

General Guides

An intelligent, unannotated, general selection of books on the fine arts is provided in E. L. Lucas, *Art Books: a basic bibliography on the fine arts* (Greenwich, New York Graphic Society, 1968), a revision of her earlier *Harvard List of Books on Art*, published in 1952. A wide-ranging but rather more mechanical selection of books is M. W. Chamberlin, *Guide to Art Reference Books* (Chicago, American Library Association, 1959). This is certainly the most extensive survey of reference works on the visual arts. Entries are annotated (Fig. 33). A useful popular narrative guide to the visual arts is N. Carrick, *How to Find Out About the Arts* (Oxford, Pergamon Pr., 1965) (Fig. 34).

It should be noted that all these 3 guides to reference materials are general in scope and place no special emphasis on the Victorian period.

structions of England. An inventory of the historical monuments in [various counties of England], 1911–(52). illus., plates, maps. 28 cm.

There are also comparable publications for Scotland and Wales. Scholarly work, well illustrated. Counties included: Buckinghamshire, 2 v.; Dorset, 1 v.; Essex, 4 v.; Herefordshire, 3 v.; Hertfordshire, 1 v.; Huntingdonshire, 1 v.; London, 5 v.; Oxford, 1 v.; Westmorland, 1 v.; Middlesex, 1 v.

Indexes, glossaries.

874

Hitchcock, Henry-Russell. Early Victorian architecture in Britain. New Haven, Yale Univ. Press, 1954. 2 v. illus., maps, plans. 28 cm. (Yale historical publications. History of art, 9)

A definitive history of architecture in England from about 1825 to 1852. Contents: v. 1, Text; v. 2, Illustrations. Index v. 1, p. 615–35.

875

Lloyd, Nathaniel. A history of the English house from primitive times to the Victorian period. London, Architectural Press; N. Y., Helburn, 1931. 487 p. illus., plates, plans, diagrs. 33 cm.

Contains 167 pages of text, divided by centuries; p. 170–469 consists of halftone illustrations and plans arranged according to type: exteriors, entrances, windows, chimneys, staircases, etc., with descriptive text. Index p. 477–87.

876

MacGibbon, David, and Ross, Thomas. The castellated and domestic architecture of Scotland from the twelfth to the eighteenth century . . . Edinburgh, Douglas, 1887–92. 5 v. illus. (incl. plans). 26 cm.

Illustrated by numerous plans and line drawings in the text. "Scottish sundials" v. 5, p. 357–514; "Early Scottish masters of works, master masons, and architects" v. 5, p. [515]–69.

Index at end of each volume and a "General index to the whole work" v. 5, p. 571–95. "Topographical index of buildings described in the whole work" v. 5, p. 597–603.

medieval church architecture in England in the light of structural analysis and comparison with the French Gothic art, and of the conditions and influences under which it was produced."—*Pref.* Index p. 229–37.

878

Nash, Joseph. Mansions of England in the olden time . . . London, M'Lean, 1839–49. 4 v. col. plates. 55 cm.

Volumes 2, 3, and 4 are called 2d, 3d, and 4th series. A smaller ed. (29 cm.), edited by Charles Holme with an introduction by C. Harrison Townsend, was published by "The Studio" in 1906; another ed., London, Heinemann, 1912.

A collection of tinted lithographs of famous Tudor and Elizabethan mansions. with representations of contemporary figures.

879

Pugin, Augustus Charles. Examples of Gothic architecture; selected from various ancient edifices in England: consisting of plans, elevations, sections, and parts at large . . . , accompanied by historical and descriptive accounts. By A. Pugin . . . the literary part by E. J. Willson . . . London, Printed for the author, Augustus Pugin, 1831–36. 3 v. plates, geneal. tables. 30 cm.

Volume 2 by A. Pugin and A. W. Pugin; text of v. 3 by Thomas Larkins Walker. Volume 3 in 3 pts. with individual title page: The history and antiquities of the Vicars' Close, Wells, [the Manor house and church at Great Chalfield, the Manor house at South Wraxhall and the church of Saint Peter at Biddestone] forming Part I–[III] of "Pugin's Examples of Gothic architecture," third series.

Carefully rendered drawings and plans.

880

Tipping, Henry Avery. English homes . . . London, Country Life, 1921–37. 9 v. illus. (incl. plans). 40 cm. (Country Life library)

A new ed. of this work, covering material down to 1840, has been issued by Christopher Hussey in three volumes, 1955–1958, 32 cm.

Each volume contains a descriptive text and excellent halftone plates of exterior and interior views of about 24 famous English country houses of the period. Each volume

FIG. 33. M. W. Chamberlin, *Guide to Art Reference Books*. (Copyright: the American Library Association.)

Chapter Fourteen

Art History: Philosophy and Study

Dewey Class 709

PHILOSOPHY OF ART

It is possible to mention here only a few of the works dealing with the philosophy of art. The bibliographies in these works can be used as guides to further sources of information.

The great pioneer work in this field was Gotthold Ephraim Lessing's *Laocoon: an Essay upon the Limits of Painting and Poetry, with Remarks Illustrative of Various Points in the History of Ancient Art.* First published in German in 1766, a revised edition was published in 1888. For standard expositions of the subject we turn to Robin G. Collingwood's *The Principles of Art,* published in Oxford, 1938, and Herbert Read's *The Meaning of Art,* of which the third edition was published in London in 1951.

Since the Second World War important works which have appeared include Susanne K. Langer's *Feeling and Form: a Theory of Art Developed from "Philosophy in a New Key",* published in London and New York, 1953, and Rudolph Arnheim's *Art and Visual Perception,* published in London, 1956, with a lengthy bibliography. A work which sums up much recent research in this field is Ernst H. Gombrich's *Art and Illusion: a Study in the Psychology of Pictorial Representation,* published in London and New York, 1960; this has many bibliographical notes.

Finally, a further guide to information in this field and the related field of aesthetics is W. A. Hammond's *A Bibliography of Aesthetics and of the Philosophy of the Fine Arts from 1900 to 1932,* of which a revised edition was published in 1934.

99

FIG. 34. N. Carrick, *How to Find Out About the Arts.* (Copyright: Pergamon Press Ltd.)

General Bibliographies

The *Universal Catalogue of Books on Art* was published in 2 volumes in 1870 (Chapman & Hall) with a supplement in 1877 (HMSO). The 3 volumes were recently reprinted (New York, Burt Franklin, 1964). The *Catalogue* aims to list books on art contained in the National Art Library in the South Kensington Museum, now the Victoria and Albert Museum, with all other books published to the date of issue of the catalogue. It includes works in all branches of the fine and applied arts. Entries are listed alphabetically by author or title and include a note on the location of copies.

The Courtauld Institute of Art compiled a 6-volume *Bibliography of the History of British Art* (CUP, 1936–56), listing books and periodical articles on the fine and applied arts published between 1934 and 1946.

The printed *Library Catalogue* of the Metropolitan Museum of Art in New York (25 vols., Boston, Hall, 1960) is a photographic reprint of the card catalogue of the library's collection. Author and subject entries are arranged in a single alphabetical sequence. Both books and periodical articles are included. The final 2 volumes list the library's large collection of sale catalogues. Regular supplements to the *Catalogue* have been published since 1962.

Bibliographies of the Victorian Period

Selective bibliographies of works devoted to the arts in the Victorian period will be found in the standard histories. T. S. R. Boase, *English Art, 1800–1870* (Oxford, Clarendon Pr., 1959), in the Oxford History of English Art, lists books and periodical articles on the fine arts and architecture. A. P. Oppé's chapter on "Art" in the second volume of *Early Victorian England, 1830–1865* (OUP, 1934) is still the best narrative survey of the early period. The essay does not include a formal bibliography but has some footnotes listing contemporary material.

J. Steegman, *Consort of Taste, 1830–1870* (Sidgwick & Jackson,

1950), though concerned primarily with the influence of Prince Albert on the arts, offers a valuable analysis of the period and some useful bibliographical material in footnotes.

Some Special Topics

The Victoria and Albert Museum has issued a list of illustrated books under the title *Victorian Book Illustration* (1967). F. Reid, *Illustrators of the Sixties* (Faber & Gwyer, 1928), includes a bibliography of illustrated books of this decade.

A. M. Hind, *An Introduction to a History of Woodcut* (Boston, Houghton-Mifflin, 1935; reprinted New York, Dover, 1963), and *A History of Engraving and Etching* (Constable, 1923; reprinted New York, Dover, 1963), both include classified lists of articles and bibliographical information about the use of these arts in book illustration.

F. Lichten, *Decorative Arts of Victoria's Era* (New York, Scribner, 1950), includes a useful selective bibliography. B. Gray, *The English Print* (Black, 1937), contains a short bibliography of books and articles. This work, more than half of which is devoted to the Victorian period, also provides concise biographical information on Victorian artists. C. Glaser, *Die Graphik der Neuzeit vom Anfang des XIX. Jahrhunderts bis zur Gegenwart* (Berlin, Cassirer, 1922), contains references to the literature.

D. Foskett, *British Portrait Miniatures: a history* (Methuen, 1963), and M. Hardie, *Water-colour Painting in Britain: the Victorian period* (Batsford, 1969), are well-illustrated guides with bibliographical references.

S. C. Hutchinson, *The History of the Royal Academy, 1768–1968* (Chapman & Hall, 1968), includes good bibliographies and biographical information. Q. Bell, *The Schools of Design* (Routledge, 1963), is a well-documented survey.

Guides to Scottish painting include J. L. Caw, *Scottish Painting Past and Present, 1620–1908* (Edinburgh, Jack, 1908), and S. Cursiter, *Scottish Art to the Close of the Nineteenth Century* (Harrap, 1949).

For the Pre-Raphaelites, W. E. Fredeman, *Pre-Raphaelitism: a bibliocritical study* (Cambridge, Harvard Univ. Pr., 1965), is an extensive bibliography with a narrative commentary (see Fig. 40).

It is perhaps appropriate here to note a few works which constitute essential narrative guides to the period and also provide a good selection of illustrations. G. Reynolds, *Nineteenth Century Drawings, 1850–1900* (Pleiades, 1949), *Painters of the Victorian Scene* (Batsford, 1953), and *Victorian Painting* (Studio Vista, 1966) are all useful. Q. Bell, *Victorian Artists* (Routledge, 1967), and J. Maas, *Victorian Painters* (Cresset Pr., 1969) also valuable.

Periodical Indexes

General indexes to periodicals are discussed in Chapter 3. These include useful materials on the visual arts in the Victorian period.

A major guide to current articles in periodicals is *Art Index: a cumulative author and subject index to a selected list of fine art periodicals* (New York, Wilson, 1929–) (Fig. 35). This is published quarterly with annual and 2-year cumulations. It indexes articles and book reviews in a wide range of English-language and foreign periodicals in the field of the visual arts. Author and subject entries are arranged in a single alphabetical sequence. Information is given about illustrations in the articles.

Periodical articles are listed by subject in the *Index to Art Periodicals*, compiled since 1907 in the Ryerson Library of the Art Institute of Chicago (11 vols., Boston, Hall, 1962). Material which appears in the *Art Index* is excluded from this catalogue.

The *Répertoire d'Art et d'Archéologie*, published since 1901, is now compiled by the Comité International d'Histoire de l'Art et Bibliothèque d'Art et d'Archéologie de l'Université de Paris. It indexes books, pamphlets, exhibition catalogues, and articles in scholarly periodicals. Since 1926 arrangement has been by subject with author and artist indexes. Before this date entries were arranged by country with author and subject indexes.

The Victoria and Albert Museum in London issues a regular list of *Library Accessions*, listing books and periodical articles added to the Library.

VERVIERS, Belgium
  Musée d'archéologie et de folklore
New sections of the Archaeological and folk-
  lore museum, Verviers, Belgium; with
  French tr. V. Bronowski and G. Hautecœur.
  il Museum (Unesco) 19 no 1:52-3 '66
VESELY. See Vézely
VESPIGNANI, Renzo
Rome: the Quadriennale—with some omissions
  repaired. J. Lucas. Arts 40:42 Ja '66
  il: Cetonia
VESTA (goddess)
Vesta sul Palatino. M. Guarducci. bibliog f il
  Deutsch Archäol Inst Röm Mitt 71:158-69 '64
VESTIBULES. See Entrances
VESTIER, Antoine
  Reproductions
Art and Music (pair of paintings)
  Connoisseur 160:LXI D '65
VESTMENTS, Church. See Church vestments
VETERINARY instruments and apparatus
  History
Pujavantes romanos esculturados: contribu-
  ción al estudio de la hipiatría antigua. A.
  Fernández de Avilés. bibliog f il Archivo
  Esp Arq 37 no 109-110:3-21 '64
VEVERS, Tony
Exhibition at Roko gallery. Art N 64:18 D '65
VEYRAC, Jacques de
Exhibition at Internationale gallery. Arts
  40:63 F '66
VEYRASSAT, Jules Jacques
  Reproductions
Moissonneurs chargeant des gerbes sur des
  charettes
  Connoisseur 160:XLV D '65

VICENTE, Esteban
Importance of being casual. N. Edgar. Art N
  64:44-5 D '65
  il: Job's Lane (col); Number 10, 1957; Black, red
  and gold
VICENTINO, Andrea. See Michieli, A.
VICKERS, Alfred
  Reproductions
Landscape with cottages
  Apollo ns 82:lxv N '65
Landscape with figures
  Apollo ns 82:lxxiii N '65
River estuary
  Art N 64:59 N '65
VICKERS, Robert
Exhibition at Galerie Internationale. Arts
  40:64 D '65
VICKREY, Robert Remsen
Exhibition at Midtown gallery. W. Berkson.
  Arts 39:64 S '65
  Reproductions
Suit of empty armor
  Am Artist (col) 30:cover S '66
VICTOR of Crete
From Damaskinos to Tzanes, some Cretan
  painters 1453-1669. A. Bryer. bibliog f
  Apollo ns 84:16 Jl '66
  il: St Catherine of Alexandria
VICTORIA, Salvador
Situation actuelle de la peinture à Madrid.
  H. Galy-Carles. il Aujourd'hui 9:64 F '66
VICTORIA, National gallery of. See Melbourne
  —National gallery of Victoria
VICTORIA and Albert museum
Catalogue of Italian sculpture in the Vic-
  toria and Albert museum, by J. Pope-
  Hennessy. Review
  Art N 64:18+ Ja '66. C. Seymour, jr

FIG. 35. *Art Index.* (Copyright: the H. W. Wilson Company.)

Encyclopedias and Dictionaries

The *Encyclopaedia of World Art* (14 vols., New York, McGraw-Hill, 1959–67) is a scholarly publication with contributions by specialists. Articles are signed and include good bibliographies. The preface states that the work covers "architecture, sculpture, and painting, and every other man-made object that, regardless of its purpose or technique, enters the field of aesthetic judgement because of its form or decoration". A large part of each volume consists of plates illustrating the text. Because of the number of biographical dictionaries for artists which exist, the number of entries under personal names is relatively small.

The nineteenth-century editions of *Encyclopaedia Britannica* are of considerable value as judgements of contemporary art. These include the eighth edition (22 vols., 1853–61) and the ninth (24 vols., 1875–89). The tenth edition, published in 1902, constituted a supplement to the ninth. The very important eleventh edition (29 vols., 1910–11) is also essential for the student of the Victorian period.

The best 1-volume dictionary is P. and L. Murray, *A Dictionary of Art and Artists*, published by Penguin Books in 1959 and reissued in an illustrated edition by Thames and Hudson in 1965. The *Dictionary* includes useful definitions of technical terms and information about art movements and individual artists.

Biographical Works

General

The most authoritative general dictionary of biography is U. Thieme and F. Becker, *Allgemeines Lexikon der bildenden Künstler von der Antike bis zur Gegenwart* (37 vols., Leipzig, Seemann, 1907–50). Articles include bibliographies with references to periodical articles and exhibition catalogues. The work is continued by H. Vollmer, *Allgemeines Lexikon der bildenden Künstler des XX. Jahrhunderts* (Leipzig, Seemann, 1953–).

E. Bénézit, *Dictionnaire critique et documentaire des Peintres, Sculpteurs, Dessinateurs et Graveurs de tous les Temps et de tous les Pays* (rev. edn., 8 vols., Paris, Gründ, 1960), also includes many minor artists. Entries usually contain a brief listing of major works and their whereabouts in public collections and references to sales and prices.

M. Bryan, *Bryan's Dictionary of Painters and Engravers*, was first published in 1816. A second edition of 1849 was supplemented in 1876 by H. Ottley. Ottley's volume incorporated answers to a questionnaire sent to Victorian artists. Later editions of the *Dictionary* appeared in 2 volumes in 1884–9 and in 5 volumes in 1903–4, revised by G. C. Williamson in 1926–34.

British

General biographical dictionaries, including the essential *Dictionary of National Biography*, are discussed below in Chapter 14.

A Dictionary of British Painters in 10–12 volumes has been announced for publication commencing in 1970 by the Paul Mellon Foundation for British Art. The work will be illustrated and will include select bibliographies.

S. Redgrave, *A Dictionary of Artists of the English School* (rev. edn., Bell, 1878), contains essential biographical information for the earlier part of the Victorian period. The edition by R. Todd of Redgrave's *A Century of British Painters* (Phaidon, 1947) is a revised version of the second edition of 1890. The work includes a bibliographical index. Todd omits the chapter on the Pre-Raphaelites which originally appeared in the earlier version of the second edition on the grounds that it was unbalanced because it did not include living painters. He does not replace the chapter, however, and the 1890 text therefore retains some value.

Several extensive lists of nineteenth-century British artists were compiled by A. Graves. *A Dictionary of Artists who have Exhibited Works in the Principal London Exhibitions from 1760 to 1893* (3rd edn., Graves, 1901) gives brief details but is of major importance for the identification of many artists. Other essential works by

Graves on the same plan include *A Century of Loan Exhibitions, 1813–1912* (5 vols., Graves, 1913–15), *The Royal Academy of Arts: a complete dictionary of contributors and their work from its foundation in 1769 to 1904* (8 vols., Graves & Bell, 1905–6), and *The British Institution, 1806–1867* (Bell, 1908).

F. Rinder and W. D. McKay, *Royal Scottish Academy, 1826–1916* (Maclehose, 1917), follows the plan of Graves's *Principal London Exhibitions* but restricts coverage strictly to academicians, associates, and honorary members of the Royal Scottish Academy and their exhibited works.

A. Cunningham, *The Lives of the Most Eminent British Painters, Sculptors, and Architects*, was first published in 1830–3. A revised edition by Mrs. Heaton (3 vols., Bell, 1879–80) adds some Victorian figures and provides an index.

R. Brydall, *Art in Scotland: its origin and progress* (Edinburgh, Blackwood, 1889), includes a section of "Biographical and critical notices of the leading deceased Scottish painters, 1800–1899".

Recent works include S. H. Pavière, *Dictionary of Victorian Landscape Painters* (Leigh-on-Sea, F. Lewis, 1968) and *Dictionary of Victorian Painters* (Leigh-on-Sea, F. Lewis, 1969). M. H. Grant has compiled *A Chronological History of the Old English Landscape Painters—in Oil—from the XVIth Century to the XIXth Century* (8 vols., the Author, 1957–61). This is the most extensive illustrated guide to the subject. The same author's *A Dictionary of British Landscape Painters, from the 16th Century to the Early 20th Century* (Leigh-on-Sea, F. Lewis, 1952) attempts "to assemble, in a single volume, the entire *corpus* of the British School of Landscape-painters". M. H. Grant has also compiled *A Dictionary of British Etchers* (Rockliff, 1952). This is a short popular guide which does not list sources. G. H. Bushell, *Scottish Engravers: a biographical dictionary* (OUP, 1949), is an authoritative 1-volume guide.

For sculpture in the early part of the nineteenth century R. Gunnis, *Dictionary of British Sculptors, 1660–1851* (rev. edn., Odhams, 1968), is an essential guide which includes many minor figures. M. H. Grant, *A Dictionary of British Sculptors from the XIIIth Century to the XXth Century* (Rockliff, 1953), is much less detailed.

B. S. Long, *British Miniaturists, 1520–1860* (Bles, 1929; reprinted Holland Pr., 1966), includes useful biographical information. H. Hubbard, *Some Victorian Draughtsmen* (CUP, 1944), is also useful.

Local

Biographical dictionaries of local artists will often be traced in the public libraries of the area. Examples of such local productions include H. C. Hall, *Artists and Sculptors of Nottingham and Nottinghamshire, 1750–1950* (Nottingham, H. Jones, 1953), H. Gibbon, *Four Centuries of Lancashire Art* (Preston, Harris Museum & Art Gallery, 1958), and G. Pyecroft, *Art in Devonshire, with the Biographies of Artists Born in that County* (Exeter, H. S. Eland, 1883).

H. C. Marillier, *The Liverpool School of Painters* (Murray, 1904), includes an account of the Liverpool Academy from 1810 to 1867, followed by memoirs of the better-known Liverpool painters of the period. A similar service is performed for Glasgow painters by D. Martin, *The Glasgow School of Painting* (Bell, 1902).

Welsh artists are listed in T. H. Rees, *Welsh Painters, Engravers, and Sculptors, 1527–1911* (Carnarvon, 1912), and Irish in W. G. Strickland, *A Dictionary of Irish Artists* (2 vols., Dublin, Maunsel, 1913).

Directories and Guides to Collections

General

The Libraries, Museums and Art Galleries Year Book (Clarke) includes a section listing museums and art galleries in the United Kingdom by location. Details are given of officers and staff, hours of opening, scope of collections, and notes on special holdings.

There is a subject index listing significant or unusual collections. The annual *Museums Calendar* (Museums Association) provides a directory of museums and art galleries.

Index Publishers produce annual guides to *Museums and Galleries in Great Britain and Ireland* and to *Historic Houses, Castles and Gardens in Great Britain and Ireland.* The National Trust publishes a detailed guide to *Properties of the National Trust.* The *Guide to London Museums* (HMSO) is a useful survey. The annual *On View* lists recent acquisitions by museums and galleries in Britain.

The Nation's Pictures: a guide to the chief national and municipal picture galleries of England, Scotland and Wales, edited by A. Blunt and M. Whinney (Chatto & Windus, 1950), is a valuable guide to the contents of major collections. D. Murray, *Museums, their History and their Use* (Maclehose, 1904), is still useful.

Individual Collections

Guides to individual collections which contain good Victorian holdings include J. Rothenstein's illustrated narrative introduction to *The Tate Gallery* (Thames & Hudson, 1958). The Tate Gallery's British catalogue and the catalogue of the National Portrait Gallery are of major importance. A. E. Popham, *A Handbook to the Drawings and Water-colours in the Department of Prints and Drawings, British Museum* (British Museum, 1938), is a guide to its rich collections. A new *Catalogue of British Drawings* (British Museum, 1960–) is in progress.

Guides to important collections in the provinces include the *Catalogue of Drawings* and *Catalogue of Paintings* of the City of Birmingham Museum and Art Gallery; the *Catalogue of Pictures* of the City of Manchester Art Gallery; the *Catalogue* of the Walker Art Gallery, Liverpool; *Pictures in the Collection* of the Harris Art Gallery, Preston; and the *Catalogue* of the Russell Cotes Art Gallery and Museum, Bournemouth. The William Morris Gallery, Walthamstow, has produced subject catalogues of its collections.

Exhibition Catalogues

Among records of notable exhibitions of Victorian art the following Royal Academy catalogues are of especial value: *Royal Academy of Arts Bicentenary Exhibition, 1768–1968* (1968), *Italian Art and Britain* (1960), *The First Hundred Years of the Royal Academy, 1769–1868* (1951–2), *Exhibition of Scottish Art* (1939), and *Commemorative Catalogue of the Exhibition of British Art, 1934* (1935).

Portrait Indexes

W. G. Singer, *Allgemeiner Bildniskatalog* (14 vols., Leipzig Hiersemann, 1930–6; reprinted 7 vols., Nendeln, Kraus, 1967), is an index of engraved portraits of all periods and countries to 1929. This was continued by Singer in *Neuer Bildniskatalog* (5 vols., Leipzig, Hiersemann, 1937–8; reprinted 2 vols., Nendeln, Kraus, 1967).

The *A.L.A. Portrait Index: index to portraits contained in printed books and periodicals*, edited by W. C. Lane and N. E. Browne (Washington, Library of Congress, 1906; reprinted 3 vols., New York, Burt Franklin, *c.* 1962), provides details of location and brief biographical notes.

F. O'Donoghue and H. M. Hake, *Catalogue of Engraved British Portraits Preserved in the Department of Prints and Drawings in the British Museum* (6 vols., British Museum, 1908–25), is an extensive descriptive guide.

Photographic Archives

For the location of large collections of reproductions in libraries and other institutions the *International Directory of Photographic Archives of Works of Art* (2 vols., Paris, UNESCO, 1950–4) gives information about 1300 collections and lists sources of supply.

ARCHITECTURE

Many of the works already noted include architecture in their terms of reference. The works listed here are limited in scope to architecture alone. No attempt is made to cover the documentary sources which are of obvious importance for the architectural historian. As in other sections of this book, the present survey is concerned almost exclusively with printed sources of information. Information about non-printed sources of information, however, is contained in the guides noted below.

Guides and Bibliographies

A good narrative guide which includes information on sources for the history of architecture is D. L. Smith, *How to Find Out in Architecture and Building* (Oxford, Pergamon Pr., 1967) (Fig. 36). H. M. Colvin, *A Guide to the Sources of English Architectural History* (Shalfleet Manor, Isle of Wight, Pinhorns, 1967), is a useful pamphlet which forms a revised version of an article on "Architectural history and its records" which the author contributed in 1955 to the periodical *Archives*. The pamphlet contains notes on printed and documentary sources for the study of royal buildings, public buildings, churches, domestic architecture, architects and craftsmen, and drawings and topographical views.

J. Harris has contributed a valuable article on "Sources for architectural history in England" to the *Journal of the Society of Architectural Historians* (vol. 24, 1965, pp. 297–300). This lists selected sources for private domestic architecture, royal buildings, and secular and ecclesiastical public buildings. Like Colvin's *Guide*, this article lists collections of drawings and some of the catalogues which have been produced for these.

The major bibliographies for the history of architecture are found in catalogues of libraries. The *Catalogue of the Library of the Royal Institute of British Architects* (2 vols., The Library, 1937–8) comprises an author list and a classified list with alphabetical subject index. The *Catalogue* lists books, pamphlets,

On this period and the nearly modern together there is a heavier-than-usual contribution from the Pelican History of Art in the form of an American's work, H. R. Hitchcock's *Architecture, Nineteenth and Twentieth Centuries* (Penguin, 1958). In the Oxford History of English Art there is *English Art, 1800–1870* by T. S. R. Boase (OUP, 1959). On nineteenth-century ideas of design, or decor in general, John Gloag has written *Victorian Taste: some social aspects of architecture and industrial design from 1820 to 1900* (Black, 1962) and *Victorian Comfort: a social history of design from 1830 to 1900* (Black, 1961). Among many accounts of the 1851 Great Exhibition may be mentioned Nikolaus Pevsner's *High Victorian Design: a study of the exhibits of 1851* (AP, 1951), and for the ending of the epoch, there is the same art historian's *Pioneers of Modern Design, front William Morris to Walter Gropius* (same publisher, 2nd edn., 1949). Also relevant to the spirit of the century is Rayner Banham's *Theory and Design in the First Machine Age* (AP, 1960).

Concise outlines of the building activities are given by R. Turnor in *Nineteenth Century Architecture in Britain* (Batsford, 1950); Sir Hugh Casson in *An Introduction to Victorian Architecture* (Art & Technics, 1948); and H. S. Goodhart-Rendel in *English Architecture since the Regency: an interpretation* (Constable, 1953); and there is a longer account in *Victorian Architecture*, edited by P. Ferriday (Cape, 1963). The 2 volumes of H. R. Hitchcock's *Early Victorian Architecture in Britain* (New Haven, Yale UP, and London, AP, 1954) offer a penetrating analysis of the opening years.

The Gothic revival and religious architecture are discussed in B. F. L. Clarke's *Church Builders of the Nineteenth Century: a study of the Gothic revival in England* (SPCK, 1938) and J. F. White's *The Cambridge Movement: the ecclesiologists and the Gothic revival* (CUP, 1962), the latter being a rare example of

Fig. 36. D. L. Smith, *How to Find Out in Architecture and Building*.
(Copyright: Pergamon Press Ltd.)

manuscripts, and typescripts in the library. The library also produces a series of *Library Bibliographies*. Although many of these deal with new buildings, some are of historical interest.

A new and most valuable listing is provided in *A Catalogue of Architectural Drawings in the Drawings Collection of the Royal Institute of British Architects* (Farnborough, Gregg, 1968–), which is currently being published in two series. The first series lists architects alphabetically and also includes an index of places and patrons, while the second comprises separate volumes devoted to special collections. The same publisher is also undertaking a *Catalogue of British Drawings for Architecture, Decoration, Sculpture and Landscape Gardening, 1550–1900, in American Collections*, edited by J. Harris.

The Catalog of the Avery Memorial Architectural Library of Columbia University (2nd edn., 19 vols., Boston, Hall, 1968) is a union list of art and architecture books and periodicals in the Avery Library and in other libraries at Columbia University. Entries are by author and subject. It is proposed to issue future supplements to the *Catalog*. The *Avery Index to Architectural Periodicals* (12 vols., Boston, Hall, 1963) indexes periodical articles, interpreting architecture in its widest sense. The first of a series of supplementary volumes listing recent articles was published in 1965.

Several books contain useful selective bibliographies. Among general histories B. F. Fletcher, *A History of Architecture on the Comparative Method*, revised and expanded by R. A. Cordingley (17th edn., Athlone Pr., 1961), and F. M. Simpson, *Simpson's History of Architectural Development* (new edn., Longmans, 1954–), should be noted. A more specific work with extensive bibliographical information is H. R. Hitchcock, *Architecture: nineteenth and twentieth centuries* (3rd edn., Penguin, 1968), in the Pelican History of Art series. The same author's *Early Victorian Architecture in Britain* (2 vols., Architectural Pr., 1954) has no separate bibliography but includes useful references to sources in the text. *Concerning Architecture: essays on architectural writers and writing presented to Nikolaus Pevsner* (Allen Lane, 1968) includes much bibliographical information about writers on architecture in the nineteenth century. An essay on "Nineteenth-century architectural periodicals" by F. Jenkins provides a useful survey of this material. The extremely well-designed index makes the work a valuable handbook to the history of the study of architecture.

Current Work

The quarterly *Library Bulletin* of the Royal Institute of British Architects records new books added to the library and also indexes significant articles from periodicals. From 1966 index entries for periodicals are cumulated in the *Annual Review of Periodical Articles*.

The Ministry of Public Buildings and Works issues a fortnightly *Library Bulletin* which provides an annotated list of books and pamphlets and an abstracting service of selected periodical articles. From this is compiled the 6-month *Consolidated Accessions List* of books and pamphlets and the annual *Consolidated Building References to Articles in Periodicals*. Although the lists deal primarily with building, they include some references of interest for the history of architecture.

Encyclopedias and Dictionaries

R. Sturgis, *Dictionary of Architecture and Building: biographical, historical, and descriptive* (3 vols., New York, Macmillan, 1901), includes much useful information and bibliographical references. *The Dictionary of Architecture*, published by the Architectural Publication Society during the period 1853–92, is valuable for the historian and contains useful biographies and bibliographical references. The German *Wasmuths Lexikon der Baukunst* (5 vols., Berlin, Wasmuth, 1929–37) includes historical information and biographical material. P. A. Planat, *Encyclopédie de l'Architecture et de la Construction* (6 vols. in 12, Paris, Dujardin, 1888–92), includes long articles by specialists on broad topics and brief biographies of great architects and builders.

Shorter dictionaries include J. Fleming, H. Honour, and N. Pevsner, *The Penguin Dictionary of Architecture* (Penguin, 1966), which contains considerable historical and biographical material, and M. S. Briggs, *Everyman's Concise Encyclopaedia of Architecture* (Dent, 1959), which includes biographies and short bibliographies.

Biographical Dictionaries

There is a great need for a biographical dictionary of British architects of the Victorian period. H. M. Colvin, *A Biographical Dictionary of English Architects, 1660–1840* (Murray, 1954), is useful for pre-Victorian architects who also worked after 1840 and sometimes for the fathers and teachers of Victorian architects. Unfortunately, there is no equivalent for the later part of the nineteenth century. For most inquiries reference will have to be made to the more general biographical dictionaries devoted to the fine arts. In addition, it is useful to note that the Library of the Royal Institute of British Architects has compiled card indexes of Fellows of the Institute and of obituary notices in *The Builder* and a few other periodicals.

The single volume of *Wyman's Architects, Engineers and Building Trades Directory*, which appeared in 1868, includes some useful biographical information.

Societies

No guide to the Victorian period could pass over the magnificent work performed by the Victorian Society under the chairmanship of Sir Nikolaus Pevsner. This Society, formed in 1958, is concerned to preserve Victorian and Edwardian buildings and to arouse interest and encourage the study of the arts and architecture of these periods and their relation to social history. The Society publishes a *Newsletter* and an *Annual Report*. There is a co-operating Victorian Society in the United States.

Other British societies which have an interest in Victorian architecture include the Society of Architectural Historians, which from 1958 has published an annual periodical, *Architectural History*, and the Society for the Protection of Ancient Buildings. Information about these and other architectural societies may be found in such general guides as the *Aslib Directory* (new edn., Aslib, 1968–) and *Scientific and Learned Societies of Great Britain* (Allen & Unwin).

The Society of Architectural Historians in America publishes a quarterly *Journal of the Society of Architectural Historians* (Philadelphia, The Society, 1942–), which includes regular book reviews.

APPLIED ARTS

The interpretation of the term "applied arts" can be almost infinite in extension. Much information may be found in the general works described above. It is proposed here to list only a selection of specific guides which are useful for the study of the Victorian period.

General

The Complete Encyclopedia of Antiques, edited by L. G. G. Ramsey (The Connoisseur, 1962), is a lavish guide to the subject. The book includes a list by subject of museums in Britain, Europe, and the United States and a useful bibliography.

L. A. and H. B. Boger, *The Dictionary of Antiques and the Decorative Arts* (New York, Scribner, 1967), is a useful guide with bibliography. M. S. Macdonald-Taylor, *A Dictionary of Marks: metalwork, furniture, ceramics* (The Connoisseur, 1962), is a handbook for identification.

Ceramics

G. A. Godden, *Encyclopaedia of British Pottery and Porcelain Marks* (Jenkins, 1964), lists signed marks alphabetically and provides pictorial indexes of unsigned marks. The work includes a glossary of terms and an extensive bibliography. The same author's *The Handbook of British Pottery and Porcelain Marks* (Jenkins, 1968) is a convenient shorter guide.

Works of identification whose scope is not limited to Britain include W. Chaffers, *Marks and Monograms on European and Oriental Pottery and Porcelain, with Historical Notices of Each Manufactory* (14th edn., Reeves, 1932; reprinted Los Angeles, Borden, 1946). J. P. Cushion and W. B. Honey, *Handbook of Pottery and Porcelain Marks* (Faber, 1956), is strong on English marks and is useful for the Victorian period.

L. M. E. Solon, *Ceramic Literature* (Griffin, 1910), is subtitled "An analytical index to the works published in all languages on the history and technology of the ceramic art; also the catalogues of public museums, private collections, and of auction sales . . .". Items are annotated. W. Mankowitz and R. G. Haggar, *The Concise Encyclopedia of English Pottery and Porcelain* (Deutsch, 1957), includes short articles and selective bibliographies.

Costume

H. and M. Hiler, *Bibliography of Costume* (New York, Wilson, 1939), lists over 8000 books and periodicals. R. Colas, *Bibliographie générale du Costume et de la Mode* (2 vols., Paris, Colas, 1933), includes over 3000 entries arranged by author with subject index.

I. S. Monro and D. E. Cook, *Costume Index: a subject index to plates and to illustrated texts* (New York, Wilson), was published in 1937 with a supplement in 1957. Its 2 volumes index nearly 1000 illustrated works either wholly devoted to costume or containing much information about the subject.

A useful guide to English costume is C. W. and P. Cunnington and C. Beard, *A Dictionary of English Costume* (Black, 1960), which covers the period from 900 to 1900. C. W. and P. Cunnington, *Handbook of English Costume in the Nineteenth Century* (2nd edn., Faber, 1966), includes many illustrations and references to source material.

Furniture and Interior Decoration

J. Gloag, *A Short Dictionary of Furniture* (Allen & Unwin, 1952), provides a useful dictionary of English-language terms used, lists of British and American makers and designers, and British clockmakers, a bibliography and tables of periods, types of furniture, materials, and craftsmen from 1100 to 1950. J. Arenson, *The Encyclopedia of Furniture* (New York, Crown, 1938), includes short articles and a brief bibliography.

The Connoisseur Period Guides to the Houses, Decoration, Furnishing and Chattels of the Classic Periods, edited by R. Edwards and L. G. G. Ramsey, include a volume on *The Early Victorian Period, 1830–1860* (The Connoisseur, 1958).

E. Aslin, *Nineteenth Century English Furniture* (Faber, 1962), contains a brief bibliography. R. W. Symonds and B. B. Whinery, *Victorian Furniture* (Country Life, 1962), though valuable for its range of reference, lacks any bibliography.

G. Lackschewitz, *Interior Design and Decoration: a bibliography* (New York, Public Library, 1961), is a selective list which includes historical references as well as twentieth-century concepts of design.

Metalwork

C. J. Jackson, *English Goldsmiths and their Marks* (2nd edn., Macmillan, 1921; reprinted New York, Dover, 1964), lists over 13,000 marks on gold and silver used by goldsmiths and plate workers in England, Scotland, and Ireland. The same author's *An Illustrated History of English Plate* (2 vols., Batsford, 1911) is also useful.

H. P. Okie, *Old Silver and Old Sheffield Plate* (New York, Doubleday, 1928), is a history of the silversmiths of Great Britain and Ireland with a detailed guide to the marks of many British, American, and European silversmiths.

W. Chaffers, *Hall Marks on Gold and Silver Plate* (10th edn., Reeves, 1922), includes much information about British work and a bibliography. H. H. Cotterell, *Old Pewter: its makers and marks in England, Scotland and Ireland* (Batsford, 1929; reprinted 1963), includes alphabetical lists of pewterers and marks.

Coins

W. Raymond, *Coins of the World: 19th century issues* (2nd edn., New York, Raymond, 1953), is an extensive list. R. S. Yeoman, *A Catalogue of Modern World Coins* (5th edn., Racine, Whitman, 1962), lists coins issued during the last 100 years.

L. Forrer, *Biographical Dictionary of Medallists* (8 vols., Spink, 1902–30), gives details of coin marks to 1900.

Photography

A. Boni, *Photographic Literature: an international bibliographic guide to general and specialized literature* (New York, Morgan, 1962), lists works on all aspects of the techniques, history, biography, and aesthetics of photography. The *Library Catalogue* of the Royal Photographic Society of Great Britain and Ireland (3rd edn., 2 vols. and supplement, The Library, 1939–53) is a valuable reference source.

Among standard histories of photography H. and A. Gernsheim, *The History of Photography from the Earliest Use of the Camera Obscura in the Eleventh Century up to 1914* (OUP, 1955), includes a selective annotated bibliography and many references in footnotes. There is a good bibliography in H. Gernsheim, *Creative Photography: aesthetic trends 1839–1960* (Faber, 1962). The same writer has also contributed *Masterpieces of Victorian Photography* (Phaidon, 1951).

B. Newhall, *The History of Photography from 1839 to the Present Day* (rev. edn., New York, Museum of Modern Art, 1964), includes an extensive bibliography of books and articles on the history of photography and on individual photographers.

CHAPTER 11

Music Literature

ATTENTION is focused in this chapter primarily on guides to
printed materials and literary information useful for the historian
of music. Such works will be useful to students of other subjects
who need to acquire information about music in the Victorian
period. The musicologist, of course, will have to study the music
itself in its printed and manuscript form and in its interpretation
on gramophone records. No attempt is made here to list the
specialized guides to the music itself. For information about such
works the reader is referred to the general guides and bibliographies noted below.

Guides and Bibliographies

The basic general introduction to research materials is V.
Duckles, *Music Reference and Research Materials: an annotated
bibliography* (2nd edn., New York, Free Pr., 1967). Entries in this
work are usefully annotated. The lists include, among other
items, dictionaries and encyclopedias, histories, guides to musicology, bibliographies of music and its literature, catalogues of
libraries and collections of musical instruments, and yearbooks.

J. H. Davies, *Musicalia: sources of information in music* (Oxford,
Pergamon Pr., 1966), is a wide-ranging narrative guide (Fig. 37).
This work includes valuable appendixes listing "the principal
music collections, formerly in private hands, and now to be found
in institutions and libraries of Great Britain", names and addresses
of music publishers and their British and American agents, music
publishers' organizations and performing rights, and collecting
societies.

CHAPTER 9

The Music Librarian

I love vast libraries; yet there is a doubt
If one be better with them or without.

J. G. SAXE, *The Library*

THE paths of the layman, the professional and amateur musician, and the musicologist having been eased in the foregoing chapters as regards sources, what remains for the music librarian—or rather the general librarian, since the majority of smaller libraries will rarely have a trained music librarian on their staff? (Of the 600 or so municipal and county library systems in Great Britain, probably not more than one-tenth have an assistant who can give his entire time to music service, even after the encouraging post-war development of gramophone record departments, and most other countries are far less well served.) Most of the reference works already discussed will be found only in libraries, and of these only the large, well-established and interested library is likely to possess the expensive and out-of-print items.

The music librarian might well become first acquainted with the basic terms of his job from C. Hopkinson's "The fundamentals of music bibliography" (*Fontes*, 1955/2) and from A. Van Hoboken's "Probleme der musikbibliographischen Terminologie" (*Fontes*, 1958/1), and then proceed to read one of the sanest short expositions (unaccountably overlooked in recent bibliographies): E. A. Savage's "One way to form a music library" in his *Special Librarianship in General Libraries* (Grafton, 1939).

Statements of problems, scope and opportunities have appeared in *Fontes* 1959/2 (A. H. King's "The music librarian and his tasks")

93

FIG. 37. J. H. Davies, *Musicalia*. (Copyright: Pergamon Press Ltd.)

G. Haydon, *Introduction to Musicology: a survey of the fields, systematic and historical, of musical knowledge and research* (New York, Prentice-Hall, 1941; reprinted Chapel Hill, Univ. of North Carolina Pr., 1959), includes bibliographies for each chapter and a general bibliography at the end of the work.

K. E. Mixter, *General Bibliography for Music Research* (Detroit, Information Service, 1962), is a good brief survey of reference works, including bibliographies, dictionaries, encyclopedias, union lists, and library catalogues.

E. C. Krohn, *The History of Music: an index to the literature available in a selected group of musicological publications* (St. Louis, Washington Univ., 1952), lists articles on the history of music in 39 leading periodicals.

L. R. McColvin and H. Reeves, *Music Libraries* (rev. edn., 2 vols., Deutsch, 1965), includes a lengthy bibliography of writings on music. It is chiefly devoted to works in English and emphasizes topics of particular British interest.

A nineteenth-century guide which is still worth noting is J. E. Matthew, *The Literature of Music* (E. Stock, 1896). This work contains a number of bibliographical essays on writings about music.

Among library collections the British Museum has published a catalogue of *Books in the Hirsch Library* (British Museum, 1959), listing over 11,500 books on music which were acquired by the library in 1946.

The Music Library Association has compiled a valuable concise *Check-list of Thematic Catalogues* (New York, Public Library, 1954). A *Queens College Supplement (1966) to the Music Library Association's Check List of Thematic Catalogues (1954)* has been issued in typescript by Queens College, Flushing, NY.

F. S. Forrester, *Ballet in England: a bibliography and a survey c. 1700–1966* (Library Association, 1968), provides a useful guide to books and periodical articles.

Theses

H. Hewitt, *Doctoral Dissertations in Musicology* (4th edn., Philadelphia, American Musicological Society, 1965), lists 1204 dissertations completed or in progress. Supplements are published annually in the *Journal of the American Musicological Society*.

The *Journal of Research in Music Education* periodically publishes a list of doctoral dissertations in music education.

Current Work

The *British Catalogue of Music* (Council of the British National Bibliography, 1957–) is a quarterly bibliography of music and books about music published in Britain (Fig. 38). Entries are cumulated annually. Like the *British National Bibliography* it is compiled from works deposited in the British Museum.

Bibliographie der Musikschrifttums (Leipzig, Hofmeister, 1936–) is an international bibliography of books and periodical articles. It indexes a large number of non-musical periodicals. There is, however, a considerable time-lag in its publication.

Histories

The New Oxford History of Music (OUP, 1954–) has not yet progressed far enough to be of use for the nineteenth century. Its predecessor, *The Oxford History of Music* (2nd edn., OUP, 1929–38), includes volumes on *The Romantic Period* by E. Dannreuther and on *Symphony and Drama, 1850–1900* by H. C. Colles.

D. J. Grout, *A History of Western Music* (New York, Norton, 1960), includes a useful bibliography and chronology.

Encyclopedias

The best English-language encyclopedia of music is G. Grove, *Grove's Dictionary of Music and Musicians*, edited by E. Blom

CLASSIFIED SECTION

This section contains entries under Subjects, Executants and Instruments according to a system of classification, a synopsis of which appears in the preliminary pages. The key to the classification and to this section is the Alphabetical Section which precedes it.

A list of music publishers and their addresses is to be found at the end of this publication.

The following are used in giving the *sizes of musical works*:—

8vo. for works up to 10½″ in height.
4to. for works between 10½″ and 12″ in height.
fol. for works over 12″ in height.
obl. indicates a work of unusual proportions.
s.sh. means a single sheet.

A—MUSICAL LITERATURE

A   MUSICAL LITERATURE

A – MUSICAL LITERATURE. GENERAL WORKS

CORBETT, Jane, *and* YELVERTON, Vera
Music for G.C.E. 'O' Level. Revised ed. London,
Barrie & Rockliff, 12/6. [dOct] 1967. *176p. illus.
(incl. music), bibliog. 18½cm. Pbk.*
Previous ed. (B61-20985) 1961.
                                        (B67-23063)

JANES, Burnett
An adventure in music. London, Baker, 36/-. Nov 1967.
3-238p. 22½cm.
                                        (B67-25482)

NEWSON, Keith R
Listening to music: with material for classroom lessons.
London, F. Warne, 12/6 (Lp.8/6). Feb 1967. *112p.
illus.(music). 25cm.*
Originally published, Wellington, (N.Z.), Reed, 1962.
                                        (B67-6450)

WILSON, Colin
Colin Wilson on music. Revised ed. London, Pan Books,
5/-. Jan 1967. *237p. 18cm. Pbk.*

A—MUSICAL LITERATURE. GENERAL WORKS—*cont.*

A(M) – Musicians

A(P) – Bernstein, Leonard. *Biographies*

EWEN, David
Leonard Bernstein. Revised ed. London, W.H. Allen,
25/-. Jun 1967. *175p. 4plates(incl.port.), 22½cm.*
Previous ed., Philadelphia (Pa.), Chilton Co., 1960.
                                        (B67-12253)

A(QU) – Notation

TOTTEN, J   , *and* TOTTEN, J   W
Totten music notation. 82 Gordon St., Glasgow, C.1,
Totten Music, unpriced. Dec 1966. *48p. illus.(music),
table, diagrs. 28½cm. Sd.*
                                        (B67-2579)

A(T) – Bibliographies

DUCKLES, Vincent [Harris]
Music reference and research materials: an
annotated bibliography; compiled by Vincent
Duckles. Revised ed. New York, Free Press;
London, Collier-Macmillan, 63/-. Jul[1967]. *xiii,385p.*

126

FIG. 38. *British Catalogue of Music.* (Copyright: the Council of the British National Bibliography Ltd.)

(5th edn., 9 vols., Macmillan, 1954). A supplementary volume to this edition appeared in 1961. Although its coverage is general, this work places special emphasis on English subjects. The *Dictionary* includes signed articles by specialists. Bibliographies of books and periodical articles are included. For the student of the Victorian period the earlier editions of this work may well be of value. Grove first published his *Dictionary* in 1879–89. The second edition, edited by J. A. Fuller-Maitland, followed in 1904–10.

The major scholarly encyclopedia of music, however, is *Die Musik in Geschichte und Gegenwart: allgemeine Enzyklopädie der Musik*, edited by F. Blume (Kassel, Barenreiter, 1949–). This contains lengthy signed articles in German and very good extensive bibliographies.

Other general encyclopedias of music include P. A. Scholes, *The Oxford Companion to Music* (9th edn., OUP, 1955), a useful 1-volume work for the non-specialist. This includes no bibliographies. H. Riemann, *Riemann Musik Lexikon*, edited by W. Gurlitt (12th edn., 3 vols., Mainz, Schott, 1959–), devotes 2 volumes to biography and the third to subjects. The work includes bibliographies. *Larousse de la Musique* (2 vols., Paris, Larousse, 1957) contains good articles by subject and brief biographical entries. Bibliographies are given at the end of each volume. *Encyclopédie de la Musique* (3 vols., Paris, Fasquelle, 1958–61) is often useful for biographical information and contains bibliographies.

Among useful encyclopedic guides to musical forms, W. W. Cobbett, *Cyclopedic Survey of Chamber Music* (2nd edn., 3 vols., OUP, 1963), includes signed articles on a wide variety of topics and persons. D. Ewen, *Encyclopedia of the Opera* (new edn., New York, Hill & Wang, 1963), and H. Rosenthal and J. Warrack, *Concise Oxford Dictionary of Opera* (OUP, 1964), are valuable 1-volume guides to opera plots, characters, terminology, and history, and to biographies of persons associated with opera. A. Loewenberg, *Annals of Opera, 1597–1940* (2nd edn., 2 vols., Geneva, Societas Bibliographica, 1955), lists nearly 4000 operas in chronological order of first performance and gives details of the history of performances, revivals, and translations of each opera. Indexes of opera titles, composers, and librettists are provided.

Biographical Dictionaries

Much biographical information may be derived from the encyclopedias listed above and from the general biographical dictionaries discussed in Chapter 14. In addition to these, T. Baker, *Biographical Dictionary of Musicians,* revised by N. Slonimsky (5th edn., New York, Schirmer, 1958), offers compact biographies with extremely good bibliographies of works by and about persons listed. This is the most comprehensive biographical dictionary in English.

F. J. Fétis, *Biographie universelle des Musiciens et Bibliographie générale de la Musique* (2nd edn., 8 vols., Paris, Didot, 1866–70), was provided with a 2-volume *Supplément et Complément,* edited by A. Pougin (Paris, Didot, 1878–80). The complete set of 10 volumes was reprinted in 1964 (Brussels, Culture et Civilisation).

A Dictionary of Modern Music and Musicians, edited by A. E. Hull (Dent, 1924), is primarily a biographical dictionary for the period 1880–1920. It includes good bibliographies.

J. D. Brown and S. S. Stratton, *British Musical Biography: a dictionary of musical artists, authors, and composers born in Britain and its colonies* (Birmingham, Stratton, 1897), includes a large number of entries for little-known Victorian musicians. The work includes useful bibliographies.

A valuable guide to 1335 dictionaries of biography and terminology is J. B. Coover, *Music Lexicography* (Denver, Bibliographical Center for Research, 1958), which is a revised edition of the author's *A Bibliography of Music Dictionaries,* published in 1952.

CHAPTER 12

English Literature

General Bibliographies and Guides

The student of English literature is well served for bibliographical information. A valuable guide to older bibliographies, including both those published separately and those included in books and periodicals, is C. S. Northup, *A Register of Bibliographies of the English Language and Literature* (New Haven, Yale Univ. Pr., 1925; reprinted New York, Hafner, 1962). This was supplemented by N. Van Patten, *Index to Bibliographies and Bibliographical Contributions Relating to the Work of American and British Authors, 1923–32* (Stanford, Univ. Pr., 1934).

An extensive guide to general bibliographies and to bibliographies devoted to periods, forms and *genres*, and subjects is T. H. Howard-Hill, *Bibliography of British Literary Bibliographies* (Oxford, Clarendon Pr., 1969). This forms the first volume of a projected *Index of British Bibliography*. Two further volumes will list bibliographies of the work of Shakespeare and non-enumerative British bibliography and textual criticism.

The basic bibliographical tool for the study of English literature is the *Cambridge Bibliography of English Literature*, edited by F. W. Bateson (4 vols., CUP, 1940). The third volume covers the period 1800–1900. Although necessarily selective, this bibliography contains an enormous amount of information. It provides an extensive list of items on all aspects of literature, and documents works by and about individual writers. The interpretation of what constitutes literature is intentionally wide. A supplementary volume, edited by G. Watson, was published in 1957. The whole work is now being thoroughly revised and a new edition, edited by

G. Watson, is being published as the *New Cambridge Bibliography of English Literature.** G. Watson has also edited the *Concise Cambridge Bibliography of English Literature, 600–1950* (CUP, 1958), a convenient 1-volume abridgement of the larger work.

There is considerable bibliographical information in the volumes of *The Cambridge History of English Literature*, edited by A. W. Ward and A. R. Waller (CUP, 1907–33). The *Oxford History of English Literature*, edited by F. P. Wilson and B. Dobrée (Oxford, Clarendon Pr., 1945–), is notable for the extensive bibliographies which are included. The volume by I. Jack, *English Literature, 1815–1832*, published in 1963, contains valuable bibliographical lists. Unfortunately, the volume for the Victorian period is not yet published.

The very useful *A Literary History of England*, edited by A. C. Baugh (2nd edn., Routledge, 1967), contains a surprisingly large amount of bibliographical information. This work was originally published in 1 volume, arranged in 4 sections corresponding to major historical periods. In the second edition each of these sections is published as a separate volume. The final section, *The Nineteenth Century and After*, is by S. C. Chew and R. D. Altick.

There are several good short general bibliographies of English literature. The most attractive and stimulating is F. W. Bateson, *A Guide to English Literature* (2nd edn., Longmans, 1967), which provides a narrative commentary on the value of editions and critical works (Fig. 39). R. D. Altick and A. Wright, *Selective Bibliography for the Study of English and American Literature* (2nd edn., New York, Macmillan, 1963), is a good basic list. D. F. Bond, *A Reference Guide to English Studies* (Chicago, Univ. Pr., 1962), is designed for research students and succeeds T. P. Cross, *Bibliographical Guide to English Studies* (10th edn., Chicago, Univ. Pr., 1951). A. G. Kennedy and D. B. Sands, *A Concise Bibliography for Students of English* (4th edn., Stanford, Univ. Pr., 1960), includes useful material on literary forms, methods and style of writing, printing and the book trade, and bibliographical and

*The new volume for 1800–1900 has recently been published since this section was written (CUP, 1969).

THOMAS BABINGTON MACAULAY, BARON MACAULAY (1800–1859). Works (9 vols., 1905–07; complete but without notes). *Lays of Ancient Rome*, edited by G. M. Trevelyan (1928); *Critical and Historical Essays*, edited by F. C. Montague (3 vols., 1903); *History of England*, edited by T. F. Henderson (5 vols., 1908). Good selection by G. M. Young (1952). The standard life is still G. O. Trevelyan's *Life and Letters* (2 vols., 1876); Arthur Bryant's *Macaulay* (1932) is a pleasant unpretentious sketch which needs supplementing by the stodgier studies by R. C. Beatty (1938), and J. R. Griffin (1964). (*CBEL*, III, 683 f.)

WILLIAM BARNES (1801?–1886). Collected poems, edited by Bernard Jones (2 vols., 1962; complete but unscholarly in presentation). Thomas Hardy's selection from Barnes's poems (1908) is much slimmer than Geoffrey Grigson's (1950; good critical Introduction). Life by Giles Dugdale (1953). (*CBEL*, III, 278 f.)

JOHN HENRY NEWMAN (1801–1890). *The Idea of a University*, edited by C. F. Harrold (1947); *Apologia pro Vita Sua*, edited by W. Ward (1913; critical text), also edited by Harrold (1947) and Basil Willey (1964); *A Grammar of Assent*, edited by Harrold (1947). Harrold – who is the author of the best modern study (1945) – has also edited several of the theological works (1948–49). Generous selection from both the prose and poetry by Geoffrey Tillotson (1957). The definitive edition of Newman's letters and diaries by C. S. Dessain and B. F. Blehl has begun with Vol. XI (1961) and progresses rapidly. The standard life is by Wilfrid Ward (2 vols., 1912). Meriol Trevor's two-volume biography – *Pillar of the Cloud* (1962) and *Light in Winter* (1963) – is the most recent life. W. E. Houghton has analysed the literary aspects of the *Apologia* in a good book (1945). (*CBEL*, III, 686 f.)

THOMAS LOVELL BEDDOES (1803–1849). Standard edition by H. W. Donner (1935; also with omissions 1950). The only modern study is also by Donner (1935). (*CBEL*, III, 248 f.)

GEORGE BORROW (1803–1881). Standard edition by Clement Shorter (16 vols., 1923–24; complete, with much from manuscripts, but next to

FIG. 39. F. W. Bateson, *A Guide to English Literature*. (Copyright: Longmans, Green & Co. Ltd. and Doubleday & Co. Inc.)

reference guides. R. D. Altick, *The Art of Literary Research* (New York, Norton, 1963), is a delightful introduction to research methods and contains much useful bibliographical information.

Two useful handbooks which contain considerable information are J. D. Cooke and L. Stevenson, *English Literature of the Victorian Period* (New York, Appleton–Century–Crofts, 1949), and T. M. Parrott and R. B. Martin, *Companion to Victorian Literature* (New York, Scribner, 1955).

J. H. Buckley, *Victorian Poets and Prose Writers* (New York, Appleton–Century–Crofts, 1966), is a very selective bibliography. An older work is the 2-volume *Syllabus and Bibliography of Victorian Literature* by H. M. Jones and others (Ann Arbor, Brumfield, 1934–5). R. F. Metzdorf, *The Tinker Library: a bibliographical catalogue of books and manuscripts* (New Haven, Yale Univ. Library, 1959), is occasionally a useful source of reference as the library has a strong emphasis on Victorian literature.

An excellent guide to works by and about the Pre-Raphaelites is provided in W. E. Fredeman, *Pre-Raphaelitism: a bibliocritical study* (Cambridge, Harvard Univ. Pr., 1965). This work (Fig. 40) includes a narrative "Survey of Pre-Raphaelite scholarship" followed by sections of annotated bibliography interspersed with short narrative introductions. The sections enumerate "Sources for bibliography and provenance", "Bibliography of individual figures", "Bibliography of the Pre-Raphaelite movement" and "Bibliography of Pre-Raphaelite illustrations".

Drama

A. Nicoll, *A History of English Drama, 1660–1900* (6 vols., CUP, 1952–9), devotes 2 volumes to the nineteenth century. The fourth volume discusses the period 1800–50 and the fifth the period 1850–1900. The historical outline in each volume is followed by appendices listing theatres in existence and plays produced during the period. The sixth volume is a comprehensive *Short-title Alphabetical Catalogue of Plays Produced or Printed in*

section most compatible with its content, nature, and purpose. Sections 80 to 85 are slight but essential categories, which, while they perhaps accommodate few items, catalogue material inappropriate to other sections in the bibliography.

In a sense, part III carries the burden of the Bibliography as a whole — and this is the principal reason for placing it after, rather than before, the Bibliography of Individual Figures. Made up of individual writers and artists, by whose accomplishments ultimately the movement must eventually be evaluated, Pre-Raphaelitism nevertheless became a thing in itself, with recognizable features and identifiable scars. This section is intended to demonstrate not only by the breadth and scope of the writings on the movement but through the variety of those writings the complexity of Pre-Raphaelitism itself.

General Discussions of Pre-Raphaelitism

Section 66

SEPARATE WORKS ON
PRE-RAPHAELITISM: GENERAL

66.1 [Ruskin, John]. *Pre-Raphaelitism: By the Author of "Modern Painters."* London: Smith, Elder, 1851.

Not until the second edition (1862) did Ruskin's name appear on the title page. For discussion of Ruskin's role in the Pre-Raphaelite Movement see Survey, pp. 9–13. Among reviews of Ruskin's pamphlet the following may be mentioned: *Leader*, II, no. 74 (23 August 1851), 803–804; *Economist*, IX, no. 417 (23 August 1851), 933–934 ("The pamphlet is only a defense of Pre-Raphaelitism if Mr. Turner be a Pre-Raphaelite."); *Builder*, X, no. 449 (13 September 1851), 571–572; *Daily News*, no. 1629 (17 August 1851), p. 3; *Athenaeum*, no. 1243 (23 August 1851), pp. 908–909; *Tait's Edinburgh Magazine*, XVIII (October 1851), 626–629; *Art Journal*, XIII (November 1851), 285–286. See also 67.4. *Pre-Raphaelitism* has been reprinted many times — in *CW* (45.3, XII, 337–393); in the Everyman's Library (no. 218), edited by Laurence Binyon (London: Dent, 1907); and, most re-

Jermyn Trevelyan (London: Longmans, 1879) contains a review of Ruskin's *Pre-Raphaelitism* reprinted from the *Scotsman*, 3 January 1852.

66.2 Rippingille, Edward Villiers. *Obsoletism in Art: A Reply to the Author of Modern Painters in His Defence of "Pre-Raphaelitism."* London: Bentley, 1852.

The Pre-Raphaelites are treated as pure copyists who fail because they imitate only nature and do not temper nature with art. "We have the consolation of knowing that the mischief produced [by Pre-Raphaelitism], whatever it may be, cannot extend very far, or lead to any very ruinous consequences; since revolutions in the arts of peace, those happy pursuits, to which men bring the best qualities of their hearts and minds, are in comparison harmless." (p. 54) A selection from Rippingille's *Reply* appeared prior to publication in *Bentley's Miscellany*, XXXI (June 1852), 598–609.

FIG. 40. W. E. Fredeman, *Pre-Raphaelitism: a bibliocritical study.*
(Copyright: Harvard University Press.)

England from 1660–1900. This includes information contained in the earlier volumes together with some additional material.

A nineteenth-century list which is still useful is R. W. Lowe, *A Bibliographical Account of English Theatrical Literature from the Earliest Times to the Present Day* (Nimmo, 1888). The British Drama League has compiled a catalogue of its collections in *The Player's Library* (Faber, 1950) and issued three supplements to this during 1951–6. D. Cheshire, *Theatre: history, criticism and reference* (Bingley, 1967), provides a good outline guide to the literature of the subject. C. J. Stratman has compiled *A Bibliography of British Dramatic Periodicals, 1720–1960* (New York, Public Library, 1962) listing 674 periodicals with locations in British and American libraries, a *Bibliography of English Printed Tragedy, 1565–1900* (Carbondale, Southern Illinois Univ. Pr., 1966), and an article on "Dramatic play lists, 1591–1963" in the *Bulletin of the New York Public Library* (March 1966, pp. 169–88). A. Loewenberg, *The Theatre of the British Isles, Excluding London: a bibliography* (Society for Theatre Research, 1950), is a guide to books and periodical articles relating to the provincial drama of Britain. The main arrangement is by place with an index of places and persons. Many of the items listed are scarce and little known.

A list of *Plays Submitted to the Lord Chamberlain, 1824–1851*, has been compiled by the Department of Manuscripts at the British Museum (British Museum, 1964). G. Rowell, *The Victorian Theatre* (Oxford, Clarendon Pr., 1956), includes a bibliography of plays and playwrights between 1792 and 1914.

Fiction

E. A. Baker's standard *The History of the English Novel* (10 vols., Witherby, 1924–39) includes brief bibliographies in each volume. E. A. Baker and J. Packman compiled *A Guide to the Best Fiction, English and American, Including Translations from Foreign Languages* (Routledge, 1932; reprinted 1967). The publishers have announced their intention of producing a supplement to this work in 1970. Baker had earlier compiled *A Guide to Historical Fiction* (rev. edn., Routledge, 1914). Both these guides include brief annotations indicating the subject of the works listed.

Guides to historical fiction are popular. D. D. McGarry and S. H. White, *Historical Fiction Guide* (New York, Scarecrow Pr., 1963), is an annotated list. J. Nield, *A Guide to the Best Historical Novels and Tales* (5th edn., Mathews & Marrot, 1929), and J. A. Buckley and W. T. Williams, *A Guide to British Historical Fiction* (Harrap, 1912), are still useful for surveying this *genre* in the nineteenth century.

A. Block, *The English Novel, 1740–1850: a catalogue* (rev. edn., Dawson, 1961), is an alphabetical list of novels, short stories, and translations of foreign fiction. I. F. Bell and D. Baird, *The English Novel, 1578–1956: a checklist of 20th century criticisms* (Denver, Swallow, 1958), is a brief but useful list of modern critical works. J. Souvage, *An Introduction to the Study of the Novel, with Special Reference to the English Novel* (Grant, Storey, 1965), includes a bibliography of writings on the novel.

A very useful extensive specialized list is L. Leclaire, *A General Analytical Bibliography of the Regional Novelists of the British Isles, 1800–1950* (Paris, Les Belles Lettres, 1954). This includes brief biographical details about each novelist, a list of relevant works, and a note on the scene of each novel.

Victorian Fiction: a guide to research, edited by L. Stevenson (Cambridge, Harvard Univ. Pr., 1964), is a narrative survey of works of bibliography, scholarship, and criticism about the major Victorian novelists. Each chapter is contributed by a specialist who provides a selection and assessment of the most important books and articles. The first chapter outlines general materials and is followed by discussions of Disraeli, Bulwer-Lytton, Dickens, Thackeray, Trollope, the Brontës, Mrs. Gaskell, Kingsley, Collins, Reade, George Eliot, Meredith, Hardy, Moore, and Gissing.

The contents of the great collection of fiction gathered by Michael Sadleir are recorded with additional information from other sources in his *XIX Century Fiction: a bibliographical record based on his own collections* (2 vols., CUP, 1951).

A collection of detective fiction is listed in *Victorian Detective Fiction: a catalogue of the collection made by Dorothy Glover and Graham Greene, bibliographically arranged by E. Osborne* (Bodley Head, 1966).

L. James, *Fiction for the Working Man, 1830–1850* (OUP, 1963), includes much bibliographical information about popular literature which often does not appear in the catalogues of major libraries.

Poetry

General bibliographical guides to poetry are rather infrequent. However, J. M. Kuntz, *Poetry Explication: a checklist of interpretation since 1925 of British and American poems past and present* (rev. edn., Denver, Swallow, 1962), is a useful index of explications published in books and periodicals between 1925 and 1959.

The Victorian Poets: a guide to research, edited by F. E. Faverty (2nd edn., Cambridge, Harvard Univ. Pr., 1968), is a narrative survey arranged on a similar pattern to L. Stevenson's *Victorian Fiction*, noted above. Chapters are devoted to General Materials, Tennyson, Robert Browning, Elizabeth Barrett Browning, Fitzgerald, Clough, Arnold, Swinburne, the Pre-Raphaelites, Hopkins, and Later Victorian Poets.

For the poets of the romantic movement, several of whom were still active in the early Victorian period, C. W. and L. H. Houtchens, *The English Romantic Poets and Essayists: a review of research and criticism* (rev. edn., New York, Modern Language Association of America, 1966), is a useful guide.

Current Work

The best general guide to twentieth-century studies of Victorian literature in books and periodicals is found in the annual "Victorian bibliography", contributed from 1932 to 1956 to *Modern Philology* and from 1957 to *Victorian Studies* (see Figs.

7–8). Although it includes much additional material, this biblio-graphy is primarily a guide to literary studies. The fourth section of the bibliography is particularly useful in listing studies of individual Victorian authors, arranged alphabetically by the author discussed. In his introduction to the collection of the bibliographies published between 1955 and 1964, R. C. Slack has noted that this section is regarded by most users as the most valuable part of the work. The other sections of this annual list have been described above in Chapter 2.

Information about recent studies, whether published separately as books or pamphlets or as periodical articles, is included in the *Annual Bibliography of English Language and Literature* (Modern Humanities Research Association, 1920/1–) and in *MLA International Bibliography* included annually in *Publications of the Modern Language Association of America*. A similar function is performed by the *Year's Work in English Studies* (Murray, for the English Association, 1919/20–), which provides a narrative commentary on works discussed.

Articles in certain periodicals are abstracted in *Abstracts of English Studies* (Boulder, National Council of Teachers of English, 1958–). This is published monthly except in July and August. Entries are listed by periodical and a subject index is provided.

Theses

A conveniently specific guide is R. D. Altick and W. R. Matthews, *Guide to Doctoral Dissertations in Victorian Literature, 1886–1958* (Urbana, Univ. of Illinois Pr., 1960) (Fig. 41). A more general bibliography of a wide range of theses compiled in several countries is L. F. MacNamee, *Dissertations in English and American Literature* (New York, Bowker, 1968).

Periodicals Devoted to Victorian Literature

Much information about current trends of thought, work in progress, and recent studies can be derived from the major modern periodicals devoted to Victorian literature. *Victorian Studies*

299. Witt, Marion W. The Elizabethan Drama in England between 1800 and 1840: Criticism, Representations, and Imitations. Wisconsin 26.
[See also 337, 382.]

V. POETRY

300. Arnold, Christine. Musik als Darstellungsobjekt der englischen Dichtung. Vienna 40.
301. Atkins, Elizabeth. The Poet's Poet: Essays on the Character and Mission of the Poet as Interpreted in English Verse of the Last One Hundred and Fifty Years. Nebraska 22.
302. Barkas, Pallister. A Critique of Modern English Prosody (1880-1930). Göttingen 35.
303. Berlage, Heinrich. Über das englische Soldatenlied in der zweiten Hälfte des 19. Jahrhunderts mit besonderer Berücksichtigung der Soldatenlieder Rudyard Kiplings. Münster 33.
304. Brewer, Joseph E. A Reëxamination of the History and Validity of the Concept "The Spasmodic School." Western Reserve 54.
305. Brown, Calvin S. The Musical Opus in Poetry. Wisconsin 34.
306. Bryant, William A. Conceptions of America and Americans by the English Romantic Poets: 1790-1850. Vanderbilt 41.
307. Burchard, Ingeborg von (geb. Heldt). Typen der englischen Flusspoesie. Freiburg 50.
308. Clark, Bruce B. The English Sonnet Sequence, 1850-1900: a Study of Fourteen Sequences. Utah 52.
309. Cunningham, James V. The Spasmodic School of Poetry. St. John's 41.
310. Davis, Arthur K., Jr. The Political Thought of Victorian Poets. Virginia 24.
311. DeSchweinitz, George W. Dipodism in English Verse in the Nineteenth and Twentieth Centuries: a Study in the Relation Between Thematics and Metrics. Iowa 49.
312. Dirlhuber, Herta. Der Einfluss von David Friedrich Strauss Leben Jesu auf die Dichter der viktorianischen Zeit. Vienna 35.
313. Doorn, Willem van. Theory and Practice of English Narrative Verse since 1833: an Enquiry. Amsterdam 32.
314. Eisner, Doris. Die Jungfrau von Orleans in der englischen Dichtung bis zur mittelviktorianischen Zeit. Vienna 27.
315. Fackler, Miriam E. Death: Idea and Image in Some Later Victorian Lyrists. Colorado 55.
316. Goodale, Ralph H. Pessimism in English Poetry and Fiction, 1847-1900. Chicago 28.
317. Gray, Donald J. Victorian Verse Humor: 1830-1870. Ohio State 56.

FIG. 41. R. D. Altick and W. R. Matthews, *Guide to Doctoral Dissertations in Victorian Literature, 1886–1958.* (Copyright: University of Illinois Press.)

(Indiana, Univ., 1957/8–) has already been noted. It includes articles and reviews on all aspects of Victorian life and thought.

The Victorian Newsletter (New York, Univ., 1952–) is edited for the English X Group of the Modern Humanities Research Association. It is published twice a year. Although its scope is not limited to articles on literature this interest is emphasized. In addition to its articles the *Newsletter* publishes very useful select bibliographies of recent books and articles, again with a strong literary bias.

Victorian Poetry (Morgantown, West Virginia Univ., 1963–) is a quarterly periodical publishing scholarly articles and reviews of new books. The summer issue includes a narrative survey of selected books and periodicals under the title "The year's work in Victorian poetry" (Fig. 42).

Nineteenth Century Fiction (Berkeley, Univ. of California Pr., 1945–) is a quarterly periodical devoted to all aspects of the fiction of the period. Originally entitled *The Trollopian*, it adopted its present title with the publication of the fourth volume.

Among periodicals devoted to individual Victorian writers, *The Dickensian* (Dickens Fellowship, 1905–) is now published three times a year. It includes articles and notes, informal and scholarly. As far as possible, it notes new books and articles on Dickens. *Dickens Studies* (Boston, Emerson College, 1965–) is published semi-annually and contains scholarly articles and book reviews.*

The Tennyson Society, based on the Tennyson Research Centre in Lincoln, commenced in 1967 an annual *Tennyson Research Bulletin*, listing research in progress, forthcoming publications, and items of general interest. The Society also publishes an *Annual Report*.

In 1968 the Armstrong Browning Library at Baylor University commenced publication of a *Browning Newsletter*. This aims to include regular surveys of research on the Brownings, reviews of new books, notes and queries, and check-lists of acquisitions of research materials by libraries. It will be published twice a year.

*From December 1969 this periodical is published by Southern Illinois University as *Dickens Studies Annual*.

on Arnold, Browning, and Tennyson and reserve discussion on other poets for a final section.

In a letter Kenneth Allott (*RES*, n.s. XV, 304-305) argues that Arnold's "Thyrsis" was conceived in the spring of 1862, begun shortly after November 28, 1863, built up in 1864 and 1865, and completed by January 23, 1866. Allott also publishes a short article on the motto of "Thyrsis" (*N&Q*, n.s. XI, 228) in which he asserts that Arnold attached a motto when he published the elegy in *New Poems* to declare his right to a poem on the subject of Lucretius. The motto is identified as being "from Lucretius, an unpublished tragedy." Arnold had heard a rumor, probably from Palgrave, that Tennyson was writing on the subject. As we know from Arnold's *Note-Books*, Arnold burdened himself almost yearly with his resolutions and plans to write a tragedy on the philosopher.

Roger L. Brooks continues as intrepid tracer of information about Arnold and his publishing habits. In an article entitled "Matthew Arnold and Ticknor & Fields" (*AL*, XXV, 514-519) he gives the American publishing history of Arnold's prose and verse to 1867. Although the firm had a good reputation for paying the authors it pirated, Arnold received very little for the use of his writing. Brooks also prints a letter from Arnold, dated November 29, 1865, to Moncure Daniel Conway. The letter has not been published before. In "The Story Manuscript of Matthew Arnold's 'New Rome,'" (*BSP*, LVIII, 295-297) Brooks announces the discovery of the album manuscript referred to in Arnold's sub-title to the poem. A torn-out page from an album is in the library at Columbia University. From this evidence, he constructs the history of the manuscript; the diary of 1873 is the first version of the poem, the album text is second, and the June, 1873, version in *Cornhill Magazine* is the last.

Herbert R. Coursen, Jr. in "'The Moon Lies Fair': The Poetry of Matthew Arnold" (*SEL*, IV, 569-581) describes Arnold's verse as "an attempt to revisit the Wordsworthian scene and to find there the transcendant significance which revealed itself to Wordsworth." He argues that the key to Arnold is the magnificent vision in *The Prelude*, XIV, 39-47 and 64-77, a vision which Arnold inverts in his own verse. In effect, Coursen explores the moonlight imagery in the poems and establishes a relationship between Arnold and Wordsworth. Strangely, the essay has nothing to say about other studies of Arnold's imagery nor about recent studies of Arnold and the Romantics. He also declares

FIG. 42. *Victorian Poetry* ("The Year's Work in Victorian Poetry").
(Copyright: the Editor.)

The Brontë Society at Haworth has since 1895 issued *Transactions* and occasional publications. The *Transactions*, now published annually, contain articles, notes, and reports on the Society.

The William Morris Society publishes a *Journal, Transactions, Newsletter,* and *Annual Report.* The Kipling Society publishes a quarterly *Journal.*

Dictionaries and Handbooks

The most useful general handbook to English literature is *The Oxford Companion to English Literature,* compiled and edited by Sir P. Harvey and revised by D. Eagle (4th edn., Oxford, Clarendon Pr., 1967). This work provides short articles about authors and works, literary societies and allusions commonly encountered in English literature. There are two valuable appendices on "Censorship and the law of the press" and "Notes on the history of English copyright" by Sir F. MacKinnon. An abridged version of this work is published as *The Concise Oxford Dictionary of English Literature.*

Originally published in 2 volumes in 1844, *Chambers's Cyclopaedia of English Literature* has undergone frequent revision and expansion. For the Victorian student its various editions are useful for the minor authors noted. The work is a chronological guide, containing a large number of entries for individual authors and articles on literary forms, subjects and periods. Short bibliographies are included.

The *New Century Handbook of English Literature,* edited by C. L. Barnhart and W. D. Halsey (New York, Appleton–Century–Crofts, 1956), is an encyclopedia of authors, titles, characters, and literary terms.

An enormous amount of information is contained in the very concise *Annals of English Literature, 1475–1950,* compiled by J. C. Ghosh and E. G. Withycombe and revised by R. W. Chapman (2nd edn., Oxford, Clarendon Pr., 1961) (Fig. 43). The sub-title describes this work as "The principal publications of each year together with an alphabetical index of authors and their works".

Austin, Alfred (1835): At the Gate of the Convent. V

Arnold (1822): Discourses in America. P

Beecher, Henry Ward (1813): Evolution and Religion. P

Birrell (1850): Life of Charlotte Brontë. P

Bridges (1844): Nero [Part II, 1894]. D
Eros and Psyche [rev. 1894]. V

Burton, Sir Richard Francis (1821): Trs. Arabian Nights [privately prtd.; concl. 1888; rev. 'for household reading' 1887–8]. P

Clifford, William Kingdon (d. 1879): Common Sense of the Exact Sciences, ed. K. Pearson.

Crawford, F. Marion (1854): Zoroaster. P

Disraeli (d. 1881): Home Letters, 1830–1 [new ed. by Ralph Disraeli 1887].

Dobson (1840): At the Sign of the Lyre. V

Ewing, Juliana H. (d. 1885): The Story of a Short Life. P

Fargus, Frederick ('Hugh Conway') (d. 1885): Called Back. P

Fiske, John (1842): American Political Ideas. P

George Eliot' (d. 1880): Life, as related in Letters and Journals, ed. J. W. Cross. P

Gordon, Charles George (d. 1885): Journals at Khartoum. P

Green, T. H. (d. 1882): Works, ed. Nettleship [later vols. 1886, 1888]. P

Greville (d. 1865): Memoirs, series II, 1837–52 [see 1874, 1887]. P

Haggard, Rider (1856): King Solomon's Mines. P

Holmes (1809): A Mortal Antipathy. P

Hudson (1841): The Purple Land. P

Lang (1844): Rhymes à la Mode. V

Lightfoot (1828): Apostolic Fathers, pt. ii [Ignatius and Polycarp].

'Mark Rutherford' (1831): Mark Rutherford's Deliverance. P

Martineau (1805): Types of Ethical Theory. P

'Owen Meredith' (1831): Glenaveril. V

Meredith (1828): Diana of the Crossways [originally in Fortnightly Review 1884–5]. P

Morris (1834): Pilgrims of Hope [in The Commonweal, 1885–6; separately 1886]. V

Pater (1839): Marius the Epicurean. P

Powell, Frederick York, and Tout, T. F.: History of England [concl. 1898]. P

Ruskin (1819): On the Old Road [collection of essays, pamphlets, &c., 1834–85].
Praeterita [concl. 1889]. P

David Herbert Lawrence b.
Ezra Pound b.
Richard Monckton Milnes,
*   Lord Houghton, d.*
Fall of Khartoum.
'Dictionary of National
*   Biography', 1st vol. (ed.*
*   Leslie Stephen 1882–91,*
*   Sidney Lee 1891 ff.).*
'The Commonweal' (con-
*   trib. by Morris, &c.)*
*   started.*
Scottish History Society
*   founded.*
Henry Sweet's 'Oldest
*   English Texts'.*
François Mauriac b.
Jules Romains b.
Victor Hugo d.
Zola, 'Germinal'.

President U.S.A.
Cleveland.

FIG. 43. *Annals of English Literature, 1475–1950.* (Copyright: Clarendon Press, Oxford.)

For each year details are given of the major works published with a note of the author's name and date of birth. In a side column are recorded the births and deaths of authors and the publication of newspapers, periodicals, translations, editions, and other works not classed as original literature. Some important contemporary events are also noted. The index provides an alphabetical list of authors, giving a brief chronological outline of their literary career.

For the theatre *The Oxford Companion to the Theatre*, edited by P. Hartnoll (3rd edn., OUP, 1967), is not confined to the British theatre but is a general encyclopedic guide. The work has a good selective bibliography.

A general guide to the identification of characters is W. Freeman, *Dictionary of Fictional Characters* (Dent, 1963). This lists some 20,000 characters from some 2000 English language novels, short stories, poems, and plays. A supplementary volume of author and title indexes, compiled by J. M. F. Leaper, was published in 1965.

E. C. Brewer, *Brewer's Dictionary of Phrase and Fable* (8th edn., Cassell, 1963), lists colloquial and proverbial phrases, biographical and mythological references, fictitious characters, and titles.

Among guides to quotations, *The Oxford Dictionary of Quotations* (2nd edn., OUP, 1953) provides a list of some 40,000 quotations. The work has a very comprehensive index. *Grainger's Index to Poetry* (5th edn., New York, Columbia Univ. Pr., 1962) indexes the contents of 574 anthologies. Entries are arranged by title and first line and there are indexes of authors and subjects. A supplement, indexing 97 anthologies published between 1960 and 1965, was published in 1967.

Biographical Works

Several of the guides listed above and the general biographical works discussed below in Chapter 14 will be found valuable. Where a standard biography exists this is, of course, the major source of information. Such biographies may be traced through the bibliographical works noted above.

The most significant work of collected literary biography for the period is S. J. Kunitz and H. Haycraft, *British Authors of the Nineteenth Century* (New York, Wilson, 1936), which includes biographies of 1000 authors. S. A. Allibone, *A Critical Dictionary of English Literature and British and American Authors* (3 vols., Philadelphia, Lippincott, 1858), includes brief biographical notes. A 2-volume supplement by J. F. Kirk was published in 1891.

CHAPTER 13

History

IT HAS already been emphasized that, since knowledge about the various aspects of a period such as the Victorian age cannot really be compartmentalized, the chapters in this book should be regarded rather as somewhat arbitrary groupings adopted for convenience than as strict divisions of the material. Inevitably, every examination of the nineteenth century is, at least in part, a historical exercise. Much of the information in other chapters is relevant to the historian. The present chapter is devoted to works on history in general, on politics and foreign expansion, and to a few sources of information about local history.

General Guides and Bibliographies

P. Hepworth, *How to Find Out in History* (Oxford, Pergamon Pr., 1966), provides a useful general guide to sources of information. There is a basic bibliography in an attractively presented short guide by V. H. Galbraith, *The Historian at Work* (British Broadcasting Corporation, 1962). G. Kitson Clark, *Guide for Research Students Working on Historical Subjects* (2nd edn., CUP, 1968) is a valuable introductory handbook.

Bibliographies of history are surveyed in E. W. Coulter and M. Gerstenfeld, *Historical Bibliographies: a systematic and annotated guide* (Berkeley, Univ. of California Pr., 1935; reprinted New York, Russell & Russell, 1965).

The American Historical Association's *Guide to Historical Literature* (New York, Macmillan, 1961) is a selective annotated bibliography arranged in broad subject and country groups

(Fig. 44). It contains an enormous amount of information about historical writings, including bibliographies, encyclopedias, dictionaries, biographies, government documents, and printed collections of sources. The work succeeds an earlier *Guide to Historical Literature*, edited by G. M. Dutcher (New York, Macmillan, 1931).

Bibliographies for all the 12 volumes of the *New Cambridge Modern History* (CUP, 1957–) are published in a single volume as *A Bibliography of Modern History*, edited by J. Roach (CUP, 1968) (Fig. 45).

An extremely useful series of bibliographical guides is the Historical Association's Helps for Students of History. This series consists of pamphlets providing authoritative handlists to the literature of selected areas of historical study.

General materials for political history are detailed in L. Burchfield, *Student's Guide to Materials in Political Science* (New York, Holt, 1935). This includes information on basic source materials, bibliographies, and other reference works.

The literature of Communism to 1962 has been listed in W. Kolarz, *Books on Communism: a bibliography* (2nd edn., Ampersand, 1963). This is an annotated guide to some 2500 books in English. It does not list periodical articles. An earlier work is J. Stammhammer, *Bibliographie der Socialismus und Communismus* (3 vols., Jena, Fischer, 1893–1909) which lists materials in various languages to 1908.

Bibliographies of British History

Volumes of the *Oxford History of England*, edited by G. N. Clark (Oxford, Clarendon Pr., 1937–), include annotated critical bibliographies. For the Victorian period, E. L. Woodward, *Age of Reform, 1815–1870*, and R. C. K. Ensor, *England, 1870–1914*, are essential guides.

The Royal Historical Society is compiling a comprehensive bibliography of *Writings on British History, 1901–1933* (Cape, 1968–). This will include books and articles published during this

434　　*Guide to Historical Literature*

VA145. Martineau, Harriet. **The history of England during the thirty years' peace, 1816–1846.** 2 v. London, 1849–50.

VA146. Bryant, Sir Arthur. **The pageant of England, 1840–1940.** London, 1941.

VA147. Young, George M., ed. **Victorian England: portrait of an age.** London, 1936. 2nd ed., Oxford, 1953. A penetrating, brief, but at the same time allusive and discursive, essay on various aspects of Victorian history and life: Valuable for its often brilliant random observations.

VA148. Aspinall, Arthur. **Lord Brougham and the Whig party.** Manchester, 1927. This and *VA149–153* give a full picture of the politics of early 19th century England and the leadership of various parties.

VA149. Brock, William R. **Lord Liverpool and liberal Toryism, 1820 to 1827.** Cambridge, Eng., 1941.

VA150. Trevelyan, George M. **Lord Grey and the reform bill.** London, 1920.

VA151. Temperley, Harold W. V. **Life of Canning.** London, 1905.

VA152. Clark, George Kitson. **Peel and the Conservative party.** London, 1929.

VA153. Davis, Henry W. C. **The age of Grey and Peel.** Oxford, 1929.

VA154. Hammond, John L., and Barbara Hammond. **The age of the Chartists, 1832–1854.** London, 1930. Though written with a strong bias, it is still the best brief social and political history of the early Victorian age.

VA155. Bell, Herbert C. **Lord Palmerston.** 2 v. London, 1936. Best recent biography of a major political figure whose life spanned the first half of the 19th century.

VA156. Benson, Edward F. **Queen Victoria.** London, 1935. Best brief, scholarly biography of the queen.

VA157. Morley, John. **Life of William Ewart Gladstone.** 3 v. London, 1903. Morley's biography is still a valuable source, though *VA158* is more recent and has the advantage of longer perspective.

VA158. Magnus, Sir Philip M. **Gladstone: a biography.** London, 1954.

VA159. Monypenny, William F., and George E. Buckle. **The life of Benjamin Disraeli.** 6 v. London, 1910–20. Rev. ed. in 2 v., 1929. Though a number of shorter single-volume biographies have appeared since

don, 1936. Useful survey of an im; half-century of British imperial histor; See also *VA80 (13, 14)*, *VA81 (7 VA83 (8)*.

The Twentieth Century

VA163. Cruttwell, Charles R. M. **tory of the great war, 1914–1918.** (1934.

VA164. Graves, Robert, and Alan **The long week end: a British social |** **1918–1939.** N.Y., 1941.

VA165. Mowat, Charles L. **Brit: tween the wars, 1918–1940.** Chicago Most useful single volume survey period.

VA166. Hirst, Francis W. **The quences of the war to Great Brita** *AG91*.

VA167. Falls, Cyril B. **The Second War: a short history.** 3rd ed., Londor Useful short summary by a military rian.

VA168. Hutchison, Keith. The decl fall of British capitalism. London, 195 and *VA169–171* deal with the vario nomic and social changes that have o in Britain since the end of World W;

VA169. Watkins, Ernest. **The c.** **revolution.** London, 1951.

VA170. Jouvenel, Bertrand de. **P! of socialist England.** London, 1949. tive essay by a French observer on th lems of Britain in the immediate post War II era.

VA171. Worswick, George D. ! Peter H. Ady, eds. **The British ec 1945–1950.** Oxford, 1952. See also relevant chapters in *VA< VA141, VA142, VA146,* and *VA162*

HISTORIES OF SPECIAL AR!

Wales

VA172. Jenkins, Robert T., and Rees, eds. **A bibliography of the his Wales.** Cardiff, 1931. New ed. in ; tion. Useful general guide.

VA173. National Library of Wales. **theca Celtica: a register of publicati**

FIG. 44. American Historical Association, *Guide to Historical Literature.* (Copyright: the Macmillan Co.)

C 1338]   BRITAIN AND THE COMMONWEALTH   313

c 1320   Willey, B. *More nineteenth-century studies* (1956); on 'a group of honest
         doubters', a sequel to:
c 190   Willey, B. *Nineteenth-century studies* (1949).
c 1321   Young, A. F. and Ashton, E. T. *British social work in the nineteenth
         century* (1956); a study of social workers.

         See also:
         c 338 Altick, R. D.

Detailed Studies

Most recent works on the period fall into the categories listed below and
include, in addition to those listed by Young and Handcock, the following:

BIOGRAPHIES

c 1322   Culler, A. D. *The imperial intellect: a study of Newman's educational ideal*
         (New Haven and London, 1955).
c 1323   Forster, E. M. *Marianne Thornton, 1797–1887* (1956).
c 1324   Hill, W. T. *Octavia Hill* (1956).
c 1325   Johnson, L. J. *General T. Peronnet Thompson, 1783–1869* (1957).
c 1326   Jones, W. D. *Lord Derby and Victorian Conservatism* (Oxford, 1956).
c 1327   Kennedy, A. L. (ed.). '*My dear Duchess*': *social and political letters to
         the duchess of Manchester, 1858–1869* (1956).
c 1328   Mueller, I. W. *John Stuart Mill and French thought* (Urbana, Ill., 1956).
c 1329   Schoyen, A. R. *The Chartist challenge* (1958); mainly a biography of
         G. J. Harney.

COMMERCIAL AND BUSINESS HISTORIES

c 1330   Addis, J. P. *The Crawshay dynasty: a study in industrial organisation and
         development, 1765–1867* (Cardiff, 1957).
c 1331   Morris, J. H. and Williams, L. J. *The South Wales coal industry, 1841–
         75* (Cardiff, 1958).
c 1332   Redford, A. *Manchester merchants and foreign trade*, vol. 2, *1850–1939*
         (Manchester, 1956); based on the activities of the Manchester chamber
         of commerce.
c 1333   Whates, H. R. G. *The Birmingham Post, 1857–1957* (Birmingham, 1957);
         the history of a great provincial newspaper.

POLITICS AND ADMINISTRATION

c 1334   Brown, L. *The Board of Trade and the free trade movement, 1830–42*
         (Oxford, 1958).
c 1335   McCord, N. *The anti-corn law league, 1838–46* (1958).
c 1336   Prouty, R. *The transformation of the Board of Trade, 1830–55* (1957).
c 1337   Whyte, J. H. *The Independent Irish party, 1850–9* (Oxford, 1958).

FIG. 45. J. Roach, *A Bibliography of Modern History*. (Copyright:
Cambridge University Press.)

period on all aspects of British history to 1914. The work will be in 7 volumes arranged to cover the main periods of British history. The final 2 volumes, at present in preparation, will list writings on the nineteenth century, 1815–1914. These volumes will provide a companion to the similar bibliographies of *Writings on British History* compiled by A. T. Milne for the years 1934–45 (8 vols., Cape, 1937–60).

The Conference on British Studies has also commenced a series of *Bibliographical Handbooks*, edited by J. J. Hecht, to cover all aspects of British history. These works will provide selective lists of printed sources, surveys, monographs, biographies, and articles. A volume on the nineteenth century by J. Altholz is planned.

The American Historical Association and the Royal Historical Society have issued some volumes of their important *Bibliography of British History* (Oxford, Clarendon Pr., 1928–). This again aims to cover all aspects of British history. Selected items are arranged in classified order with author index. Books, pamphlets, document material, and periodical articles are included. Unfortunately, no volume for the nineteenth century has yet appeared.

S. R. Gardiner, *Introduction to the Study of English History* (4th edn., Kegan Paul, 1903) includes bibliographical essays on sources, excluding manuscripts, and secondary works and is still useful. S. B. Chrimes and I. A. Roots, *English Constitutional History: a select bibliography* (Routledge, 1958), is a valuable guide.

The *Cambridge History of the British Empire* (8 vols. in 9, CUP, 1929–59), includes good bibliographies in each volume. J. E. Flint, *Books on the British Empire: a guide for students* (OUP, 1966), lists some additional material and provides a reliable selection of books.

F. M. Gardiner, *The Indian Mutiny* (Library Association, 1957), is a select bibliography. Naval history in the nineteenth century is well covered in G. E. Manwaring, *A Bibliography of British Naval History: a bibliographical and historical guide to printed and manuscript sources* (Routledge, 1930).

Guides to parliamentary papers have been discussed in Chapter 4. For the student of foreign affairs *A Century of Diplomatic Blue Books, 1814–1914*, edited by H. Temperley and L. M. Penson (CUP, 1938; reprinted Cass, 1966) (see Fig. 19), and M. I. Adams, *Guide to the Principal Parliamentary Papers Relating to the Dominions, 1812–1911* (Edinburgh, Oliver & Boyd, 1913), are particularly useful.

Wales

The history of Wales is well documented in *A Bibliography of the History of Wales*, edited by R. T. Jenkins and W. Rees (2nd edn., Cardiff, Wales Univ. Pr., 1962). A supplement was published in 1963.

Scotland

G. F. Black, *A List of Works Relating to Scotland* (New York, Public Library, 1916), includes extensive references for the history of Scotland. A. Mitchell and C. G. Cash, *A Contribution to the Bibliography of Scottish Topography* (2 vols., Edinburgh, Univ. Pr., 1917), is a detailed record of books and periodical articles on Scottish history, life, and culture. This is continued by P. D. Hancock, *A Bibliography of Works Relating to Scotland, 1916–1950* (2 vols., Edinburgh, Univ., Pr. 1959–60).

A short bibliographical guide to Scottish history is J. D. Mackie, *Scottish History* (National Book League, 1956). A fuller list is provided in H. W. Meikle and others, *Scotland: a select bibliography* (CUP, 1950).

A useful list by C. S. Terry, *Catalogue of the Publications of Scottish Historical and Kindred Clubs and Societies, and of the Volumes Relative to Scottish History Issued by His Majesty's Stationery Office, 1780–1908* (Glasgow, Maclehose, 1909), was continued for 1908–27 by C. Matheson (Aberdeen, Milne & Hutchinson, 1928).

Ireland

A. R. Eager, *A Guide to Irish Bibliographical Material: being a bibliography of Irish bibliographies and some sources of information* (Library Association, 1964), is a basic guide to the literature. T. P. O'Neill, *Sources of Irish History* (Dublin, Library Association of Ireland, 1958), C. Maxwell, *A Short Bibliography of Irish History* (Historical Association, 1921), and the *Bibliography of Irish History, 1870–1921*, compiled by the National Library of Ireland (2 vols., Dublin, Stationery Office, 1936–40), provide useful additional lists.

Local History

A basic guide which is packed with bibliographical information is W. G. Hoskins, *Local History in England* (Longmans, 1959). J. L. Hobbs, *Local History and the Library* (Deutsch, 1962), contains very valuable information on printed and manuscript sources and lengthy sections on the treatment, arrangement, recording, and exhibition of materials in local history collections. Both these books give guidance on the use in local collections of such essential materials as directories, newspapers, census returns, parliamentary papers, maps and manuscript materials.

English Local History Handlist: a short bibliography and list of sources for the study of local history and antiquities, edited by F. W. Kuhlicke and F. G. Emmison (Historical Association, 1965), is a good introduction to a wide range of materials designed to help the student "to an understanding of such matters of historical and antiquarian interest as he may encounter in his local studies. It is not designed to be a guide to original materials, printed or manuscript, for local history."

There is, of course, an enormous amount of bibliographical information in the volumes of *The Victoria History of the Counties of England* (Univ. of London, Institute of Historical Research, 1899–) and in the many works compiled by local historians. Valuable guides to sources may be found in the periodical *Amateur Historian* and in the publications of local historical societies. P. Hepworth, *How to Find Out in History* (Oxford, Pergamon Pr., 1966), lists many bibliographies devoted to local areas.

A very useful series of leaflets entitled "Short guides to records", edited by L. M. Munby, are included in the periodical *History* and are also issued separately. These leaflets are published by the Historical Association. The series includes brief guides to records of particular interest to the local historian, such as rate books, poll books, and wills.

W. R. Powell, *Local History from Blue Books: a select list of sessional papers of the House of Commons* (Historical Association, 1962), provides a convenient list of parliamentary papers for local historians.

It is obviously impossible to place a limit on the local historian's range of reference. Among other topics of interest, general guides to parliamentary papers and to manuscript sources are discussed in Chapter 4. Sources of biographical information are noted in Chapter 14.

Municipal History

The literature of municipal history has been well documented in C. Gross, *A Bibliography of British Municipal History, Including Gilds and Parliamentary Representation* (2nd edn., Leicester, Univ. Pr., 1966) (Fig. 46). This work was originally published in 1897, the second edition being a photographic reprint with the addition of a preface by G. H. Martin. In his original preface Gross notes: "This bibliography comprises books, pamphlets, major articles, and papers of learned societies, relating wholly or in part to British municipal history; in other words, to the governmental or constitutional history of the boroughs of Great Britain, including gilds and parliamentary representation. Town histories which do not deal with any of these topics, purely topographical works, and parish histories are omitted." Altogether the bibliography lists 3092 items. G. H. Martin is preparing a continuation of Gross's work to list material published since 1897.

485. WILLIAMS, JOSEPH. Parliamentary reformation, examined under the following articles: extending the right of election, abolition of boroughs; qualification of members; abridging the duration of Parliament. . . . London, 1782. 4°.

486. WORDSWORTH, C. F. F. The law and practice of elections (for England and Wales) as altered by the Reform Act, etc., including the practice of election petitions. With a copious appendix, containing all the acts on elections; with the reform, and the division of counties and boundary of borough acts; new forms to be used in elections; lists of boroughs, etc., etc. London, [1832.] 8°.

487. † WYVILL, CHRISTOPHER. Political and historical arguments proving the necessity of parliamentary reform. 2 vols. York, 1811. 8°.

488. —— Political papers, chiefly respecting the attempt of the county of York and other considerable districts, commenced in 1779 and continued during several subsequent years, to effect a reformation of the Parliament of Great Britain. 6 vols. York, [1794–1802.] 8°.

Many of these papers discuss borough representation.

489. —— A summary explanation of the principles of Mr. Pitt's intended bill for amending the representation of the people in Parliament. London, 1785. 8°.

The Reform of 1867.

30 & 31 Vict. c. 102: an Act further to amend the laws relating to the Representation of the People in England and Wales.
The fullest account is that of Cox (No. 496).

490. ANSTEY, T. C. Notes upon "The Representation of the People Act" 1867 (30 & 31 Vict. c. 102). With appendices con-

FIG. 46. C. Gross, *A Bibliography of British Municipal History*. (Copyright: Leicester University Press.)

Current Work

Since 1911 the Historical Association has published an *Annual Bulletin of Historical Literature* which contains articles by specialists surveying in narrative form the major publications of the last year. Although coverage is general, the emphasis is on British history. Books and periodical articles are noted.

The International Committee of Historical Sciences compiles an annual *International Bibliography of Historical Sciences*

(OUP, 1926–). This is a selective list arranged in classified order. The term "historical sciences" is interpreted in a wide sense to include political, constitutional, religious, cultural, economic, and social aspects of history. The International Committee of Historical Sciences has also compiled an *International Bibliography of Historical Articles in Festschriften and Miscellanies, 1880–1939* (Paris, Colin, 1955).

The quarterly periodical *Historical Abstracts, 1775–1945* (Santa Barbara, Clio Pr. with International Social Science Institute, 1955–) provides abstracts of the world's current periodical literature on the history of the period 1775–1945. Entries are arranged in classified order with author and subject indexes.

In 1947 L. B. Frewer compiled a *Bibliography of Historical Writings Published in Great Britain and the Empire, 1940–1945* (Oxford, Blackwell). This is a record of books and periodical articles on all aspects of history. In 1957 J. C. Lancaster compiled a similar list of books only, entitled *Bibliography of Historical Works Issued in the United Kingdom, 1946–1956* (Univ. of London, Institute of Historical Research). This was succeeded by similar bibliographies for 1957–60 and 1961–5, both compiled by W. Kellaway (Fig. 47).

Information about political history may be derived from the annual *International Bibliography of Political Science*, published from 1953 to 1959 by UNESCO and then by the Tavistock Press, and from the quarterly *International Political Science Abstracts* (Oxford, Blackwell, 1952–).

Current periodicals are listed in E. H. Boehm and L. Adolphus, *Historical Periodicals: an annotated world list of historical and related serial publications* (Santa Barbara, Clio Pr., 1961). This work lists more than 4500 current periodicals, arranging them by area and country with an index of titles. The list covers history and auxiliary fields as well as serials in other subjects if they include historical articles. An older list of periodical titles is P. Caron and M. Jaryc, *World List of Historical Periodicals* (New York, Wilson, 1939). This is still useful as a guide to titles which are now discontinued.

THOMSON, David. England in the 19th century, 1815-1914, [new edn.]. 1910
Cape, 1964. 30s.

LEAN, Garth. Brave men choose. Blandford, 1961. 12s. 6d. 1911

CROOK, D. P. American democracy in English politics, 1815-50. Oxford: 1912
Clarendon P., 1965. 35s.

GASH, Norman. Reaction and reconstruction in English politics, 1832-52 1913
(Ford lectures, 1964). Oxford: Clarendon P., 1965. 30s.

SOUTHGATE, Donald. The passing of the Whigs, 1832-86. Macmillan, 1914
1962. 50s.

LONGFORD, Elizabeth, *Countess of.* Victoria R. I. Weidenfeld & 1915
Nicolson, [1964]. 63s.

BOLITHO, Hector. Albert: Prince Consort. Parrish, [1964]. 30s. ·1916

CONNELL, Brian, *ed.* Regina v. Palmerston: the correspondence between 1917
Queen Victoria and her Foreign and Prime Minister, 1837-65. Evans,
1962. 42s.

RAMM, Agatha, *ed.* The political correspondence of Mr. Gladstone and 1918
Lord Granville, 1876-86. 2 vols. Oxford: Clarendon P., 1962. 8 gns.

DEACON, Richard. The private life of Mr. Gladstone. Muller, 1965. 25s. 1919

ARNSTEIN, W. L. The Bradlaugh case: a study in late Victorian opinion 1920
and politics. Oxford: Clarendon P., 1965. 50s.

JENKINS, Roy. Sir Charles Dilke: a Victorian tragedy, rev. edn. Collins, 1921
1965. 36s.

AKERS-DOUGLAS, E. A., *3rd Viscount Chilston.* W. H. Smith (Studies in 1922
political history). Routledge & K. Paul, 1965. 63s.

NAYLOR, L. E. The irrepressible Victorian: the story of Thomas Gibson 1923
Bowles, journalist, parliamentarian and founder editor of the original
'Vanity Fair'. Macdonald, 1965. 40s.

FOWLER, W. S. A study in radicalism and dissent: the life and times of 1924
Henry Joseph Wilson, 1833-1914. Epworth P., 1961. 35s.

JAMES, R. R. Rosebery: a biography of Archibald Philip, 5th Earl of 1925
Rosebery. Weidenfeld & Nicolson, [1963]. 50s.

20th Century

DICTIONARY OF NATIONAL BIOGRAPHY. The concise dictionary, pt. 2. 1926
1901-50. O.U.P., 1961. 42s.

BUTLER, D. E., *and* FREEMAN, Jennie. British political facts, 1900-60. 1927
Macmillan, 1963. 40s.

MAGNUS, *Sir* Philip. King Edward the Seventh. Murray, [1964]. 50s. 1928

GERNSHEIM, Helmut, *and* GERNSHEIM, Alison. Edward VII and Queen 1929
Alexandra: a biography in word and picture. Muller, 1962. 75s.

MINNEY, R. J. The Edwardian age. Cassell, 1964. 36s. 1930

FIG. 47. W. Kellaway, *Bibliography of Historical Works Issued in the
United Kingdom, 1961–1965.* (Copyright: University of London
Institute of Historical Research.)

Theses

The Institute of Historical Research in London University has
since 1931/2 published, as a supplement to its *Bulletin*, an annual
guide to theses completed during the year and theses in progress
in universities of the United Kingdom. Before 1931 lists were

published in the periodical *History*. The guide now appears in 2 parts, arranged in broad chronological and topographical groups with indexes of authors.

American theses are listed in the annual *List of Dissertations in History now in Progress or Completed at Universities in the United States*. This commenced in 1909 and is now published in Washington by the American Historical Association. The list is arranged by field of study with indexes of authors and universities.

W. F. Kuehl, *Dissertations in History: An Index to Dissertations Compiled in History Departments of United States and Canadian Universities, 1873–1960* (Kentucky, Univ. Pr., 1965), is a useful cumulated list of American and Canadian theses.

Research Locations and Catalogues

G. Kitson Clark and G. R. Elton, *Guide to Research Facilities in History in the Universities of Great Britain and Ireland* (2nd edn., CUP, 1965), is a useful handbook to research locations. *Historical, Archaeological and Kindred Societies in the British Isles: a list*, edited by S. E. Harcup (rev. edn., Institute of Historical Research, Univ. of London, 1968), is a convenient guide for the research worker.

E. Lewin, *Subject Catalogue of the Library of the Royal Empire Society, Formerly Royal Colonial Institute* (4 vols., The Society, 1930–7), lists books, pamphlets, and periodical articles and is arranged by subject within country divisions. There is an author index to each volume.

The *Catalogue of the Colonial Office Library, London*, has been printed photographically (15 vols., Boston, Hall, 1964) and constitutes an invaluable source of reference. A. R. Hewitt, *Guide to Resources for Commonwealth Studies in London, Oxford and Cambridge, with Bibliographical and other Information* (Athlone Pr., 1957), is a useful guide to materials mainly in history and the social sciences in libraries and other institutions in the 3 locations listed. A. R. Hewitt has also compiled a *Union List of Commonwealth Newspapers in London, Oxford and Cambridge* (Athlone Pr., 1960), indicating holdings in 62 libraries and

newspaper offices of newspapers published in Commonwealth nations.
D. H. Simpson has compiled a well-indexed *Biography Catalogue of the Royal Commonwealth Society* (The Society, 1961), listing both books and periodical articles.

Chronological Outlines

Guides to dates sometimes provide information which is not readily available elsewhere. F. M. Powicke and E. B. Fryde, *Handbook of British Chronology* (2nd edn., Royal Historical Society, 1961), lists chronologically rulers, officers of state, archbishops and bishops, dukes, marquises and earls, parliaments, and provincial and national councils of the Church in England. Useful bibliographical sections are included. C. R. Cheney, *Handbook of Dates for Students of English History* (Royal Historical Society, 1945), includes complementary information on calendars and chronological reckoning. The *Cambridge Modern History* (14 vols., CUP, 1902–12) includes extensive genealogical tables and lists in volume 13.

Among comparative tables of events S. H. Steinberg, *Historical Tables, 58 B.C.—A.D. 1963* (7th edn., Macmillan, 1964), offers a chronological guide to political, constitutional and economic history, natural science and cultural life. There are several other similar publications.

A useful guide to nineteenth-century events is provided by the *Annual Register: a review of public events at home and abroad* which has been published in London since 1761. This contains information on contemporary developments in many fields, including politics, economics, religion, science, law, and the arts. Extracts from political speeches are included. The nineteenth-century volumes are strong in biographical information in the obituary sections. This periodical still continues, having been published since 1890 by Longmans. Since 1954 it has been entitled *Annual Register of World Events.*

CHAPTER 14

General Biographical Works

BIOGRAPHIES of individual Victorians may be traced through the bibliographies listed in preceding chapters. Some works of collected biography whose scope is limited to specific fields of interest are discussed above by subject. The present chapter surveys some general guides to biographical information.

Bibliographies of Biography

R. B. Slocum, *Biographical Dictionaries and Related Works* (Detroit, Gale, 1967), provides a comprehensive listing of materials. It is described as "an international bibliography of collective biographies, bio-bibliographies, collections of epitaphs, selected genealogical works, dictionaries of anonyms and pseudonyms, historical and specialized dictionaries, biographical materials in government manuals, bibliographies of biography, biographical indexes, and selected portrait catalogs". This work is arranged in three main sections, covering universal biography, national or area biography, and biography by vocation arranged in broad subject groups. Many entries include brief annotations. Very full author, title, and subject indexes are appended.

An extensive index of the contents of biographical dictionaries and similar works is provided by P. M. Riches, *An Analytical Bibliography of Universal Collected Biography* (Library Association, 1934). This bibliography indexes the contents of works of collected biography published in English in Britain, Ireland, America, and the British Dominions. Biographies of persons of various nationalities and periods are indexed in a single alphabetical sequence. There is also a chronological list, by century, of persons indexed and author and subject bibliographies of biographical dictionaries.

Recent material is recorded in the periodical *Biography Index: a cumulative index to biographical material in books and magazines* (New York, Wilson, 1946–) (Fig. 48). This is published quarterly with annual and 3-year cumulations. It is particularly useful in including articles in approximately 1600 periodicals as well as biographical material in books in the English language.

The *Essay and General Literature Index* (New York, Wilson) was originally published in 1934 and covered the period 1900–33. Since then regular cumulative supplements have continued the work. It indexes essays and articles published in collections and includes many useful references to biographical material.

Occasional help may be obtained from H. Hefling and E. Richards, *Index to Contemporary Biography and Criticism* (rev. edn., Boston, Faxon, 1934), which indexes some 420 collections of biography and criticism of persons born since the middle of the nineteenth century. A. M. Hyamson, *A Dictionary of Universal Biography of All Ages and of All Peoples* (2nd edn., Routledge, 1951), offers a guide to the location of biographical information in 24 standard biographical dictionaries.

D. H. Simpson, *Biography Catalogue of the Library of the British Commonwealth Society* (The Society, 1961), is an index of books and periodical articles of biographical value contained in the library.

Two very useful bibliographies which serve both as guides to biographical sources and themselves also act as brief sources of biographical information have been compiled by W. Matthews. *British Diaries: an annotated bibliography of British diaries written between 1442 and 1942* (Berkeley, Univ. of California Pr., 1950) lists published and manuscript diaries in a chronological sequence. The contents of each are briefly noted and there is an author index. *British Autobiographies: an annotated bibliography of British autobiographies* (Berkeley, Univ. of California Pr., 1955)

BIOGRAPHY INDEX

148

DEWEY, John—*Continued*
McCaul, R. L., Dewey in college, 1875-79.
  Sch R 70:437-56 Winter '62
McCaul, R. L. Dewey's school days, 1867-
  75. El Sch J 63:15-21 O '62

Bibliography
Thomas, Milton Halsey. John Dewey; a cen-
  tennial bibliography. Univ. of Chicago press
  '62 370p por

DEWEY, Lloyd Ellis, 1897-1960, economist
Biography
  NCAB por autograph 45:289 '62
DEWEY, Melvil, 1851-1931, librarian
  Library, hall of fame. (In Marshall, John
  David, ed. American library history reader.
  Shoe string press '61 p451)
DEWEY, Nelson, 1813-1889, governor

Fiction
Derleth, August William. Shadow in the
  glass. Duell '63 471p maps
DEWEY, Thomas Edmund, 1902- ex-governor
Ray, R. F. Thomas E. Dewey; the great
  Oregon debate of 1948. (In Reid, Loren, ed.
  American public address. Univ. of Mo.
  press '61 p245-67)
Turkus, B. B. and Feder, S. Almost-
  assassination of Thomas E. Dewey. (In
  Congdon, Don, ed. Thirties. Simon &
  Schuster '62 p247-67)
DEWEY, William Sabin, 1860-1945, lawyer
Biography
  NCAB por autograph 46:341 '63
DEWHURST, Colleen, Canadian actress
Pryce-Jones, A. Cleo in the park, pors Thea-
  tre Arts 47:16-18 Jl '63
DEWI, Saint, See David
DEWIEST, Roger J. M, engineer
Civil engineer wins Freeman fellowship. por
  Civil Eng 33:44 Ag '63
DE WILDE, Brandon, 1942- . actor

DIAZ, Justino, singer
Daniels, R. D. Winners two; Justino Diaz,
  Joann Grillo. il por Opera N 28:29 Ja 11 '64
Look at the future. por Mus Am 73:9 Jl '63
DIAZ Porfirio, 1830-1915, Mexican general and
  president
Cosio Villegas, Daniel. United States versus
  Porfirio Diaz; tr. by Nettie Lee Benson.
  Univ. of Neb. press '63 259p bibliog
DIAZ DEL CASTILLO, Bernal, 1492-1584. Span-
  ish explorer and historian
Cerwin, Herbert. Bernal Diaz, historian of
  the conquest. Univ. of Okla. press '63 229p
  bibliog il
DIAZ ORDAZ, Gustavo, 1911- Mexican politi-
  cal leader
Armstrong, R. Viva el candidato! il pors Sat
  Eve Post 237:73-7 Je 20 '64
Presidential ritual. por Newsweek 62:56 N 18
  '63
DIBELIUS, Otto, 1880- German bishop
Dibelius, Otto, bp. in the service of the Lord;
  autobiography; tr. from the German by
  Mary Ilford. Holt '64 280p il pors
DIBRELL, Louis Nelson, 1885-1956, business
  executive
Biography
  NCAB por autograph 43:111-12 '61
DICEY, Edward James Stephen, 1832-1911,
  English journalist
Waller, J. O. Edward Dicey and the Ameri-
  can Negro in 1862; an English working
  journalist's view. N Y Pub Lib Bul 66:31-
  45 Ja '62
DICHTER, Ernest, 1907- Austrian-American
  psychologist
Biography
  Cur Biog Yrbk por 1961:130-2 '62
Boyle, R. H. Not-so-mad doctor and his liv-
  ing lab. il Sports Illus 15:50-6 Jl 24 '61
DICK, Albert Blake, 1894-1954, manufacturer
Biography
  NCAB por autograph 45:226 '62

FIG. 48. *Biography Index.* (Copyright: the H. W. Wilson Co.)

includes brief biographical notes on each author and contains a useful subject index.

National Biography

Dictionary of National Biography

The most important general guide to British biography is the *Dictionary of National Biography*. Itself a product of the Victorian genius for large-scale planning and persevering effort, it was published by Smith, Elder & Co. in 63 volumes during the period 1885–1900. During the twentieth century it has been reprinted and extended by the addition of further supplementary volumes. The first supplement was devoted primarily to biographies of persons who died between 1885 and 1900. Later volumes have concentrated on biographies of persons who have died since 1900. The *Dictionary* is now published by OUP.

Selection in the *Dictionary* is extremely wide and, despite its inevitable imperfections, the work is invaluable for the student of the Victorian period. The sixty-third volume includes a "statistical account" of the main work in which it is stated that the *Dictionary* contains biographies of 29,120 persons: "It is believed that the names include all men and women of British or Irish race who have achieved any reasonable measure of distinction in any walk of life. . . . No sphere of activity has been consciously overlooked. . . . The principle upon which names have been admitted has been from all points of view generously interpreted."

Corrections are published in the *Bulletin of the Institute of Historical Research* and have been cumulated in *Dictionary of National Biography Corrections and Additions, Cumulated from the Bulletin of the Institute of Historical Research* (Boston, Hall, 1966).

The *Concise Dictionary of National Biography*, like the main work, was originally published by Smith, Elder & Co., but is now revised at intervals and published by OUP. It contains entries for all names about which substantial information is given in the main work. An epitome is provided of the most significant facts and dates in each biography and volume and page references to the main work are noted. The *Concise Dictionary* thus constitutes both an index to and an abstract of entries in the full work.

Contemporary Biography

The student of the Victorian period is fortunate in having several other collections of contemporary biography. Many of these, however, do not appear in a very satisfactory or useful form until rather late in the nineteenth century. The annual publication *Who's Who*, for example, was first published by Black in 1849. Until 1896, however, this included lists of names rather than biographical details and was essentially a handbook of titled and official classes. In 1897 it assumed its present character of a biographical dictionary of prominent living persons.

The first volume of *Who Was Who* contained biographies of persons who died during the period 1897–1915. The first edition was published by Black in 1920 and reprinted details which had previously appeared in *Who's Who*. Later editions include additions and corrections.

In 1901 *Who's Who* incorporated *Men and Women of the Time* (Routledge). From 1852 to 1887 this was published as *Men of the Time: or, sketches of living notables*. The work was retitled *Men and Women of the Time* in the thirteenth edition of 1891. The first edition included 300 biographies of living persons. By 1899 the work was in its fifteenth edition and contained more than 3400 biographies. The 1899 edition includes a useful supplement listing persons who had died and noting the latest edition of the work in which biographies of them appeared.

T. H. Ward, *Men of the Reign* (Routledge, 1885), is sub-titled "a biographical dictionary of eminent persons of British and colonial birth who have died during the reign of Queen Victoria". This provides concise biographies of some 3000 figures. Much of its information is stated by the compiler to be derived from volumes of *Men of the Time*.

A. T. C. Pratt, *People of the Period* (2 vols., Beeman, 1897), is described as "a collection of the biographies of upwards of six thousand living celebrities". It contains short biographies of a wide range of contemporary figures and is not limited to those of British birth.

Other contemporary collections of biography most often merely repeat facts about eminent persons which are easily found elsewhere. Thus Lord Brougham "and other distinguished authors" compiled a fulsomely laudatory volume of *Old England's Worthies* (Sangster, no date) which includes a supplement giving biographies of Prince Albert, Wellington, Peel, Macaulay, Nelson, and George and Robert Stephenson. In *A Book of Memories of Great Men and Women of the Age from Personal Acquaintance* (Virtue, 1871), S. C. Hall compiled "a series of written portraits" of more than 120 of his literary acquaintances who died before 1871. The book is an uninspiring combination of fact and reminiscence.

More helpful are the obituary notices in the *Annual Register: a review of public events at home and abroad*, which has been published in London since 1761. Another useful but short-lived biographical magazine of the later nineteenth century is *The Biograph and Review* (7 vols., 1879–82).

The Victorian period saw the development of illustrated biographical magazines. Examples of these include *Portraits of Men of Eminence*, edited by L. Reeve and E. Walford (6 vols., 1863–7); *Men of Mark*, edited by T. Cooper (7 vols., 1876–83); *Men and Women of the Day* (7 vols., 1888–94); and *The Vanity Fair Album: a show of sovereigns, statesmen, judges and men of the day*, edited by "Jehu Junior", the pseudonym of T. G. Bowles (35 vols., 1869–1903).

Details of persons of rank may be traced in standard works such as *Burke's Peerage* (1826–), *Debrett's Peerage* (1803–), *Walford's County Families of the United Kingdom* (1860–), and Kelly's *Handbook to the Titled, Landed and Official Classes* 1880–). Parliamentary figures are included in *Dod's Parliamentary Companion* (1833–), until 1864 entitled *Parliamentary Pocket Companion*, and in *Debrett's Illustrated House of Commons and the Judicial Bench* (1867–).

It will be noted that the works listed above are generally limited to biographies of eminent figures. The most useful national collected biography for tracing persons of lower rank and position is F. Boase, *Modern English Biography* (6 vols., Truro, Netherton, 1892–1921; reprinted Cass, 1965). Entry is restricted to persons who died between 1851 and 1900. The work is indexed by subjects and by "important, curious and interesting facts". The range of persons covered is very wide, some 30,000 biographies being included. Biographies contain a note of sources in which more complete details may be traced. The criterion of entry adopted by Boase was simply that a person should have been well known, whatever his occupation or status. The work includes entries for foreigners who spent their lives in England and there are a few entries for natives of the colonies. In his preface Boase notes the increased interest in biography revealed during the latter part of the nineteenth century in newspapers, periodicals and in dictionaries of collected biography.

Scotland

A useful older guide for Scottish figures is *A Biographical Dictionary of Eminent Scotsmen*, edited by R. Chambers. First published by Blackie in 1835 this was revised and expanded by T. Thomson for later editions in 1855, 1868–70, and 1875. W. Anderson, *The Scottish Nation: or, the surnames, families, literature, honours and biographical history of the people of Scotland* (3 vols., Edinburgh, Fullarton, 1862–3), includes a large amount of biographical material. The work was expanded by supplementary volumes.

Ireland

Information about sources of biographical information for Irish figures may be obtained from A. R. Eager, *A Guide to Irish Bibliographical Material* (Library Association, 1964). The best collected biography for the Victorian period is J. S. Crone, *A Concise Dictionary of Irish Biography* (rev. edn., Dublin, Talbot Pr., 1937).

Wales

The basic guide to Welsh biography was compiled under the auspices of the Honourable Society of Cymmrodorion. It was published in Welsh in 1953 as *Y Bywgraffiadur Cymreig hyd 1940*. An English edition appeared as *The Dictionary of Welsh Biography down to 1940*. This edition, published by the Society in 1959, is not a mere translation but includes the results of later research and many corrections. It contains some 3500 articles. For persons who were born in Wales but whose lives were mostly passed elsewhere emphasis is placed on their Welsh descent and background and the reader has to refer to other sources for details of their later career. Although most persons in the book were Welsh by birth, some non-Welshmen who exercised a strong influence on the country's history have also been included.

Newspapers

It should be noted that much biographical information may be derived from obituary notices in newspapers. *Palmer's Index to the Times Newspaper,* covering the period from 1790, is an invaluable guide to that newspaper. Obituary notices are listed under the heading "Deaths" and frequently supply biographical material not available from other sources.

Obituaries of persons of major importance are reprinted in *Eminent Persons: biographies reprinted from The Times*. The first volume of this series was published by Macmillan and *The Times* in 1892 and included some of the biographies which appeared between 1870 and 1875. Both British and foreign figures are included.

Encyclopedias

For major figures some information may be obtained from encyclopedias. Modern editions, of course, will not usually add much to information obtained from the major collected biographies, such as the *Dictionary of National Biography*. A nineteenth-century edition of *Encyclopaedia Britannica* or *Chambers's*

Encyclopaedia, however, may provide a useful indication of the Victorian estimate of a contemporary figure.

Encyclopaedia Britannica was first published in 3 volumes in 1768–71. There were several nineteenth-century editions, the latest being the ninth, published in 24 volumes during 1875–89. The tenth edition, published in 1902, formed a supplement to the ninth, with a combined index to both the main work and the supplement. The eleventh edition, published in 29 volumes during 1910–11, is of great importance. It should be noted, however, that until the twentieth century the work concentrated on lengthy scholarly monographs rather than shorter articles under specific headings, and did not include biographies of living persons.

Chambers's Encyclopaedia was first published in 1859–68. The first edition was published by William Chambers in 520 weekly parts, comprising 10 volumes, and was the work of more than 100 contributors. A new edition, published in 1888–92, was also in 10 volumes.

Local Biography

County Biographical Dictionaries

The major series of illustrated county biographical dictionaries of the 1890s and the early twentieth century are well described in a valuable article by H. J. Hanham, "Some neglected sources of biographical information: county biographical dictionaries, 1890–1937", in the *Bulletin of the Institute of Historical Research* (vol. 34, 1961, pp. 55–63). This includes a list of dictionaries by county with notes of their present locations. Hanham notes two major series. Pike's New Century Series (Brighton, W. T. Pike) covers persons of local importance and volumes include many names not found in other biographical dictionaries. The series published by C. A. Manning Press and Ernest Gaskill is less useful because of its much less extensive coverage.

Less significant series published late in the nineteenth century include the British Biographical Company's *Leading Men of*

London and the Biographical Publishing Company's *Men of the Period*, including volumes of Yorkshire and Lancashire. At the beginning of the twentieth century imitations of Pike's New Century Series were published notably by J. & G. Hammond & Co. of Birmingham and by the London & Provincial Publishing Company.

The publication of unillustrated series of county biographies on the pattern of *Who's Who* is a later development, dating initially from the years immediately before 1914.

Biographical Magazines

A number of magazines devoted to local biography were published during the later nineteenth century. Good examples are *Birmingham Faces and Places* (1888–94) and *Manchester Faces and Places* (1889–96).

Directories

The major guide to early examples of local directories is J. E. Norton, *Guide to the National and Provincial Directories of England and Wales, Excluding London, Published before 1856* (Royal Historical Society, 1950). This work contains useful introductory chapters on the origin and development of directories and on authorship, methods of composition, and tests of reliability. For London the standard guide is C. W. F. Goss, *The London Directories, 1677–1855: a bibliography with notes on their origin and development* (Archer, 1932).

The second half of the nineteenth century is rich in directories and it should not be difficult to find information about the inhabitants of most places in a town or county directory. William White published an especially useful series beginning with Yorkshire in 1831 and including many counties and individual towns.

J. E. Norton notes that by the 1850s directories had become fairly uniform. Developments in the postal service, the telegraph and the railways improved the opportunities for personal intercourse and contributed to make the publication of directories profitable. In 1845 Kelly's *Post Office Directory* for Birmingham noted that "the increased and rapidly increasing facilities of communication seemed to indicate a necessity for more extended and elaborate works of the present description than had been before attempted".

Index

Abstracts *see specific topics*
Adult education 77
Anglican biography 59
Anonymous authors
  books 18, 20–21
  periodical articles 22
Applied arts 118–21
Architecture 113–18
  bibliographies 113–16
  biography 117
  current work 116
  dictionaries 116–17
  encyclopedias 116–17
  guides 113–16
  societies 117–18
Archives 44, 46–48
Astronomy 96
Autobiographies 159, 161

Ballet 124
Banking 64, 71
Baptists 55–57
Bibliographies 4–13, 15–17
  see also specific topics
Biographical magazines 163, 167
Biography 158–68
  bibliographies 158–61
  local 166–8
  national 161–6
  see also specific topics
Biology 98
Birds 99
Blue Books 44–45, 75, 77, 150, 152
Book illustration 104
Botany 98

British Empire 149–50, 156–7, 159
Building 113–18
  bibliographies 113–16
  biography 117
  current work 116
  dictionaries 116–17
  encyclopedias 116–17
  guides 113–16
  societies 117–18
Business archives 48
Business history 64

Ceramics 118–19
Chamber music 127
Chemistry 96–97
China 118–19
Christian Church 54–59
  abstracts 56
  bibliographies 54–56
  biography 59
  current work 56–57
  dictionaries 57–58
  encyclopedias 57–58
  guides 54–56
  theses 57
Church of England biography 59
Church of Scotland 55, 59
Coins 121
Colonial history 149–50, 156–7, 159
Communism 146
Costume 119–20
County biography 166–7
County records 48
Current work (indexes and bibliographies) 10–17
  see also specific topics

Decorative arts 104, 118–21
Dentistry 92
Detective fiction 136
Devonshire artists 110
Diaries 159
Dictionaries *see specific topics*
Diplomatic papers 44–45, 150
Directories 167–9
see also specific topics
Dissertations 17–19
see also specific topics
Drama 132, 134, 143
Drawings 105
Dress 119–20

Ecclesiastical history 54–59
abstracts 56
bibliographies 54–56
biography 59
current work 56–57
dictionaries 57–58
encyclopedias 57–58
guides 54–56
theses 57
Ecclesiastical records 48
Economic history 60–72
abstracts 68
bibliographies 61–65
current work 65, 68
dictionaries 72
encyclopedias 72
guides 60
research collections 71
theses 68, 70–71
Ecumenical movement 55
Education 73–83
abstracts 79
bibliographies 73–77
biography 81–83
current work 79–80
dictionaries 79, 81
encyclopedias 79, 81
guides 73–77
theses 77–79
Educational administration 77
Educational psychology 77–78
Electrical engineering 96

Empire 149–50, 156–7, 159
Encyclopedias 165–6
see also specific topics
English literature 129–44
abstracts 137
bibliographies 129–36
biography 143–4
current work 136–7
dictionaries 141, 143
encyclopedias 141, 143
guides 129–36
handbooks 141–3
periodicals 137, 139–41
theses 137–8
Engraving 104, 108–10
Etching 104, 108–10

Festschriften 64, 154
Fiction 134–6, 139
Fictional characters 143
Finance 64, 71
Fine arts 100–13
bibliographies 100–5
biography 104, 107–10
collections 110–12
dictionaries 107
directories 110–12
encyclopedias 107
guides 100–2
periodical indexes 105–6
photographic archives 112
portrait indexes 112
Fishes 99
Furniture 120

Geology 97–98
Glasgow artists 110
Goldsmiths' marks 120–1
Government libraries 40–42
Government publications 42–44,
75, 77, 150, 152
Guides *see specific topics*

Historical fiction 135
History 145–57
abstracts 154

History (*cont.*)
  bibliographies 145–53
  chronological outlines 157
  current work 153–5
  guides 145–6
  research locations 156–7
  theses 155–6

Imperial history 149–50, 156–7, 159
Indian Mutiny 149
Interdisciplinary studies 2–3
Interior decoration 120
Irish artists 110
Irish biography 164
Irish botanists 98
Irish history 151

Judges 163

Lancashire artists 110
Landed classes 163
Landscape painting 109
Law
  bibliographies 61–63
  biography 163
  encyclopedias 72
  guides 60
  research collections 71
  theses 68, 71
Learned societies 41
Library catalogues 6, 8–9
  see also specific topics
Literature 129–44
  abstracts 137
  bibliographies 129–36
  biography 143–4
  current work 136–7
  dictionaries 141, 143
  encyclopedias 141, 143
  guides 129–36
  handbooks 141–3
  periodicals 137, 139–41
  theses 137–8
Liverpool artists 110
Local artists 110

Local biography 166–8
Local history 46, 151–2
Local novelists 135

Manuscripts 44, 46–48
Mathematics 95–96
Medallists 121
Medicine 91–95
  bibliographies 91–92
  biography 93, 95
  current work 92–94
  guides 91–92
Metalwork 118, 120–1
Methodists 57
Miniatures 104, 110
Municipal history 152–3
Municipal records 48
Music 122–8
  bibliographies 122–4
  biography 128
  current work 125–6
  dictionaries 125, 127–8
  encyclopedias 125, 127–8
  guides 122–4
  histories 125
  theses 125
Music education 125

National biography 161–6
Naval history 149
Newspapers (Victorian) 22–38, 165
  indexes 28–35
  lists 23, 25–28
  obituary notices 165
  studies 36–38
Nonconformist archives 48
Nottingham artists 110
Novels 134–6, 139
Numismatics 121
Nursing 92

Opera 127–8

Painting 100–13
  bibliographies 100–5
  biography 104, 107–10
  collections 110–12
  dictionaries 107
  directories 110–12
  encyclopedias 107
  guides 100–2
  periodical indexes 105–6
  photographic archives 112
  portrait indexes 112
Parliamentary biography 163
Parliamentary papers 42–44, 75, 77, 150, 152
Peerage 163
Periodicals (Victorian) 22–38
  indexes 28–35
  lists 23, 25–28
  studies 36–38
Periodicals (20th century) 10, 13–17, 22–38
  indexes 10, 13–17
  lists 23, 25–28
Pewter 121
Philosophy 49–53
  bibliographies 49–51
  biography 53
  current work 51
  dictionaries 51–52
  encyclopedias 51–52
  guides 49–51
Photographic archives 112
Photography 121
Physics 96
Plays 132, 134, 143
Poetry 136, 139, 143
Politics
  bibliographies 61–65, 145–53
  biography 163
  current work 65, 153–5
  encyclopedias 72
  guides 60, 145–6
  research collections 71, 156–7
  theses 68, 71, 155–6
Population 64, 68
Porcelain 118–19
Portrait indexes 112
Portrait miniatures 104, 110

Pottery 118–19
Pre-Raphaelites 105, 132–3
Prints 104
Pseudonymous authors
  books 18, 20–21
  periodical articles 22
Psychology
  bibliographies 49–51, 61–63
  dictionaries 52, 72
  encyclopedias 52, 72
  guides 49–51, 60
  research collections 71
  theses 68, 71
Public Records 46–47

Quakers 56–57, 59
Quotations 143

Railways 65–67
Record repositories 44, 46–48
Regional novelists 135
Religion 54–59
  abstracts 56
  bibliographies 54–56
  biography 59
  current work 56–57
  dictionaries 57–58
  encyclopedias 57–58
  guides 54–56
  theses 57
Research collections 39–48
  see also specific topics
Roman Catholics 56, 58–59

Science 84–99
  bibliographies 84–86, 90–91
  biography 89–91
  current work 86–89
  encyclopedias 89
  guides 84–86
  see also specific sciences
Scientific education 77
Scientific societies 41
Scottish art 104, 109–10, 112
Scottish biography 164

Scottish church history   55, 59
Scottish education   83
Scottish history   150
Sculpture   109–10
Sheffield plate   120
Silver   120–1
Social sciences   60–72
  bibliographies   61–67
  current work   65, 68–69
  dictionaries   72
  encyclopedias   72
  guides   60
  research collections   71
  theses   68, 70–71
Socialism   146
Society of Friends   56–57, 59
Special collections   39–48
  see also specific topics
Statutes   42

Technical education   77–79
Technology   84–91
  bibliographies   84–86
  biography   89–91
  current work   86–89
  encyclopedias   89
  guides   84–86
Theatre   132, 134, 143
Thematic catalogues   124
Theses   17–19
  see also specific topics
Titled classes   163

Trade unions   64
Tragedy   134
Transport   65–67

Urban history   64, 68–69

Visual arts   100–21
  bibliographies   100–5
  biography   104, 107–10
  collections   110–12
  dictionaries   107
  directories   110–12
  encyclopedias   107
  guides   100–2
  periodical indexes   105–6
  photographic archives   112
  portrait indexes   112

Water-colour painting   104
Welsh artists   110
Welsh biography   165
Welsh educationists   83
Welsh history   150
Welsh politicians   83
Woodcuts   104
Working class fiction   136
Working classes   64

Zoology   98–99